Expository Commentary on HEBREWS

Expository Commentary on HEBREWS

J.C. Macaulay

MOODY PRESS
CHICAGO

Formerly entitled *Devotional Studies in the Epistle to the Hebrews*

MOODY PRESS EDITION 1978

Library of Congress Cataloging in Publication Data

Macaulay, Joseph Cordner, 1900-
Expository commentary on Hebrews.
Published in 1948 under title: Devotional studies in the Epistle to the Hebrews.
1. Bible. N.T. Hebrews–Commentaries. I. Title.
BS2775.3.M28 1978 227'.87'07 78-7848
ISBN 0-8024-2422-8

Printed in the United States of America

CONTENTS

PREFACE

These studies do not pretend to be an exhaustive, much less a critical, commentary on the epistle to the Hebrews. The purpose throughout is devotional and practical. Problems of introduction do not enter, but there has been no studied avoidance of difficulties met with in the text.

The writer cannot hope that his interpretation will find universal acceptance, but he has sought to approach every passage in the spirit of the young champion of the Scottish Kirk who sat in the Westminster Assembly with the prayer in his heart and on his notebook, *Da lucem, Domine!*

I have followed my usual custom of dealing freely with the words of the text, in order to be more rigid with the meaning. Therefore I have not bound myself to any one version, nor to the exact words of a version, where clarity and force demanded some substitution.

As in the case of my former works on St. John's gospel and the Acts, these studies have been given as Sunday morning messages to a congregation able to digest strong meat as well as milk. I am quite prepared to agree with some of the saints that it was rigorous discipline in spots, but the gracious Holy Spirit has rewarded us with fresh glimpses of our glorious High Priest, and many are praying that the reading of the following chapters will bring a like blessing to not a few.

> Eternal Voice! which, as in ages past,
> May still be heard;
> More than a timeworn record, writ by scribes,
> The *living* Word!
> Eternal Christ! Who walked among us here
> To bless and heal!
> Whose unseen presence on our stony way
> We inly feel!

We turn in our perplexity to Thee!
  Thou, ever true!
To us, by false lights duped, by lies distraught,
  Speak Thou anew!
So our bewildered age may prove afresh
  Thou still art here,
As in the ship, on storm-tossed Galilee,
  Our bark to steer
To calmer waters, where, beyond this stress,
  The billows cease,
And our earth, bleeding from a thousand wounds,
  At last finds peace!

—MAX REICH*

*Quoted by permission of *Moody Monthly*.

1

LISTEN! GOD SPEAKS!

HEBREWS 1:1-3

In this opening chapter we contemplate:

1. The kindness and mercy of God's total word
2. The authority and incompleteness of God's former word
3. The superiority and finality of God's latter word

"HEAR, O HEAVENS, and give ear, O earth: for the LORD hath spoken" (Isa 1:2). But while heaven hearkens and bows down at the voice of the Almighty, earth shuts her ear and is deaf to the word. We listen to the scientist, to the philosopher, to the statesman, to the economist as if they were divine oracles, nor does our passionate confidence fail when their words turn to ashes again and again; while the only word that will outlive heaven and earth, the word which is life and health to all who receive it, is given scant hearing. In the tense days of national and international crisis, when the President of our country, or the prime minister of Great Britain had something to say to the people, the channels of the air were cleared for all to listen. How much more should we silence other voices to hearken to the word of the living God!

God hath spoken. Not otherwise could we know Him. It is true that "the heavens declare the glory of God" (Psalm 19:1), and all things created have a voice to utter, "The hand that made us is Divine." "For the invisible things of him from the creation of the world are clearly seen, being understood by the things that are made, even his eternal power and Godhead" (Rom 1:20). History also carries its ever expanding testimony of God, declaring His sovereignty, His justice, His truth. Within our own breasts there is that wounded but invincible monarch whose witness to the holiness of God, stifled as it is, stirs in us a restlessness which we cannot altogether allay. But creation and history and conscience all together cannot bring us to a sufficient knowledge of God. "Canst thou by searching find out God? canst thou find out the Almighty unto perfection?" (Job 11:7). If God is to be known, He must sovereignly reveal Himself; He must speak. And in infinite grace He has spoken.

The Voice of God's Creation found me
  Perplexed 'midst hope and fear;
For though His sunshine flashed around me,
  His storms at times drew near;
And I said–
  O that I knew where He abideth!
    For doubts beset our lot,
  And lo! His glorious face He hideth,
    And men perceive it not.

The Voice of God's Protection told me
  He loveth all He made;
I seemed to feel His arms enfold me,
  And yet was half afraid;
And I said–
  O that I knew where I might find Him!
    His eye would guide me right:
  He leaveth countless tracks behind Him,
    Yet passeth out of sight.

The Voice of Conscience sounded nearer,
  It stirred my inmost breast:
But though its tones were firmer, clearer,
  'Twas not the voice of rest:
And I said–
  O that I knew if He forgiveth!
    My soul is faint within,
  Because in grievous fear it liveth
    Of wages due to sin.

It was the Voice of Revelation
  That met my inmost need;
The wondrous message of salvation
    Was joy and peace indeed:
And I said–
  O how I love the sacred pages
    From which such tidings flow,

As monarchs, patriarchs, poets, sages,
Have longed in vain to know!

What does it signify that God has spoken to men? This—that God made man capable of comprehending His speech, receiving His revelation, and entering into a sympathetic and understanding communion with Him. Indeed, God made man with the express design of having a creature to whom He might communicate Himself, with whom He might share Himself. "Let us make man in our image, after our likeness" (Gen 1:26), for only to such a being could God make Himself known. We were made for the knowledge of God, made to hear the word of the Lord; and only as we hearken, only as we "follow on to know the LORD" (Hos 6:3), can the purpose of our being be realized. We have not sufficiently contemplated this twofold grace of God, in creating us with a capacity to know Him, and in bringing this knowledge of Himself to us in a glorious self-revelation.

But the creature that God made for glory and honor fell, through unbelief, disobedience, rebellion, and became a sinner, depraved and despoiled in every part of his being. What does it mean that God has spoken to man, the sinner? It means mercy! He who spoke in gracious communion to unfallen man, came again to fallen man with His wooing call, "Where art thou?" (Gen 3:9). Adam, the sinner, was afraid of the voice of God, but David, wiser than the ancients, was more alarmed at the thought of the silence of God. "Be not silent to me," he cried out, "lest, if thou be silent to me, I become like them that go down into the pit" (Psalm 28:1). The silence of God in face of our sin would have spelled irrevocable ruin and eternal doom. But He has not so left us to the despair of voiceless gloom. Ever since the breeze of evening wafted the voice of the Lord to the guilty pair in Eden, God has spoken in mercy, whether amid the thunders of Sinai or the rending rocks of Horeb or the lovely stillness of Olivet. Even His sharpest rebukes, His severest chastenings, His most fearful threatenings are mercy. It was James McKendrick who said to Wendell P. Loveless, during the Scottish evangelist's visit to the WMBI studios in Chicago, "Remember, brother, everything outside the lake of fire is mercy; every drop of water is pure grace." It is because God has spoken that there is an answer to our question, a solution to our problem, hope for our end.

"In many portions and in many ways God spoke of old time to the fathers in the prophets, but in the last of these days He spoke to us in one who is a Son" (Heb 1:1-2, author's trans.). So God's self-revelation is in two great movements—the former and the latter, the old and the new, the preparatory and the final. The record of what God spoke in old time to the fathers in the prophets is what we call the Old Testament, and the record of this great, complete, and final revelation is given in our New Testament.

Now the first thing we notice in this apostolic statement is the equal claim of both to divine authorship and authority. God spoke to the fathers in the prophets; God spoke to us in the Son. Many who are fully convinced of the divine revelation in Christ are not so sure that what we have in the Old Testament is unmixed revelation, and they regard the inspiration of our Old Testament as of an entirely different and decidedly lower sort than that of the New Testament. That is not the view of the Scriptures themselves. Not only do the Old Testament Scriptures come to us with a claim to be the divinely inspired record of a divinely given revelation, but the New Testament Scriptures consistently grant, and indeed press, the claim. It was of the Old Testament that our Lord said, "The scripture cannot be broken" (John 10:35). It was of the Old Testament that Peter wrote, "Holy men of God spake as they were moved by the Holy Ghost" (2 Pet 1:21); and Paul declared, "All scripture is given by inspiration of God" (2 Tim 3:16). The Christian faith does not claim to displace the older as false, but to fulfill it as true. It does not say of that long line of Hebrew prophets and the ancient Hebrew system, "These were but the gropings of men, but now God has spoken;" rather, it stands champion for "the divine commission of Jewish prophets, the divine sanction of Jewish institutions," and adds, "These all have found their meaning and fulfillment in the new word which God has spoken." The great statement of Augustine regarding the relation of the two has been repeated in many forms: "The New Testament is latent in the Old, the Old is patent in the New."

For all the dignity and authority and divinity of the former revelation, it had its limitations, of necessity. It was fragmentary, "in many portions," for God was speaking to a people who could receive only "precept upon precept, precept upon precept; line upon line, line upon line; here a little, and there a little" (Isa 28:13). Using men as His channels, men with their limitations in understanding, He added fragment to fragment, always in accord with the need of the moment and the suitability of the vessel.

In keeping with the fragmentary character of the revelation were the many forms and ways in which it was imparted. A dream, a vision, an angel visitant, a voice, a burden, an ecstatic experience; by such divers means were the prophets given their messages, with Moses, towering over them all, receiving his in open, face to face conversation. Then they delivered their oracles in divers ways—by a parable, by a prediction, by a dramatic representation, by a song, by a proverb, by a history, by a law, by the institution of a ritual.

The fragmentary and varied character of the Old Testament revelation makes more divinely wonderful its complete unity, as it moves on in orderly progression, through fifteen centuries of recording and at the hands of thirty or more writers, to its goal in the new and more glorious manifestation, God speaking in the Son, God manifest in the flesh. All that went before was preparatory to this. Not that all who received the earlier oracles understood their preparatory nature. The prophets themselves, living in the shadows and sensing some better thing to come, only dimly perceived its nature, "searching what, or what manner of time the Spirit of Christ which was in them did signify, when it testified beforehand the sufferings of Christ, and the glory that should follow" (1 Pet 1:11).

At last it came. "In the fulness of time God sent His Son, made of a woman, made under the law, to redeem them that were under the law" (Gal 4:4-5, author's trans.). "God . . . spake to us in His Son" (Heb 1:1-2, author's trans.). All the fragments and all the forms are now gathered together in one, complemented and accomplished in the one perfect manifestation. Now the meaning of the shadows is plain. They were the heralds of the coming Son, in whom God was about to utter His full and final word. It is as if one were walking across a plain at eventide, away from the setting sun. A shadow, not his own, catches up with him. It resembles a man's head, then a man's head and shoulders, but the identity is obscure. Finally the entire shadow has passed, and the traveler finds beside him a beloved companion. The mystery of the growing shadow is solved, and its promise has given way to perfect realization. Now the shadow itself is full of interest, and actually suggests features and characteristics that might otherwise not be observed.

One evening, as we were driving through the Arizona desert, the moving shadow of our car, cast by a low sun, fascinated us. As I was not driving at the time, I impulsively reached for my camera, turned it to slow motion, and took a picture of that moving shadow. It turned out to be one of our most interesting pictures, and gave us a view of our own car such as we never could have had otherwise. So we are in Christ, the place of unspeakable privilege, but we do not despise and neglect the shadows. "[These] are they which testify of me" (John 5:39), said our Lord, and from our vantage point "in Christ," we take these under review in order to acquaint ourselves with the manifold offices and character of our blessed Lord. Indeed, to us they are scarcely shadows anymore, but details of particular features of our glorious Redeemer. Till we find ourselves moving through this Old Testament gallery with the exclamation ever breaking from our lips, "It is the Lord! It is the Lord!" I hope you have learned to read your Old Testament, and to see Jesus there.

The vast superiority of the new revelation lies in the superiority of the Messenger. The prophets were men "of like passions" (Acts 14:15) with ourselves, but the Son is "holy, harmless, undefiled, separate from sinners, and made higher than the heavens" (Heb 7:26). Let the Spirit of inspiration present the unspeakable excellence of the Son: "Whom he appointed heir of all things, through whom also he made the ages; who, being the outshining of his glory and the exact impress of his substance, and upholding all things by the word of his power, when he had made purification of sins, sat down on the right hand of the Majesty on high" (Heb 1:2*b*-3, author's trans.). Do you notice that whatever Jesus touches, in that He holds the place of undisputed preeminence? Does He touch the vast realm of things created? He walks in the midst of it as sole Heir. Does He enter the stream of history? It is as the Maker and Molder of the ages. Does He sustain a relation to God? He shares the very substance of God and carries the rays of the divine glory out to view. Has He a place in this material universe and the moral realm which embraces it? It is to bear aloft and along all things to the predetermined consummation. Does

He touch sin? It is to do what none other could: "put away sin by the sacrifice of himself" (Heb 9:26). Has He a place in heaven? "He . . . sat down on the right hand of the Majesty on high." Surely we are handling things too vast, too glorious for thought, and how can words express them! Behold the Messenger of the new covenant—the Son, Creator, Heir, Upholder, Redeemer, Lord!

If this is God's Messenger, there is place for no other beside Him. Some time ago I visited the B'Hai temple in Winnetka, Illinois, with several friends, being interested solely in the building, for it is indeed a piece of exquisite tracery in stone. I asked our guide what place they gave to Jesus Christ. She answered that He was one of the world's great teachers and saviors, along with Confucius and Buddha and Muhammad and others. In New York there is a magnificent cathedral housing a professed Christian church, where the gallery of figures assigns a like place to Jesus, one among many, perhaps in some sense primus inter pares! This is nothing short of blasphemy; it is wickedness. Not so does the Scripture of truth present Him. When Peter suggested the building of three booths on the Mount of Transfiguration, one for Jesus, one for Moses, and one for Elijah, so placing the Lord on a parity with the others, God withdrew the ancient prophets from view and spoke to the disciples out of the cloud, "This is my Son, my chosen: hear ye him" (Luke 9:35, author's trans.). "And when the voice was past, Jesus was found alone" (v. 36). How remarkable, how significant! Not even the divinely commissioned prophets of the divinely instituted order could stand beside Jesus. When they had given their witness to Him, their work was done, and they must retire to leave Him in sole view.

The superiority and finality of the revelation is in this also, that not only is Jesus the Messenger; He is the message. It is not a matter of the sayings of Jesus being so much greater and better and completer than the sayings of Isaiah, but that Jesus is Himself the Word, the revelation. "He that hath seen me hath seen the Father" (John 14:9), and "no man cometh unto the Father, but by me" (v. 6).

Listen! God speaks! He is speaking in His Son. And what is He saying? "Come unto me, all ye that labour and are heavy laden, and I will give you rest" (Matt 11:28). "Him that cometh to me I will in no wise cast out" (John 6:37). Have you heard? Have you come?

2

BETTER THAN THE ANGELS

Hebrews 1:4-14

Here we view the superiority of Jesus:

1. As God the Son, whom angels worship
2. As God the King, whom angels obey
3. As God the Creator, whom angels serve

We still have with us the sons of the Sadducees, who regard belief in the existence of angels as a piece of childish credulity, on a par with superstitions about fairies, pixies, and hobgoblins. If, however, we accept the Bible as an authoritative record of divinely revealed truth, we have no choice in the matter. The biblical references to angels are too numerous to deal with here, but they consistently present to us spiritual beings of a high order, far above men in strength, intelligence, and beauty, who serve God with perfect obedience and loving devotion.

Surely it cannot be thought unreasonable that God would surround Himself with a great host of glorious creatures to enjoy His presence, to obey His commands, and to serve His purposes. If He created the human race, we certainly cannot affirm a priori that we are the only moral and intelligent beings in the whole creation! That we have neither seen nor heard angels does not disprove their existence. Have you heard the song of the bat? Yet by the echo of its song that strange creature guides its flight. Its notes are just out of range of the human ear. And what if God has decreed that His angels should for the most part be unseen and unheard by us? It is better so, better for faith, better for discipline.

They must be noble creatures indeed, when the pen of inspiration deems them at all worthy of mention alongside our risen, exalted Lord. For the sacred writer, moved by the Holy Spirit, no sooner shows us Christ, seated "on the right hand of the Majesty on high" (Heb 1:3), than he exclaims, "Better than the angels!" (1:4*a*).

Just how much better than the angels is Jesus? We are given a remarkable answer to that question: "having become by so much better than the angels, as he hath inherited a more excellent name than they" (1:4, ASV). But what is the "more excellent name"? It must be the same as that referred to in the second chapter of the Philippian letter, where the apostle, after describing the progressive self-abasement of our Lord, declares: "Wherefore also God highly exalted him, and gave unto him the name which is above every name; that in the name of Jesus every knee should bow . . . and that every tongue should confess that Jesus Christ is Lord" (Phil 2:9-11, ASV). This name bestowed upon Jesus is of such transcendent dignity that He who bears it receives universal homage and worship. There is only one such name, the ineffable name, God's own all-glorious name, which the Man, Christ Jesus, shares with the Father—Jehovah, great I Am!

What's in a name? Among us, not very much. My family name indicates relationship, and identifies me with a gang of ruffians who lived recklessly and lawlessly in the wild Hebrides of Scotland a thousand years ago. My Christian name (as we call it), betokens the friendship of my parents with a certain Presbyterian minister. But my name tells nothing about my character, my rank, my purpose in life, or my destiny. Any real significance which our names may have had in the beginning has been lost. It is not so with the name which Jesus bears. That name not only marks His oneness with God, but tells us that all God is, He is; the character of God is His character; the attributes of God are His attributes. "In him dwelleth all the fulness of the Godhead bodily" (Col 2:9).

All divine glories are included in this name which God said was His memorial forever; and when the holy name is compounded to present some special character of God, that also is the name of Jesus. Jesus is Jehovah-Tzidkenu, the Lord our righteousness. Jesus is Jehovah-Shalom, the Lord our peace. Jesus is Jehovah-Ropheka, the Lord our Healer. Jesus is Jehovah-Jireh, the Lord our Overseer and Provider.

Jesus is Jehovah-Shammah, our ever present Lord. Jesus is Jehovah-Rohi, the Lord our Shepherd.

Jehovah is not only the name of eternal being, but the name which gathers up into itself all that God is, all that God is for us, and Jesus is just that. Jesus was the name given Him in the day of His humiliation, in the day of His coming into our flesh; but we must remember that this same Jesus, exalted at God's right hand, bears the august, holy, terrible name, Jehovah. Thus the name Jesus, in itself suggestive of the meekness and lowliness of the days of His flesh, nevertheless is vested with all the glory and all the majesty of the ineffable name, and calls for the submission and homage of all creatures.

The greater excellency of the name which Jesus bears is the index of His superiority over the angels. This vast superiority is now presented with the help of Old Testament Scriptures, in a threefold character. He is the divine Son, the divine King, and the divine Creator.

First, Jesus is God the Son, and as such receives the worship of the holy angels. "For unto which of the angels said he at any time, Thou art my Son, this day have I begotten thee?" (Heb 1:5). The answer is, of course, "To none of them." Angels are, indeed, called sons of God, but in a very inferior and general sense, as being creatures of His hand who stand close to Him, doing His bidding continually. Here we are dealing with the only begotten, "declared to be the Son of God with power, according to the spirit of holiness, by the resurrection from the dead" (Rom 1:4).

The unique and transcendent sonship of Jesus was made the basis of one of the most important decrees ever issued from the eternal throne. "I will declare the decree: the LORD hath said unto me, Thou art my Son; this day have I begotten thee. Ask of me, and I shall give thee the heathen for thine inheritance, and the uttermost parts of the earth for thy possession. Thou shalt break them with a rod of iron; thou shalt dash them in pieces like a potter's vessel" (Psalm 2:7-9). The decree of universal sovereignty rests upon the divine sonship.

To confirm the witness, a second Scripture is referred to: "And again, I will be to him a Father, and he shall be to me a Son" (Heb 1:5*b*). To which of the angels was this spoken? To none of them. Actually, the words were spoken to David concerning his son, who should be king after him. They refer primarily to Solomon, though only conditionally, if he would obey the voice of the Lord; but David, by prophetic insight, saw their farther and ultimate fulfillment in the Messiah. From the day that Nathan spoke these words to David from God, all the prophets looked for "great David's greater son" as the promised Messiah, and knew, though they could not comprehend the mystery, that He should also be the Son of God. The generation of Jews to whom Jesus came knew that one who claimed to be the Son of God in the Messianic sense, "[made] himself equal with God" (John 5:18). It was for that claim that they sent Him to the cross. But the claim stands.

Our Lord's entry into this world, humble and obscure as it was, was announced by heavenly messengers, and there can be no doubt that angels hovered over the manger bed, adoring the divine mystery, "God . . . manifest in the flesh" (1 Tim 3:16). Another entry of the first begotten into the world is here contemplated when, on command from the eternal throne, the innumerable host of angels will bring their adoration to His feet. "And when he again bringeth in the first-born into the world he saith, And let all the angels of God worship him" (Heb 1:6, ASV). Surely this is part of the cosmic pageant of worship, when

> In the name of Jesus every knee shall bow,
> Every tongue confess Him King of Glory now.

Thus He who as Son bears the highest name receives the homage of all who as messengers carry the lesser name.

God the Son is also God the King, to whom the angel hosts render obedience as servants. "Of the angels he saith, Who maketh his angels spirits, and his ministers a flame of fire. But unto the Son he saith, Thy throne, O God, is for ever and ever: a sceptre of righteousness is the sceptre of thy kingdom. Thou hast loved righteousness, and hated iniquity; therefore God, even thy God, hath anointed thee with the oil of gladness above thy fellows" (Heb 1:7-9).

This statement about the angels, taken from Psalm 104, has disturbed and puzzled the scholars, until we are left with many conflicting opinions as to the exact sense. We need not try to solve the fine problems here, but be satisfied with the use which the Holy Spirit is making of the passage in the Hebrews letter. The angels are still regarded as glorious beings, swift and mysterious as the wind, bright and strong as flaming fire. Nevertheless, like the elements with which they are compared, they are servants—messengers sent forth on the wings of the wind, ministers to wait before God with burning devotion. Beyond that we need not go.

Upon whom do these glorious spirits wait, to do His royal bidding? Upon the Son, Jesus, for He is God, the King. To Him are the words of Psalm 45 addressed: "Thy throne, O God, is for ever and ever: a sceptre of righteousness is the sceptre of thy kingdom" (1:8). We are well acquainted with the threefold office of our Lord, as Prophet, Priest, and King. Some have drawn the difference in terms of time, declaring that He was Prophet in the days of His flesh; He is Priest now at God's right hand; and He will be King in the millennial age. We need to be careful about such sharply drawn distinctions. Jesus is King now! This whole passage in Hebrews, arguing the superiority of Christ over the angels, views Him as He is now, exalted at the right hand of the Majesty on high. The Old Testament Scriptures cited to enforce that superiority are regarded as applying to Him now, not in some future age. It is as the Son ascended on high from His earthly travail that He is addressed in these majestic words: "Thy throne, O God, is for ever and ever." So we heartily join in the words which open the second part of the *Te Deum*: "Thou art the King of glory, O Christ. Thou art the everlasting Son of the Father."

This divine kingship of Christ is secured for eternity, exercised in righteousness, and blessed with gladness. His is the one stable throne, His the only scepter unstained with deeds of violence and trickery, His the anointing which guarantees eternal joy. Upon such a King the myriads of angels attend, consecrating all their powers to His blessed will and service.

Finally our Lord is acclaimed the eternal Creator, the ascription of Psalm 102 being applied to Him. Heaven and earth owe their being to Him, and when, their purpose fulfilled, they pass away, He shall abide; when their form is changed for other uses, He is "the same yesterday, and to day, and for ever" (Heb 13:8). He is above all change. The withering of age cannot touch Him. Disintegration comes not near Him. Death cannot breathe upon Him. When ten million million years have passed, "Thou hast the dew of thy youth" (Psalm 110:3).

This eternal Son, eternal King, eternal Creator, sits on "the right hand of the throne of the Majesty in the heavens" (Heb 8:1), as our triumphant Saviour, not only served by the heavenly host, but sending them forth to minister on behalf of the heirs of salvation. So dear are we to Him, through His precious blood, that the highest ministry available is none too good. The angels ministered to Him in the days of His flesh, and the lowliest believer will not lack the service of heaven's own messengers all his pilgrim journey. Better still, He who is "better than the angels" (1:4*a*) has said, "I will never leave thee, nor forsake thee" (13:5*b*).

3

BEWARE OF THE DRIFT

Hebrews 2:1-4

In this chapter we press a solemn warning:

1. In view of the steadfastness of the former witness
2. In view of the superiority of the latter witness
3. In view of the certain doom of neglect

The meanest messenger, if he bear God's message, must command attention. Outcast lepers brought the good news of deliverance to beleaguered Samaria. A slave girl gave the word of salvation to her renowned, but leprous, master. To have refused heed on the ground of the baseness of the witnesses would have doomed a city to starvation and a great soldier to a leper's grave.

When God makes a choice of messengers of high dignity, it must be a word of special import that He has to communicate, and the demand to give heed is the more urgent. The prophets were men who bore the stamp of God upon them, and their words carried the weight of divine authority. But a messenger of higher rank has brought the final word from the eternal throne. "God, who at sundry times and in divers manners spake in time past unto the fathers by the prophets, hath in these last days spoken unto us in his Son. Therefore we ought to give heed more abundantly" (Heb 1:1-2; 2:1, author's trans.).

Among all the former words spoken to the fathers through the prophets, one stands out with unique grandeur—the Law of Sinai. The prophet in this case was, of course, Moses; but in order to add the strength of more lofty sanction to the word of the Law, God gave His angels a part in the solemn transaction. Several Scriptures mention this fact. In his last blessing upon the children of Israel, Moses said,

"The LORD came from Sinai, and rose up from Seir unto them; he shined forth from mount Paran, and he came with ten thousands of saints: from his right hand went [forth] a fiery law for them" (Deut 33:2). The word "saints" here signifies "holy ones," a designation applied to the holy angels.

Stephen, in his magnificent statement before the Sanhedrin, speaking of the great lawgiver, said, "This is he, that was in the church in the wilderness with the angel which spake to him in the mount Sina, and with our fathers: who received the lively oracles to give unto us" (Acts 7:38). He also addressed the Jews as those who had "received the law by the disposition of angels" (v.53).

The apostle Paul declares that the Law "was ordained by angels in the hand of a mediator" (Gal 3:19*b*)—the mediator being Moses. The part played by angels added considerably to the profound awe in which the Jews held the Law of Moses, and rightly so.

Any word of God is steadfast, spoken by the lowliest mortal or the most exalted angel. But one will expect that where God has impressed the importance of a message in such an unusual fashion, its authority will be jealousy guarded. That "the word spoken by angels was stedfast" (Heb 2:2*a*) is made evident by the fact that "every transgression and disobedience received a just recompense of reward" (v. 2*b*). Witness the defiance of Nadab and Abihu in bringing strange fire to the altar, and the swift retribution of devouring fire from the presence of the Lord. Witness the blasphemy of the Egyptian half-breed, with the command to stone him, and the like punishment upon the Sabbath breaker.

Will the word brought by the Lord of the angels be any less steadfast? We have seen how much "better than the angels" is the Son, God's final Messenger, God's final message. If, then, a mighty sanction accompanied the word of the Law given through angels, certainly "we ought to give heed more abundantly to the things that were heard" (Heb 2:1, author's trans.), the things pertaining to grace and life and salvation and holiness, brought to us by Jesus Christ; and "how shall we escape, if we neglect so great salvation?" (2:3*a*).

One should like to dwell on this "so great salvation." It is not surprising, nor is it improper, that preachers should frequently isolate this phrase, holding up the sparkling jewel of salvation, with its radiant facets, before their people. Its greatness is manifold. It is great in its origin, in its plan, in its cost, in its scope, in its operation, in its effectiveness, in its simplicity, in its freeness, in its end. Yet it is to none of these that the apostolic writer appeals as demonstration of the greatness of this salvation, but rather to the Messenger who brought it, and the manner of its heralding. This salvation is of such paramount importance that the triune Godhead is united in its declaration: "having at the first been spoken through the Lord . . . God also bearing witness . . . by gifts of the Holy Spirit" (Heb 2:3*b*-4, ASV). God the Father, God the Son, and God the Holy Spirit join their tireless energies in making effectual the testimony of this salvation at the lips of chosen vessels. It must be an unspeakably great, an unimaginably great, salvation!

We certainly cannot deny the evangelist's right to apply these words to the unsaved. There is nothing in all the world so urgent as the gospel. For one thing, the issues at stake are infinite. No market prince ever transacted so big a piece of business as this; no scientist ever made a discovery comparable in importance; no statesman ever arranged an alliance so vital. If men were wise, they would be willing to lay all worldly business aside to hear the voice of the Son of God. "We ought to give heed more abundantly," for "what shall it profit a man, if he shall gain the whole world, and lose his own soul?" (Mark 8:36).

Many have been brought and held under the influence of the gospel in early days, but instead of giving heed and following through to living faith, have neglected, with the result that in later years they seemed as dark and ignorant of divine things as if they had never heard. They had drifted away. The longer the neglect, the farther the drift. This is a sequence of cause and effect, from which there is no escape.

Some have seen here the picture of a ship drifting away from its moorings, to be inevitably caught in the rapids and dashed to destruction. It is an apt figure. Gospel truth has a way of holding even neglecters to some measure of stability of conduct, but persistent neglect tends to loosen that restraint, till the moorings are severed, and the life is wrecked in sin. Any rescue mission will produce a goodly number of such cases. We can be thankful that some of these, like Augustine, seek again the truth they long neglected, and by earnest heed become fastened to the Rock for ever. But how much sorrow and shame might have been averted had more earnest heed been given in the beginning! Some, alas, never turn again, but neglect till they are caught in the last tide of death, and swept out to judgment. "How shall we escape if we neglect so great salvation?"

Yes, this is a great text for the evangelist, yet it was addressed to believers. "Give heed more abundantly lest we drift! How shall we escape if we neglect?" There are altogether too many neglecting Christians, paying the price of their neglect in loss of joy and peace and power, in a life of pitiable defeat, and whose works shall be burned up as wood, hay, and stubble in the great day of reckoning.

"I have neglected Thee, O God!" cried so sinning and so penitent Bishop Andrewes in his private devotions, and Alexander Whyte adds, "I trembled as I heard him cry it. And I have never come upon that awful word from that day to this without a shudder." This is the cardinal sin of the Christian, and from it stems all the other sins of the saints that bring so much dishonor and reproach. Do you see that saint neglecting God? There is no sin that you may be quite sure he will not commit, whether he be a new babe in Christ or a saint of ripe years. And if you yourself are that saint, think not that there is any sin too gross or too vile for you to stoop to. A neglected God is a neglected salvation, and a neglected salvation means that the defenses are lowered.

Pastor Hsi, that great saint of China, was something of a farmer as well as a preacher. One severe winter, some of his sheep died, and the heathen round about him chided him, saying, "Why did your God not protect your sheep?" These words of reproach distressed the good man, and drove him to prayer. Then he remembered that the sheep which had died were the thin ones; the sheep that had not eaten enough when eating was good, and so had not fattened themselves against the cold of winter. This was the theme of his next sermon. He told his people how sheep must not neglect feeding in season, for they need an excess of fat to protect them from the cold. Had not his sheep paid the price of neglect? Then he continued: "Here we are in the green pastures of our Middle Eden. Every opportunity is given us for feeding on the Word of God and for growing strong in spiritual things. It will not always be so. This is our year of grace. The time will come when we will be scattered, and exposed to persecution and trial in the cold world without. Those who are careless now, and slothful, will then inevitably fail. How are we using our opportunities? You who neglect private prayer, and are inattentive at worship, what will happen to you later, when trouble comes? Your souls, half starved, will be unable to sustain the cruel frosts the devil is sure to send."

Let us heed the godly Chinese pastor's sermon, and his text, "How shall we escape, if we neglect so great salvation?"

4

LORDS OF CREATION

HEBREWS 2:5-10

In this chapter we see:

1. The divine intention
2. The divine frustration
3. The divine realization

WHAT A CONTRADICTION is man! Look at him from one angle and he is a bedraggled creature, "wretched, and miserable, and poor, and blind, and naked" (Rev 3:17), as the Spirit of God describes the Laodiceans. But look again, and you see the stuff of kings in him, some remnant of majesty rebelling against his degradation. This very contradiction appears in one of Robert Burns's more philosophical works. At one point he makes the aged man of the poem say:

> I've seen yon weary winter-sun
> Twice forty times return,
> And ev'ry time has added proofs
> That man was made to mourn.

A few stanzas later the sage reveals the undying protest of his soul:

> If I'm designed yon lordling's slave–
> By nature's law designed–
> Why was an independent wish
> E'er planted in my mind?

One moment, "made to mourn," the next, made to reign! Is there an answer to the riddle? Like all the other really big problems, this finds its answer in the Holy Scriptures, and only there; and the passage before us gathers up the whole answer and gives it to us in a few terse sentences.

"What is man?" (Heb 2:6), cried the psalmist as he contemplated the expanse of heaven; and his words were at once an exclamation and a question. The apostolic writer takes up the cry, to press to its ultimate answer of revelation—he is a king. "Thou madest him a little lower than the angels" (v. 7*a*). The phrase here translated "a little" could grammatically be given the temporal sense as well as the thought of degree, giving us this: "Thou madest him for a little while lower than the angels." Some adopt one reading, some the other. Which is correct? Since the truth lies in both directions, we can well believe that the Holy Spirit had both senses in mind.

We have already been reminded of the exalted nature of the angels, high spiritual intelligences whose proper dwelling is the very presence of the Most High God, and who, because of their nearness to God, share the designations of holiness and divinity. They rank next to God Himself, and now we are informed that man was made but a little lower than they. "And God said, Let us make man in our image, after our likeness" (Gen 1:26). Such a creature could not be much lower than the angels. What a noble creature the first man must have been, as, still untouched by the blight of sin, he walked in holy, intimate communion with God his Maker!

Now consider the divine intention for this man. That phrase "for a little while" suggests that his inferiority to the angels is but a temporary arrangement, and the rest of the passage definitely looks to ultimate superiority. "Thou crownedst him with glory and honor, and didst set him over the works of thy hands: thou didst put all things in subjection under his feet" (Heb 2:7*b*-8*a*, ASV). Now the psalmist's view of the "all things" so subjected to man is limited to the creatures in the air, in the sea, and upon the earth. But that the divine intention went beyond that, to include all created beings, is evident in this additional declaration in the Hebrews passage before us: "Now indeed in subjecting all things to him, he left nothing unsubjected to him" (v. 8*b*, author's trans.). In another place, where the apostle Paul is speaking of a like subjection of all things to Christ, he specifies that the only exception is the One who effects the subjugation: "it is manifest that he is excepted, which did put all things under him" (1 Cor 15:27). So it must be here. The divine intention is to have man stand in rank next to Himself, that man should be lord of all creation, owning one Superior only, God Himself.

When an heir apparent to a throne is born, he is committed to the care of nurses for a time, then to tutors and instructors. While the intention is that he should one day mount the throne, yet during this period of child training he is inferior, at least in the matter of obedience, to those very nurses and masters who one day will offer their homage and service and submission to him as superior. So man was "made a little lower than the angels." Yet are they servants, "sent forth to do service for them who are about to inherit salvation" (Heb 1:14, author's trans.); and when the day of our promotion is come, then will they yield place to those whom they have helped to prepare for the higher rank and dignity.

"But now we see not yet all things subjected to him" (2:8*b*, ASV). Back we come to the contradiction in man. He is both victor and victim, both king and slave. See him in his conquest of nature. He has set himself to have "dominion over the fish of the sea, and over the fowl of the air, and over the cattle, and over all the earth, and over every creeping thing that creepeth upon the earth" (Gen 1:26*b*), till he claims amazing mastery in all the realms of nature.

In the sphere of exploration, man has refused to consider any section of the globe a closed door to him. Torrid deserts and icy wastes are alike beaten to submission. Men will die rather than admit defeat, and others will come after to press the conquest. I have been reading the heroic story of man's grim fight with Mount Everest, the highest peak on this globe. What painstaking organization, what arduous toil, what indomitable courage, what agonies of endurance, what refusals to give up! Then that last glorious but tragic episode—Mallory and Irvine seen for the last time through a break in the mist, within eight hundred feet of their goal, two black spots moving upward, a few steps at a time, then the falling of the curtains of mist upon the lone figures. Was it triumph or tragedy? Did they conquer Everest before Everest beat them to the draw? God alone knows. "The reward of Everest is that the spirit of man has proved itself greater and higher than herself." When a friend asked Mallory, previous to his last attempt, why he was so bent on climbing this mountain, he replied simply, "Because it is there." Aye, that's it. Whatever is, is to be conquered. The stuff of kings is there.

It would be superfluous to dwell on man's conquests in the realm of scientific research, engineering, and such. The bowels of the earth, the depths of the sea, the air, and regions beyond the air have all been forced to yield secrets and render service to man. The long, tragic but glorious story of man's duel with nature substantiates the revelation of God's intention, that man was made to reign.

Yet the story is not one of simple, consistent victory. "We see not yet all things put under him" (Heb 2:8*b*). Nature fights back. Up to a point, the air will submit to bear man up and on in his winged carriage, then she piles herself up into a stone wall to crush him. Or again the atom will yield a little bit of its secret to prying man, only to mock him by becoming an instrument of self-destruction in his hands. Cures for disease and preventives against it are multiplied, but man still returns to the dust whence he came.

There is a strange futility attached to all man's triumphs. Continually advancing, he arrives nowhere. Every new era, hailed as a millennial age, leaves him disillusioned. Is there a reason? Yes, a big reason, but spelled in three letters: S-I-N. Man goes forth conquering but not to conquer, because he has failed to conquer himself, and failing to do that, has become the bondslave of sin. For all the boasted advance of civilization, man himself is not improved. It must still be said of him as God complained of ancient Israel: "The whole head is sick, and the whole heart faint. From the sole of the foot even unto the head there is no soundness in it; but wounds, and bruises, and putrifying sores: they have not been closed, neither bound up, neither mollified with ointment" (Isa 1:5*b*-6). Buchenwald and Dachau are vivid and livid demonstrations that this is so. In view of the wickedness which these names denote, Howard Vincent O'Brien wrote a telling article in the *Chicago Daily News* of October 16, 1946. I quote a few sentences:

> I feel that I have been rudely awakened from a pleasant dream. I had thought that 2,000 years of the Christian faith must surely leave some imprint on the granite of man's nature. And I had believed fondly in the gentle attrition of education.
>
> I had thought that the boundaries of cruelty were slowly being

> pushed back to primitive men, and that the area of enlightenment was increasing.
>
> Now I must face the harsh fact that men who had espoused all the principles of Christ, men who were most learned in the arts and sciences, men who were familiar with ethics and philosophy, men who, on the surface, appeared to be the perfect flowering of what we call civilization, could be more vicious than any creature of the jungle, and as devoid of morals as a stone.*

But this statement made me shudder: "I find myself looking into the faces of people I pass on the street, wondering what dark caverns of bestiality are hidden behind their friendly exterior." Even today "the heart is deceitful above all things, and [it is] desperately wicked" (Jer 17:9). For all the outcroppings of kingliness, indications of high destiny, man is a slave, a minion, a victim. His name is Ichabod, "the glory has departed," and Enosh, "child of weakness."

Does this mean that God's high purpose for man has been frustrated? The divine intention must and will be realized. But how? "We see not yet all things subjected to him. But we behold him who hath been made a little lower than the angels, even Jesus" (Heb 2:8*b*-9*a*, ASV). The answer to all this riddle is—Jesus!

"We behold him who hath been made a little lower than the angels." After telling us all this time how much greater is Jesus than the angels! We were made lower than the angels in our original creation, but He by an act of supreme condescension. What a spectacle it must have been for the angels to behold their Lord rise up from eternal glory to take the form of a servant, to regard Him wrapped in the helpless flesh of a little babe, to see Him enduring hunger and thirst and weariness in our nature, to look upon Him in the unspeakable humiliation and anguish of death!

But—He stoops to conquer! Where fallen man has won half victories with much effort and pain, a word from His lips brought instant obedience; and where we have yielded shameful submission, He triumphed gloriously.

Consider His mastery in the physical realm. With a word He hushed the tempest and calmed the raging waters. By a touch of His hand the leper was cleansed. In His hands the bread and fishes were

*Used by permission.

multiplied for distribution to the hungry multitude. All manner of diseases responded instantly to His touch or command, and even death itself withdrew, yielding up its victims, at His presence.

In other realms His triumphs were even more notable. Demons cringed and fled before Him. The tempter left the field in defeat at every attack, finding no point of weakness in His pure soul. Surrounded on all sides by sin, "in him is no sin" (1 John 3:5), and He did no sin. Having won skirmishes with death in the raising of the daughter of Jairus, the son of the widow of Nain, and Lazarus (and doubtless others unrecorded), He entered the lists with death for Himself, and overcame.

Death cannot keep its prey—
Jesus, my Saviour!
He tore the bars away,
Jesus, my Lord!

Then, as He ascended on high, He despoiled the hosts of hell, principalities and powers, and pursued His victorious way through the heavens, past all ranks of angels, to the throne, where He "sat down on the right hand of the Majesty on high" (Heb 1:3), highly exalted a Prince and Saviour, both Lord and Christ, "being made by so much better than the angels, as he hath inherited a better name than they" (v. 4, author's trans.). This is God's King, the Man Christ Jesus!

Lo, He sits on yonder throne!
Jesus rules the world alone!
Hallelujah!

And when all His enemies shall be made His footstool, when dawns the day of the restitution of all things, when the world that is, with its travail and its curse, gives place to the world that is to be, God's Kingdom perfected and manifested, then

At the name of Jesus every knee shall bow,
Every tongue confess Him, King of glory now;
'Tis the Father's pleasure we should call Him Lord,
Who from the beginning was the mighty Word.

"Not unto angels hath he committed the world to come . . . but we see Jesus" (2:5-9, author's trans.). The lost crown has been recovered, and adorns the worthy brow of Jesus.

Does this mean that the Son of God has taken advantage of our downfall to increase His own glory, seizing our forfeited crown by the subtlety of the incarnation, so that now it is hopelessly and irretrievably lost to us? A thousand times, no! For what does our passage say? "For it became him, for whom are all things, and by whom are all things, in bringing many sons unto glory, to make the captain of their salvation perfect through sufferings" (2:10). All this conflict and conquest was on our behalf. He wrought as our Champion to open for us the way to glory which our sin had blockaded beyond all hope of our breaking through. Consider that "suffering of death" because of which He was "crowned with glory and honour" (2:7, ASV). It was not just to demonstrate His own power over the grave; He was tasting "death for every man" (2:9*b*). All the bitterness of death, of death for sin, of death as judgment, He tasted, for He would not leave death's claim over a single soul unsettled. No man will ever be able to say, "The payment of Calvary did not cover me!" It was there that the Captain of our salvation broke through and opened the highway of victory for us. Let our faith lay hold of the mighty Conqueror at God's right hand, and we shall begin our triumphant climb to the throne. The divine intention is secured; man, in the person of Christ Jesus the Lord, is even now exalted above the high estate of the angels; man, restored in Christ, will yet attain to that lofty place.

We may not press too far the question of the nature of that kingship which we shall exercise in union with our blessed Lord. One thing is certain—our sovereignty will be moral and spiritual. The dominion committed to Adam, and defined again by the psalmist, is but a parable of the vaster, grander dominion for which we are being prepared. God is not leading us this long, costly way of redemption and discipline and sanctification to make us only keepers of immense gardens and vast zoos. God's future for us is commensurate with the stupendous processes of preparation by which He is bringing us to glory. "The world to come" (2:5*b*) is more than this little earth that men are now circling in a few hours. It is all creation, restored and renewed, the everlasting Kingdom of God, in which we shall exercise authority with Christ.

"Not unto angels . . . but we behold . . . Jesus . . . and we shall . . . reign" (2:5*a*-9; 2 Tim 2:12, author's trans.). And here is the secret: we reign in life as we behold Him!

5

A BROTHER TO THE RESCUE

HEBREWS 2:11-18

We consider here:

1. The common bond which made help imperative
2. The common substance which made help possible
3. The common experience which made help real

WHEN ABRAHAM received the news that Lot had been taken in battle with all his household and his substance, the patriarch did not stop to consider his nephew's selfishness, inordinate ambition, and ingratitude. The bond of blood left no place for recrimination or revenge in the day of affliction, but demanded instant action for the release of his brother and the recovery of his goods. Such a bond unites us and Christ, that all consideration of our unworthiness must be swept aside. His brethren need Him—that is the great imperative that fastens upon Him.

The nature of this bond which holds our Lord under obligation to us is declared in these remarkable words: "For both he that sanctifieth and they who are [being] sanctified are all of one" (Heb 2:11). Of one what? The rest of the verse gives the answer: "for which cause he is not ashamed to call them *brethren*" (italics added). Why does He call us brethren? Because He and we are from one *Father!* What a lovely message was that which our Lord sent to His disciples after His resurrection: "Go to my brethren, and say unto them, I ascend unto my Father, and your Father; and to my God, and your God" (John 20:17), as much as to say, "What God is to Me, He is to you also—the Father; and we are brothers!"

Two things must be said about this common bond. First, it does not embrace all men, but only those "who are being sanctified." There is nothing here to warrant such teaching of the universal fatherhood of God and universal brotherhood of man, as we sometimes hear, to the expulsion of the redemptive work of Christ and the regenerative work of the Holy Spirit. Only they who are being sanctified have common parentage with the Sanctifier.

How and when was this relationship established? We read in John's first chapter, "As many as received him, to them gave he power to become the sons of God, even to them that believe on his name" (John 1:12). That has to do with our personal experience of the holy relationship. There is another, and very wonderful, aspect of this truth—the Godward aspect. The heavenly Father has not been wondering all these ages how many sons He would receive from among the children of men, and who they would be! He had His whole family made up beforehand. The divine counsels not only decreed the redemptive work of our Lord Jesus, but its total effect. So the apostle Paul gives us this: "Blessed be the God and Father of our Lord Jesus Christ, who hath blessed us with all spiritual blessings in heavenly places in Christ: according as he hath chosen us in him before the foundation of the world, that we should be holy and without blame before him in love: having predestinated us unto the adoption of children by Jesus Christ to himself, according to the good pleasure of his will" (Eph 1:3-5). From God's side, then, this common parentage existed before the worlds were created, and it was this gracious decree of God that laid the eternal Son under bond to come to the rescue of His brethren, who as yet did not know Him.

How could the eternal Son, "being in the form of God" (Phil 2:6), honor this bond with the chosen sons of earth, held as we were in the captivity of sin, in the yoke of the devil, and in the terror of death? He must reach us where we are, even as Abram went right to the spot where Lot was held captive. Such help as we required must be rendered by one who, while greater than we, is yet one of us, and after our own order. "Forasmuch then as the children are partakers of flesh and blood, he also himself likewise took part of the same" (Heb 2:14*a*). From "the form of God" to the fashion of a man—that was the first stage in the awful descent which our Brother must make to fulfill that obligation which the infinite grace of God to us imposed on Him.

To assume the form of an angel were condescension enough for the Lord of glory, but He passed by their exalted, though to Him inferior, estate, and swept on down to the virgin's womb and the manger of Bethlehem. "For verily not of angels doth he take hold, but of the seed of Abram doth he take hold" (2:16, author's trans.). "The Word was made flesh" (John 1:14).

The ultimate reason for this assumption of our flesh was that Jesus might die. Such was our condition that only an all-covering death could prevail to recover us. His was that death, which purchased back for us all that we had forfeited by our sin.

But a certain specific feature of the redemptive work of Christ is here emphasized. He took our flesh and went forth to death, that, among other benefits secured for us, "he might destroy him that . . . had the power of death, that is, the devil; and deliver them who through fear of death were all their lifetime subject to bondage" (Heb 2:14*b*-15).

Now it is not said here that the death of Christ annihilated the devil, nor that even the ultimate effect of the death of Christ will be the annihilation of the devil. The final destiny of this prince of iniquity is to be "tormented day and night for ever and ever" (Rev 20:10) in the lake of fire. Our text is simply telling us that the devil's occupation as holder of the dominion of death is over by the death of Christ.

In what respect did Satan ever hold the dominion of death? "The wages of sin is death" (Rom 6:23), and so long as he kept men sinning, and so long as the atoning death of Jesus had not been accomplished, Satan could rightly demand the payment of the wages. Perhaps he could be likened to the paymaster. At any rate, while he held the dominion of death, he did not spare its terror. His minions who had served him in sin must feel its sting, its bitterness, its blackness, its hopelessness, and even life itself was tormented by the haunting terror of what lay at the end.

All that is changed for the children of God. Their death is "precious in the sight of the LORD" (Psalm 116:15), and blessed to themselves, as it is written, "Blessed are the dead which die in the Lord from henceforth: Yea, saith the Spirit, that they may rest from their labours; and their works do follow them" (Rev 14:13). And so complete is the saint's deliverance from the fear of death that it is replaced by a sense of exultation at the prospect. "I am in a strait betwixt two," declares the apostle, "having a desire to depart, and to be with Christ; which is [very] far better" (Phil 1:23). This prospect of laying aside the tent of clay for the "house not made with hands, eternal in the heavens" (2 Cor 5:1*b*), is a far cry from the pangs of hell which Satan, as holder of the dominion of death, laid upon the soul drawing nigh unto the grave.

A missionary in China, J. W. Vinson, one of the noble army of martyrs, was asked by his captors if he were afraid. He replied, "No! If you shoot, I go straight to heaven." His heroic testimony inspired the pen of a fellow missionary, a Mr. Hamilton. Two verses of the poem which he wrote express our thought here:

Afraid? Of what?
To feel the spirit's glad release?
To pass from pain to perfect peace,
The strife and strain of life to cease?
Afraid?—of that?

Afraid? Of what?
Afraid to see the Saviour's face,
To hear His welcome, and to trace
The glory gleam from wounds of grace?
Afraid?—of that?

The other verses bear more specifically on the martyrdom. It is of interest to recall that this very poem proved a great encouragement to John and Betty Stam in the dangerous days preceding their own capture and death. "Fear not," says our Lord to us. "I am the . . . Living one; and I was dead, and behold, I am alive for evermore, and I have the keys of death and of Hades" (Rev 1:17-18, ASV). By His one all-covering death He has wrested the dominion of death from our great adversary, and robbed death of its terrors, till we are able to sing, "For through its portals we enter into the presence of the living God. . . . O death, where is thy sting, O grave, where is thy victory!"

The common bond demanded the common substance, and the common substance demanded a common experience. "Wherefore in all things it behoved him to be made like unto his brethren, that he might be a merciful and faithful high priest in things pertaining to

God, to make reconciliation for the sins of the people" (Heb 2:17). Our Lord did not so come into our flesh as to exempt Himself from the severer disciplines of men. He was true man, and was subject to all the natural limitations and distresses of this world. He made Himself so, for our sakes.

Whatever we in this country think of royalty, we shall appreciate the manner in which the king and queen of England shared the privations of their subjects during World War II. When the windows of the king's private apartments in Buckingham Palace were shattered in an air raid, he waited his turn like any private citizen to have them repaired. The royal family received the same ration coupons as any other, and the queen, like many other housewives, saved her meat coupons for a Sunday roast. The blue line around the bathtubs marked the five-inch limit of water for the inhabitants of the palace, the same as allowed to any other Londoner. The great park at Windsor Castle did not escape the plow for growing wheat. Even the king's carriage horses were sent to farm work. The queen personally drove around with a station wagon, gathering paper, bones, and scrap metal in the national drives. She ordered sixty suites of furniture from Windsor Castle to be delivered to poor families in their damaged homes after a specially heavy raid. The poor of London learned not to be surprised to see the king and queen walking among the rubble of their bombed homes. One Londoner said to an American reporter: "They share the same dangers and privations I do. Their home was bombed just like mine."

One is not surprised that this royal couple occupied a place in the hearts of their people. But their touching devotion to their people, and their attempts to be one with them in all the hardships of war, pale before the divine condescension of our Lord, who, emptying Himself of the form of God, took upon Him our flesh, and followed through His humiliation to a complete partnership in all our sorrows, afflictions, and temptations. Hunger, thirst, weariness, disappointment, misunderstanding, calumny, scorn, misrepresentation, persecution, loneliness—all entered into His lot, and in full measure. And all "that he might be a merciful and faithful high priest" (Heb 2:17). If He is going to represent struggling, bewildered, suffering, tempted men before the throne of God, He will do so out of an understanding and sympathy which only experience can give.

Is there any one can help us, one who understands our hearts
When the thorns of life have pierced them till they bleed:
One who sympathizes with us, and in wondrous love imparts
Just the very, very blessing that we need?

Yes, there's one, only one,
The blessed, blessed Jesus, He's the one.
When afflictions crush the soul,
And waves of trouble roll,
And you need a friend to help you, He's the one!

Of special value to us are our Lord's temptations, "For in that he himself hath suffered being tempted, he is able to succour them that are tempted" (2:18). Robert Burns finishes his "Address to the Unco Guid" with these lines:

What's dune we partly may compute,
But know not what's resisted.

That cannot be said of our Lord, who "was in all points tempted like as we are, yet without sin" (4:15*b*). In every case He resisted the full force of temptation, and came off Conqueror. That is why He not only can sympathize, but give effectual aid. The untempted can have no compassion. The conquered can lend no assistance. But the tempted and triumphant Saviour is "our refuge and strength, a very present help in trouble" (Psalm 46:1).

Temptation was no light matter to Jesus. It was positive, downright suffering. His pure soul writhed in the torture of it. What made Him turn so sharply on Simon Peter that day with, "Get thee behind me, Satan" (Matt 16:23) if it were not that Peter's suggestion to avoid the way of the cross constituted a temptation which pained Him to the heart? So our temptations are no light matter to Him, but are His peculiar concern, and He stands ready to champion us against every onslaught. Is it not wonderful to know that all the resources of spiritual power by which our Lord Jesus overcame temptation are ours because we have Jesus Himself? He knows our weakness, but His strength is made perfect in weakness, and we are "more than conquerors through him that loved us" (Rom 8:37).

He was made like us that we might be made like Him; He was made like us in our weakness that we might be made like Him in His power; He was made like us in our sorrows that we might be made like Him in His joy; He was made like us in our temptations that we might be made like Him in His triumphs. Wherefore let us consider Him, our Leader, our Sanctifier, our Brother, our High Priest—the sympathizing Jesus! Bring your burdens to Him, and He will bear them; bring your griefs to Him, and He will assuage them; bring your fears to Him, and He will banish them; bring your temptations to Him, and He will conquer them; bring your sins to Him, and He will blot them out.

There's not a friend like the lowly Jesus,
No, not one!

6

BETTER THAN MOSES

HEBREWS 3:1-6

In this passage we learn that Jesus is greater than Moses:

1. As the Builder is greater than the house
2. As the Son is greater than the servant

IT WAS DIFFICULT for a Jew to contemplate a greater man than Moses. Throughout the long centuries of their changing fortunes, no rival had ever arisen to challenge his supremacy. Samuel, David, Solomon, Elijah, Isaiah, Daniel, the Maccabees—none of these could overshadow the greatness of Moses, nor dim the luster of his name. In the days of our Lord they were still boasting, "We are Moses' disciples" (John 9:28), and coupling the name of Moses with that of God as demanding equal, or nearly equal, reverence. "We have heard him speak blasphemous words against Moses, and . . . God" (Acts 6:11), they declared in framing their accusations against Stephen.

It was no small demand to make upon a Jew, therefore, to ask him to acknowledge Jesus as better than Moses. The miracles of the Galilean might mark Him "a teacher come from God" (John 3:2), as Nicodemus early confessed, but He had wrought no great national deliverance as had Moses. Indeed, He had left His nation as much under the Roman yoke as He found it. While "he taught them as one having authority, and not as the scribes" (Matt 7:29), yet there was no such terrifying sanction of His teaching as accompanied the giving of the Law at Sinai. Jesus had added nothing to the solemn and inspiring ritual of the Temple services, which were only an elaboration of the sacrificial system imposed upon them by the great lawgiver.

Even the Hebrew Christians found themselves falling back upon

Moses, fascinated by his grandeur which the passing of the centuries only enhanced. Under pressure of persuasion or persecution, many of them were sorely tempted to abandon their Christian faith. How could such defections be avoided, and professors of the name of Jesus be kept from apostasy? This remarkable letter gives the answer in two words: Consider Him!

Why all our weakness, all our backsliding, all our ineffectiveness, all our confusion, all our gullibility? Why do so many professing Christians go back to their old ways or turn aside to strange doctrines? Because there is so little occupation with Christ. If all believers would heed the exhortation to consider Him, to set our minds down upon Him in earnest study of His person, character, offices, and ministries, the church of Jesus would go forth "fair as the moon, clear as the sun, and terrible as an army with banners" (Song of Sol 6:10). Dwelling on earthly things, our souls turn to clay; occupied with systems, we run to tangents; considering Him, we become "stedfast, unmoveable, always abounding in the work of the Lord" (1 Cor 15:58).

> What doth strip the seeming beauty
>   From the idols of the earth?
> Not a sense of right or duty,
>   But a sight of Peerless Worth.
>
> 'Tis that look that melted Peter,
>   'Tis that face that Stephen saw,
> 'Tis that heart that wept with Mary
>   Can alone from idols draw,—
>
> Draw and win and fill completely,
>   Till the cup o'erflows its brim.
> What have we to do with idols
>   Since we've companied with Him?

All that has been said of Jesus in the first two chapters of the epistle is preparatory for the consideration to which we now come. It is neither prophets nor angels, but Moses, who is proving the unwilling rival of the Lord Jesus, the Mosaic system, which is holding men from the full freedom of the Christian faith. Jesus, then, must finally be set forth in His superiority to the older economy.

"Consider the Apostle and High Priest of our confession . . . Jesus"

(Heb 3:1, ASV). These two titles immediately throw Jesus and Moses into comparison. For Moses also was the apostle of God to the nation of Israel to deliver it from sore bondage, and to lead it out to freedom; and it was under the hand of Moses that the priesthood was established in Aaron and his sons. Even before Moses is mentioned, however, Jesus gains by the suggested comparison. While Moses exercised priestly functions during the period of organization, he was commanded to hand over the sacred office of the priesthood to another. Thus, in the old order the apostolate and the priesthood were divided. In Jesus, the final apostolate and the perfect priesthood combine.

When the inspired writer finally introduces the name of Moses, it is with the utmost deference and consummate courtesy. Indeed, the superiority of Jesus is never secured, throughout this epistle, by derogatory suggestions concerning others, as is so much the way with men. You know how political campaigns are carried on, for instance: Mr. Brown goes out to prove that Mr. White is black, while Mr. White demonstrates that Mr. Brown is yellow. That is the principle. Not so in the Word of God. In demonstrating that Jesus is better than the prophets, there is no slight cast upon the prophets; God spoke through them also. Likewise the angels are not despised in order to exalt Jesus; they are swift as the winds, mighty as consuming flames. So the first thing said about Moses is that he was a pattern of faithfulness, even for the Son of God! Notice how remarkable is the order: not, "Moses was faithful, as was Christ," but, "Christ was faithful, as was Moses" (Heb 3:1*a*-2, author's trans.). Here is high commendation indeed!

Now one would think that, where the superiority of Jesus is being argued, this would be a logical place to bring in the failures and mistakes of Moses, but there is not a word of them here. Some years ago I preached three sermons at the Canadian Keswick Conference on "The Mistakes of Moses." They were the mistake of haste in his youth, the mistake of hesitancy in middle life, and the mistake of heat in old age. Dr. R. V. Bingham, who was still with us then, remarked rather facetiously, "What about the mistakes of Joseph?" (My name is Joseph!) A good thought that, when we are given to criticism of others for purposes of self-exaltation! Here the Spirit of holiness, in exalting Jesus so far above all others, has not a word to say about the weaknesses of the prophets, the rebellion of some of the angels, or the mistakes of

Moses. "Let your speech be always with grace, savored with salt" (Col 4:6, author's trans.).

The essential element in the superiority of Jesus over Moses in all the house of God is His superior relationship to it. "This man was counted worthy of more glory than Moses, by how much he who established the house has more honor than the house" (Heb 3:3, author's trans.). A man is always greater than his work. Shakespeare is greater than his plays; Sir Christopher Wren is greater than St. Paul's Cathedral; Rembrandt is greater than his portraits; Bach is greater than his fugues. The man expresses himself in his works, pours himself into them, yet remains apart from them, a potential of yet greater accomplishment. Let us say, then, that Moses was greater than his actual labors. The fact still remains that, however honorable his place in the house of God, he was still part of it. On the other hand, Jesus, however closely identified with the house of God, is yet its Builder, and therefore transcends it.

The transcendent greatness of Jesus is further indicated by a most suggestive verse: "For every house is built by somebody, but he who built all things is in his very nature God" (Heb 3:4, author's trans.). As much as to say: men build things according to their own nature and ability, but are dependent on One greater than themselves to establish the works of their hands; and there are some things beyond the range of human power and skill, and in these we are dealing solely with One who in essence and nature is very God. The house of God is just such an institution. Human hands may labor within the building, as part of it, but the Builder is God. Thus by implication the sacred writer is informing us that the supremacy of Jesus ultimately rests on this: that Jesus is God.

As the builder is greater than the house, so is Christ greater than Moses. That would seem sufficient, but the argument is pressed still further. The excellency of Jesus over Moses is that of a son over a servant in the Father's house. In developing this point, the same respectful attitude toward Moses is maintained. Not only is the faithfulness of this great servant given repeated emphasis, but the very word for "servant" is an exceedingly honorable one. It is not *doulos,* indicating the bond servant, nor *diakonos,* one appointed to run on errands, nor even *huperetes,* a subordinate, but *therapon,* one who renders free service, constrained by duty or love. Only here is this word used in the New Testament, being taken over from the Septuagint version of Numbers 12:7, where God is defending Moses against the complaints of Miriam and Aaron: "If there be a prophet among you, I the LORD will make myself known unto him in a vision, and will speak unto him in a dream. *My servant Moses is not so, who is faithful in all* . . . [my] *house.* With him will I speak mouth to mouth, even apparently, and not in dark speeches; and the similitude of the LORD shall he behold: wherefore then were ye not afraid to speak against my servant Moses?" (Num 12:6-8, italics added). The writer to the Hebrews remembered this, and gave Moses every honor due. But however free, honorable, and faithful the service rendered, it left Moses still a servant in the house, while Jesus rules over the house as Son and Lord.

But what is the house of God? It is both interesting and instructive to notice that no distinction is drawn between the house of God in which Moses served and the house of God over which Christ rules. I cannot accept the suggestion that His "house" means first the tabernacle in the wilderness, then the material universe, then the New Testament church. That is reading a system of doctrine into the text. The house of God is one. It was in process of building before Moses came on the scene, but under his hand it took a form and received an expression till then unknown. All the time the Word, who was with God and was God, was the Builder. Then He Himself came, and added yet another form to the house of God, of which the former was the promise and type. He is still building, and when the New Jerusalem comes down from heaven, the completed work will be seen, the house of God, the city of God, the Kingdom of God, the economy of God, whose twelve gates carry the names of the twelve ancient tribes, and whose twelve foundations bear the names of the twelve apostles of the new covenant.

Moses served in *all* the house. He served those who went before and those who came after. He served the new covenant even in administering the old covenant. Likewise the sonship of Jesus establishes Him as Lord, not only of the New Testament house, but of the whole house. He is Moses' Lord, and Elijah's Lord. There are no rival houses in the Kingdom of God. This whole passage is dead against the idea that Moses built one house and Jesus built another. There is one house, of which Jesus is the Builder and over which, as Son, He rules, while Moses, as part of the building, is an honored servant—so honored, indeed, that the completed house will resound with "the song of Moses the . . . [man] of God, and the song of the Lamb" (Rev 15:3).

"Whose house are we" (Heb 3:6), in company with all the saints, "built upon the foundation of the apostles and prophets, Jesus Christ himself being the chief corner stone; in whom all the building fitly framed together groweth unto an holy temple in the Lord: in whom ye also are builded together for an habitation of God through the Spirit" (Eph 2:20-22).

Yes, all that "if we hold fast the confidence and the boast of hope" (Heb 3:6, author's trans.). For there is a confession of Christ which is spurious, shallow, fickle, which is not the work of the Holy Spirit. The test of a true confession is its permanence. Confidence in Christ endures when mere profession of religion gives way before the pressure of temptation, persecution, and affliction. Much shale lies around the house of God, but only granite is in the building. Many so-called "backsliders" are resting in the false security of a spurious "once saved, always saved" doctrine, mistaking some emotional experience, now evaporated, for salvation. Equally deluded are the "saved today, lost tomorrow" variety. Whatever you have today which can be lost tomorrow may be religion, may be reformation, but it is not salvation. God is not building living stones into His house to pull them out again. "The gifts and calling of God are without repentance" (Rom 11:29). Permanence is the mark of God's work. "Whose house are we, if we hold fast the confidence and the rejoicing of the hope" (Heb 3:6).

Jesus is greater than Moses, as the Builder is greater than the house, as the Son is better than the servant. What an encouragement to the wavering faith of those first-century Hebrew Christians! And what a fortifying of our faith in this confused twentieth century! By such assurances the "holy brethren, partakers of a heavenly calling" (3:1, ASV), are sustained as living stones in the everlasting temple.

7

THE HEART THAT KNOWS NOT REST

HEBREWS 3:7-19

We learn that the heart without rest is:

1. The erring heart that misconstrues God
2. The hardened heart that provokes God
3. The unbelieving heart that abandons God

REST IS A CONDITION of the heart. It is the reposc of the spirit in God. It is first an attribute of God, and then the gift of God, reserved for those who seek after Him, wait upon Him, and fully trust Him. George Herbert poetically imagines God pouring His rich bounties upon His creature, man, out of "a glass of blessings," until only one was left.

When almost all was out, God made a stay,
Perceiving that alone of all His treasure,
  Rest in the bottom lay.

  For if I should (said He)
Bestow this jewel also on my creature,
He would adore my gifts instead of Me,
And rest in Nature, not the God of Nature,
  So both should losers be.

  Yet let him keep the rest,
But keep them with repining restlessness:
Let him be rich and weary, that at least,
If goodness lead him not, yet weariness
  May toss him to My breast.

All of which is the poet's way of telling us that rest is found, not in God's bounties, but in God Himself.

From the beginning God has been calling men to rest, to share the deep repose of His own infinite nature in a life of communion with Him. To this rest He called Israel in the days of Moses and Joshua. He called them in David, and in the prophets. Listen to His plaintive cry in Jeremiah 6:16: "Thus saith the LORD, Stand ye in the ways, and see, and ask for the old paths, where is the good way, and walk therein, and ye shall find rest for your souls." Then hear Him in the beloved Son, calling, not to Israel alone, but to all men: "Come unto me, all ye that labour and are heavy laden, and I will give you rest. Take my yoke upon you, and learn of me; for I am meek and lowly in heart: and ye shall find rest unto your souls" (Matt 11:28-29).

But Israel under Moses did not enter into rest; nor under Joshua; nor at the pleadings of Jeremiah; nor at the call of the Saviour Himself. And to this day multitudes hear the word, but it falls strangely on their ears. They seek rest and find it not, yet turn away from Him who longs to bestow it. Surely the heart of man is given over to folly.

"He brought them out that He might bring them then in." Out of sore bondage He brought them, that they might be God's free men; out of deep humiliation, that they might "walk on their high places" (see Hab 3:19); out of grinding poverty, that they might possess the land "flowing with milk and honey" (Exod 3:8); out of wearisomeness without respite that they might enter into the rest of God. With strong hand He brought them out, and with a mighty arm would He bring them in. The wonders that He showed in Egypt, the way by which He led them through the sea, the miraculous provision which He made for them in the wilderness, the wall of protection that He threw around them, all bespoke His power and His faithfulness to fulfill His promises to this people whom He had chosen for Himself. Yet they entered not in. Not only so, we hear God taking an oath that they shall not enter in. "But as truly as I live, all the earth shall be filled with the glory of the LORD. Because all those men which have seen my glory, and my miracles, which I did in Egypt and in the wilderness, and have tempted me now these ten times, and have not hearkened to my voice; surely they shall not see the land which I sware unto their fathers, neither shall any of them that provoked me see it" (Num 14:21-23). It is this reversal of decision, this "breach of promise," that is recalled in the ninety-fifth Psalm, which in turn is quoted in our Hebrews passage: "So I sware in my wrath, They shall not enter into my rest" (Heb 3:11), or, "if they shall enter into my rest," for the Greek follows the Hebrew idiom of the conditional in an oath. Why the failure to enter in? And why the solemn oath barring their entrance? In answering this question the Holy Spirit mentions three states of heart which logically follow one another, and end in spiritual disaster.

Look at the first—not first mentioned, but first in order of development: the erring heart that misconstrues God. "They did not recognize my ways" (3:10, author's trans.). Immediately we think of that word of the psalmist, "He made known his ways unto Moses, his acts unto the children of Israel" (Psalm 103:7). The acts of God were perfectly evident to the children of Israel. They saw His wonders of judgment in Egypt. They saw the sea stand on heaps to give them an highway as on dry land. They saw the mighty walls of water close down on their pursuers. They saw the manna morning by morning lying like white dew throughout all their camp. They saw the waters gushing forth from the rock in response to the smiting rod of Moses. They saw the defeat of warlike Amalek in that so unequal battle. They saw Mount Sinai all afire with the presence of God. Yes, the acts of God they saw, but they did not see the ways of God in all these. They failed to mark the direction in which all these pointed. They could not read the character of God and the purposes of God in all these. They lacked the synthetic sense. They could not put two and two together. They discerned no pattern in these manifestations of divine power and bounty and faithfulness. Moses, the man of the mountains, the man in communion with God—he saw the pattern, the direction, the unity of the acts, and walked in the majesty of a great calm, while the multitude of the people failed to catch the vision of the far horizons. What they saw of God's works they did not build into a great assurance of faith. The letters which read for Moses, as afterward for Paul, "All things work together for good to them that love God, to them who are . . . called according to his purpose" (Rom 8:28), were only a mixed alphabet to those spiritually incapable people.

With what result? They always erred in their hearts. Every fresh test, every new trial, instead of being filled with expectancy, was made an occasion for new murmuring and repining, till even the blessings were despised. They never carried over remembrance of former mercies and bounties and deliverances and providings as bulwarks against fear and faithlessness in presence of a new need. Therefore, when they might have been forestalling Cowper in singing,

> His love in time past
>   Forbids me to think
> He'll leave me at last
>   In trouble to sink;
> Each sweet Ebenezer
>   I have to review
> Confirms His good pleasure
>   To see me right through—

they were filling all the camp with their desolate complaints and rebellious speeches. How could such enter into rest?

A short time ago I was requested to go to a certain hospital to inform an elderly patient of the death of her husband, also a patient in the same hospital. Both had been there many months. A young lady, closely connected with the family, accompanied me. On the way to the hospital, she expressed the wish that she could have the faith of the one we were going to see. When I told her that she could, and tried to show her the way, she replied that she could have no faith after seeing what this old couple, who never harmed anyone, had suffered in the past several years. That was the erring heart that misconstrued God. Despite many gospel opportunities, she was blind to the ways of God with His children, and so assumed a wrong attitude, a rebellious attitude, toward God. It was evident enough that she had no rest of heart.

We proceeded to the hospital. I had never met the lady, but quickly saw that she was a most kindly soul. Of course the news I had to impart was heavy news to her, all the more so for being unexpected. She was overwhelmed for a few minutes, but before I left that hospital ward, she was quietly singing the great hymns of assurance, while the others in the room sobbed, and I could not restrain the tears. When I saw her again a few days later, she was so gentle. She said, "My dear Ed is just upstairs. That is how I think of him. Upstairs with Jesus! And I'll go upstairs soon." Then she started to sing, "Face to face with

Christ my Saviour." She knew God's ways, and her heart was at rest.

From the erring heart that misunderstands God there develops the hardened heart that provokes God. "Today, if ye shall hear his voice, harden not your hearts, as in the provocation, according to the day of temptation, when your fathers tempted me, in putting me to the proof" (Heb 3:7-9, author's trans.). This passage, like the psalm from which it is quoted, looks back to two incidents in Israel's wilderness journeys, one before they arrived at Sinai, and the other near the end of the years of wandering. The first took place at Rephidim, where no water was found. Instead of taking this as an occasion to wait upon the Lord in humble expectancy, considering how wonderfully He had provided the daily manna, the people not only gave way to fear and anxiety, but bitterly upbraided Moses, accusing him of incompetence and insincerity. "Wherefore is this that thou hast brought us up out of Egypt, to kill us and our children and our cattle with thirst?" (Exod 17:3). They even accompanied their taunts with threatening gestures, so that Moses cried to God, "They be almost ready to stone me" (v. 4). See how completely they had forgotten God, seeing only Moses! Nevertheless, God was long-suffering, and gave them water out of the flinty rock at the hand of Moses. "And he called the name of the place Massah, and Meribah, because of the chiding of the children of Israel, and because they tempted the LORD, saying, Is the LORD among us, or not?" (v. 7). For *Massah* signifies *temptation,* and *Meribah* means *chiding,* or *strife.*

The later incident also concerned water for the congregation. This time Aaron shared with Moses the bitter reproaches of an ungrateful, hardened people, who chided them with failure to make good the promises of a land abounding in figs and vines and pomegranates. "There is not even water to drink," they railed, "and we are brought here to perish!" (see Num 20:2-5). This place also was called Meribah, on account of the strife of the people.

These two incidents are taken up by the Holy Spirit as typical of the hardness of heart which the children of Israel manifested throughout all God's dealings with them. The Hebrew psalm recalls the events under the very names given to the two places: "Today, if ye shall hear his voice, harden not your heart, as at Meribah, as in the day of Massah in the wilderness" (Psalm 95:7-8, author's trans.).

The Hebrews passage, following the Greek version of the psalm, translates the proper names: "Today, if ye shall hear his voice, harden not your hearts, as in the embitterment, according to the day of temptation in the wilderness" (Heb 3:7-8, author's trans.).

How did such hardness of heart affect God? "I was disgusted with that generation" (3:10, author's trans.), He declares. Such forgetfulness of His bounties, such rebellion against His disciplines, such refusals to be corrected, such distrust of His ways, such thwartings of His purposes, He could not endure. His long-sufferings are wonderful, His mercy is great, but at last there comes the solemn oath, "They shall not enter into my rest" (3:11).

It is no light thing to provoke God, and nothing so much provokes Him as the hardened heart. When a man starts hardening his heart, God is provoked to help along the hardening process, to that man's destruction. That is what happened to Pharaoh. He hardened his heart against God's commands. Then God hardened his heart, in preparation for the judgments which came upon him. "It is a fearful thing to fall into the hands of the living God" (10:31). Beware of the hardened heart which provokes God!

On the basis of this Old Testament example, the New Testament writer issues his solemn warning to the Hebrews of the first century A.D., and to all men of this age of grace. "Beware of the erring heart that misconstrues God, and of the hardened heart that provokes God, lest, as a consequence of these, there be in anyone among you a wicked heart of unbelief manifested in a definite departure, an act of apostasy, from the living God" (3:12, author's trans.). The others are indeed stages of unbelief, bearing their own bitter fruit; and part of this fruit is this final stage of unbelief, in which there are not merely misconceptions of God which lead to false attitudes, and rebellion against God's ways in murmurings and disobedience, but a definite casting of God out of the life, a refusal to know Him or have any dealings with Him. Beware, then, of unbelief in its incipient stages, and it will not get you in its final damnation.

Some regard unbelief as a mark of superior intellect, but God defines it as a mark of the wicked heart. Following the declarations of Scripture, Principal Cairns of Edinburgh used to insist that "the causes of unbelief were chiefly of a moral and spiritual nature, having their home in man's heart, and removable only by the grace of God." An outstanding American lawyer, Irwin Linton, who used to write valuable articles for the *Sunday School Times,* declared after many years of experience with agnostics and atheists that he had never yet dealt with one who had examined the case for Christianity. They had read Tom Paine, Bob Ingersoll, and others of that school, but were ignorant even of the existence of such works as Paley's *Evidences* and Nelson's *Cause and Cure of Infidelity.* Everything hinges on the state of the heart. The word of Jesus still stands as a challenge to all unbelief: "If any man wills to do His (God's) will, he shall know of the doctrine, whether it be of God" (John 7:17, author's trans.).

Unbelief is the supreme sin, and it is violently deceptive. It is this particular sin against whose trickery we are warned. It does not make a frontal attack and suddenly overthrow the citadel of the soul, but enters the heart hidden in some Trojan horse of fair desire. That desire being incompatible with the lordship of Jesus Christ in the life, there arises conflict, which finally must be settled by the expulsion of one or the other—the sinful desire or God. Then it is that unbelief makes its bold encounter, not from without, but from within, proposing itself as the only way to end the struggle. The heart, married to its sin, falls for the deceit, and the breach is made: the wicked heart of unbelief apostatizes from God, departs from Him, and the ruined soul sinks to its eternal doom. Beware of this cunning of unbelief, lest, despising the tender offers of mercy, you be embraced in the awful oath of God: "They shall not enter into my rest" (Heb 3:11). But the rather, "To day, if ye will hear his voice, harden not your hearts" (3:7-8). Today, if you shall hear Him say, "Come unto me, all ye that labour and are heavy laden, and I will give you rest," hasten to Him, "and ye shall find rest unto your souls" (Matt 11:28-29).

8

GOD'S REST FOR GOD'S PEOPLE

HEBREWS 4:1-11

In this brief meditation we consider:

1. The nature of the divine rest
2. The secret of the divine rest
3. The realization of the divine rest

"HE HAD FOR WEARY FEET the gift of rest." Such was William Watson's explanation of Wordsworth's fascination, despite his lack of many qualities possessed by other poets. "But," says Dr. Jowett, "his gift of rest is a holiday; we want the rest of the eternal, the changeless rest."

It is this changeless rest that God is offering men, even pressing upon us with gracious urgency. For it is no product of man. It is God's own rest, which issues from the utter perfections of His character. He is able to view with limitless complacency the works of His hands and pronounce them "very good"; He is able to contemplate His purposes with complete certainty, "declaring the end from the beginning" (Isa 46:10), knowing that no part will fail of realization.

There can be no perfect rest without such complacency and such certainty, and these we cannot know in considering our own works and our own purposes. Our past and our future can afford us little rest. In this we may allow Robert Burns to be our spokesman:

> But och! I backward cast ma e'e
> On prospects drear;
> An' forward, though I canna see,
> I guess, an' fear.

The way of rest, then, is turning from ourselves, with our imperfect works and our uncertain plans, and looking to God in all trust and obedience. That was the way for the Israel that went out of Egypt with Moses, but, not accepting the way, they fell in the wilderness. The same way of rest was offered the Israel that entered Canaan with Joshua, but they too failed, and instead of rest found constant strife, as the book of the Judges testifies. The same way of rest was offered to Israel under David, but despite many mercies they plunged into the ways of disobedience and apostasy.

Such failure after failure to enter into rest is enough to make us wonder if the way of rest is now closed. "No," urges our apostolic writer, "it is more open than ever, but the danger of missing it is just as great as ever." So he would stir in us a holy fear of losing out by copying the unbelief of those whose perverse behavior called forth the oath of God barring them from the divine rest. For the fault lay not in the message delivered them, but in the lack of the "mixing" element of faith. Hearing plus believing equals rest.

The corollary of this insistence on faith as the way into rest is that we do not enter into rest by our own works, but only as we abandon them. This suggests the thought of a Sabbath keeping, to which we are introduced, not in the Law of Moses, but in God's own rest after the work of creation. "God did rest the seventh day from all his works" (Heb 4:4*b*). In this case the cessation of work was not based on the futility of all the labor, but on the completion of the task, and delight in the finished product. It was a glad Sabbath which God kept.

We know how stringent were the rules governing the Sabbath in Israel. Our modern blue laws cannot compare with the strictness of the ancient observance. All that was not without its value as a parable of New Testament truth. It tells us that God's rest is realized only as we completely abandon our own works, because of their futility, because the stain of sin is upon them. So while we cease from our own works, "as God . . . from his" (4:10*b*), it is for an altogether different reason.

But rest must be based on work. God's rest was the crown of His own work, and if we are to enter into rest, it must be on the ground of some accomplished work: if not our own, then another's. We cease from our own works to rest in God's. We turn from our own imperfect, unavailing labors to find our perfect rest in the finished work of the cross, and our certainty in the sure purposes of God.

> Not the labors of my hands
> Can fulfill Thy law's demands;
> Could my zeal no respite know,
> Could my tears forever flow,
> All for sin could not atone;
> Thou must save, and Thou alone!

John Barridge, a close friend of George Whitefield in the days of the great awakening, was a vicar in the Church of England, deeply devoted to his church and to his parishioners. He strove to live an exemplary life, and tirelessly exhorted his people to the same. But for all his preaching and labor, his congregation continued in a most unsanctified state. In his discouragement he began to wonder if he were right himself, so he gave himself to prayer, on this order: "Lord, if I am all right, keep me so; if I am not right, make me so." One day as he meditated and prayed, the voice of the Spirit spoke within his mind: "Cease from thy works and believe only." The failure of his life and ministry was immediately spread before him. From that hour, restless striving gave place to trustful rest, and he went forth in the strength of the Lord to new victory and usefulness.

To cling to our own works is an act of unbelief and disobedience which must have the same consequences as befell the unbelieving Israelites of other days. No diligence should be wanting to see that we are not clinging to false hopes, but that we have found the true rest of God.

If rest, in all its fullness and perfection, were realized here, we should have little desire for "the better land." Such a danger is not allowed to beset us. However deeply we may experience God's rest in our hearts, we are still exposed to temptations, toils, and tribulations while we sojourn in this world, enough to give a future tense to the verse, "There remaineth therefore a Sabbath-keeping to the people of God" (Heb 4:9, author's trans.).

> I thank Thee, Lord, that Thou hast kept
> The best in store.
> We have enough, yet not too much
> To long for more,

A yearning for a deeper peace
  Not known before.

I thank Thee, Lord, that here our souls,
  Though amply blessed,
Can never find, although they seek,
  A perfect rest,
Nor ever shall, until they lean
  On Jesus' breast.

9

WE HAVE AN HIGH PRIEST

HEBREWS 4:14-16

In this chapter we contemplate:

1. The dignity of our High Priest
2. The compassion of our High Priest
3. The sufficiency of our High Priest

THE HIGH PRIESTHOOD of Jesus is the main theme of this letter to the Hebrews, yet the writer comes up to it slowly and by degrees. His first hint is a reference to the priestly function of making purification of sins, given in the opening verses of the book where Jesus is presented as the full and final revelation of God. Not before the end of the second chapter is the office of high priest referred to specifically, where the qualifications of Jesus are under review. The third chapter opens with a call to contemplate Him in His twofold office as Apostle and High Priest, but immediately comparison is drawn between Him and Moses, the apostle of the old covenant; and not till after the long digression on entering God's rest are we recalled to the proposed consideration of Jesus, our High Priest.

Before opening his main topic, the sacred writer has brought us face to face with our need of a great high priest. He has made us tremble before the sharp, penetrating, searching Word of God and laid us low beneath the inescapable eyes of the Almighty. We can defend ourselves with some success against the criticisms of our fellows. We can at least throw the stones back that they hurl at us. But the Word of God is a critic which finds us out, strips us of our defensive coverings, and leaves us "naked and exposed unto the eyes of him with whom we have to do business" (Heb 4:13, author's trans.). It is a terrible picture. We can almost feel our necks bared for the stroke of the avenging sword! Then immediately the scene changes, and we behold our great High Priest, Jesus, the Son of God. That is the end of fear. From here on our vocabulary stresses new words. Sympathy, confidence, grace, mercy, help—these give a new tone to the passage, and become the big words in our experience.

At last, then, we come to "consider the . . . High Priest of our confession" (3:1, ASV), and the first thing we are here asked to ponder is His exalted state. "We have a great high priest, that is passed through the heavens" (4:14, author's trans.).

The high priest of ancient Israel passed through the veil into the holiest of all one day in the year, the great Day of Atonement. It was a solemn moment, both for himself and for all Israel, when he drew aside that curtain and entered the inner sanctuary, where the Shekinah glory rested upon the Mercy Seat of the Ark of the Covenant. There he presented the blood of atonement, and thence returned to the people with the benediction of God. That act laid a dignity upon the high priest which lifted him above all others of the nation. Even the king waited upon that mediatorial work.

Enlightened Hebrews realized the temporariness of such an arrangement. After all, that was but a veil of cloth, woven, however skillfully, by human hands, and it gave access to a holy place made with hands, which could not be regarded as the real residence of the living God, who fills all things. All this Solomon freely expressed at the dedication of the Temple, that magnificent and beautiful structure. Then, too, the great solemnity of the occasion could not hide the fact that the high priest entered that holy place for but a few moments, to await the passing of another year before repeating the same ministry.

If the first-century Hebrew Christians were inclined to look longingly back to the elaborate and stirring ritual of the Day of Atonement, here was a word to assure them that, so far from losing anything in the changeover from the Temple to the church, they had gained immeasurably. As the heavens exceed a curtain in glory, by so much is Jesus greater than the high priests of old. They passed through the veil, He through the heavens. The better thing had come with Jesus.

The Jews were wont to talk about seven heavens, though without scriptural warrant. The apostle Paul speaks about the third heaven, into which he was caught up on the occasion of very special exultation and revelation. In the same passage he tells also of being caught up into Paradise, where he heard things "unlawful for a man to utter" (2 Cor 12:4, author's trans.). Whether he means to identify the third heaven with Paradise or to distinguish the two is not quite clear. Attempts have been made to define the three heavens as aerial, sidereal, and celestial: the atmospheric heaven, the element of all flying things; the region of the stars, much vaster than we can comprehend; and above all (if we can use prepositions in such a case!), the abode of God and the holy angels, where also the redeemed have their eternal home.

However this may be, there are the heavens, and there is a realm "far above all heavens" (Eph 4:10), which is yet known as "heaven itself" (Heb 9:24). The passage of Jesus, our great High Priest, was "through the heavens" (4:14, ASV), "far above all heavens," into "heaven itself," where the eternal glory of God enswathes the throne of infinite majesty.

Think of the magnificent and complete triumph involved in that passage "through the heavens." Remember that He came into this world with respect to sin. Himself knowing no sin, He yet took upon Him a world's sin. That means that the heaven of heavens is barred and bolted and locked against Him until He has made away with that awful burden. Unless He can offer a sacrifice for sin sufficient to cover all, He must be the everlasting derelict, heaven's vagabond, filling the vaults of the universe with an eternal cry, "My God, my God, why hast thou forsaken me?" (Matt 27:46). But that cry is only for an infinite moment, while the sacrifice is being offered, the price paid, reconciliation effected; and then, having "put away sin by the sacrifice of himself" (Heb 9:26), He passes through the heavens, amid the Hosannas of the celestial hosts, to His seat at the Father's right hand.

His procession through the heavens marks also His triumph over death and hell, and all the powers of darkness. He has met death in its own tilting ground, and come forth the Victor. He has put His boast beyond dispute: "I am the resurrection and the life; if a man believe in me, though he die, yet shall he live; and whosoever liveth and believeth in me shall never die" (John 11:25-26, author's trans.). As Vanquisher of death, He mounts the stairway of the skies, Forerunner of the multitudes of the redeemed snatched from the jaws of death.

The Captain of our salvation did not ascend to His seat of glory without grim encounter with the prince of darkness and his hosts. Again and again the great enemy came to the attack, only to be hurled back in defeat. Then came the ascent to the cross, and as He went, our conquering Saviour shouted His battle cry, "Now is the judgment of this world: now shall the prince of this world be cast out" (John 12:31). Then He stooped to conquer, and turned His own cross into a battle-ax for the destruction of the kingdom of Satan. Now the risen Redeemer of man mounts the ascension chariot. The baffled hierarchy of hell raises futile opposition, but He thrusts them from Him as one would scorn a polluted garment, and passes through the heavens. "Lift up your heads, O ye gates; even lift them up, ye everlasting doors; and the King of glory shall come in. Who is this King of glory?" (Psalm 24:9-10*a*). He is Jesus, the Son of God, our great High Priest!

Lest we should think that such exaltation would set a distance between us and our High Priest, we are now reassured of His tender and understanding sympathy. "We have not an high priest unable to suffer along with our weaknesses, but one who has been tempted in all ways in keeping with his likeness (to us), without sin" (Heb 4:15, author's trans.). This is the very point that was made in that first definite reference to the priesthood of Jesus, back in the second chapter of the epistle: "Wherefore in all things it behoved him to be made like unto his brethren, that he might be a merciful and faithful high priest in things pertaining to God" (2:17). Only now it is shown that being made like us involved Him in a round of temptations which gives Him experimental knowledge of our conflicts, so that His sympathy is not just the pity of an omniscient onlooker, but the compassion of a fellow sufferer. "In all things" He was made "like unto his brethren," and every point of likeness meant such temptations as beset us at that point. Sinless flesh was exposed to all the temptations of sinful flesh, and they were all the more poignant and grievous to Him by reason of His keener perception and perfect recoil and complete resistance.

"Without sin." That means more than that He did not sin by responding to the temptations. It means that the temptations left His sinlessness intact, unshaken, undisturbed. The story of the temptation in the wilderness reveals how desperately Satan tried to break through the defenses of our Saviour's soul, but not a breach was made in them, not a flaw was discovered in His spiritual armor. He shared our natural weaknesses, and these were targets of the adversary, occasions of temptation, but never causes of sin. See, then, how He is exactly the High Priest we need—one with us in our infirmities, that He may suffer with us; but without infirmity, that He may prevail in our behalf.

Dr. Stuart Nye Hutchison has given us the story of a boy who had lost his right hand, and was so humiliated that he wanted nobody to see him. When his father suggested bringing the minister, the boy rebelled. The father, however, followed his own counsel and brought the minister. As the visitor entered the house, the boy noticed that he had no right hand. There was an immediate bond of sympathy between the two, and when the minister said, "I know how it feels," the boy knew he had a friend indeed. Now that is a beautiful example of the power of common suffering to draw hearts together, but it will never do as an illustration of our High Priest. Assuredly we must have one who has been through the battle, the thickest and the hottest of it, and scars there may be, but if He be maimed as I am, He needs my help as much as I need His. He must know the heat of temptation, but if He be seared by it, He can do me no good. But it is not thus with Jesus. He has been "in all points tempted like as we are, yet without sin" (Heb 4:15*b*). He knows how it feels, but He has not lost His right hand. He is mighty to save.

Thus, in a few words our High Priest is presented to us for our earnest contemplation, in His divine dignity and His tender compassion. What will be our answer to a vision like that? Surely it is calculated to steady wavering saints. The exhortation to "hold fast our confession" (4:14, ASV) is so much in place that it is almost out of place, so logical and consistent as to seem unnecessary. Who could consider such an High Priest and do otherwise? Yet the Holy Spirit adds the exhortation to help our infirmity, to strengthen our purpose, and save us from the danger which lurks around us.

For the first-century Hebrew Christian, under pressure of persecution, and missing the carnal help of the elaborate ritual of the Temple, there was real peril of drifting back. Here, however, was the recall of faith. In the light of Jesus, the Son of God, passing through the heavens to the fulfillment of His priestly mediation, the shadowy things of the Temple would lose their attraction. Divinely ordered as they were, and full of significance while they served their purpose, they could now appear only trivial and meaningless. Who would abide in the foreshadowings when the substance had been found?

Whether we be Jew or Gentile, the remembrance of Jesus passing through the heavens to take up our case in unceasing intercession is surely incentive to more boldness and steadfastness in our confession of Him. Such vision of our ascended Lord will sustain us in apostolic confidence: "I know whom I have believed, and am persuaded that he is able to keep that which I have committed unto him against that day" (2 Tim 1:12).

Having such a High Priest, exalted and compassionate, we have a rare privilege: "Let us therefore come boldly unto the throne of grace, that we may obtain mercy, and find grace for timely help" (Heb 4:16, author's trans.). With Jesus standing there, the eternal throne is the throne of grace. For all the infinite majesty and glory and splendor of it, for all the justice and judgment and power that characterize it, it is for us the place of mercy and love and bounty and help. When that throne is set for judgment, heaven and earth will flee before it, and sinners will be dumb as, prostrate, they hear the doom of the unrepentant and unbelieving pronounced upon them; but with Christ there for us, that awful throne becomes the place where we freely and frankly unburden our hearts, spell out our needs, take mercy upon mercy, and find the exact help at the exact moment for every sort of need. There sins are confessed and forgiven; there sorrows are poured out and comforted; there weakness is exchanged for strength; there questioning gives place to certainty.

The heathen have their many gods, which are no gods, and they must learn to apply to the right god for various needs—one god to give rain, one god to keep from sickness, one god to prosper them in battle, one god to give sons, and so on. We pity their ignorance, but multitudes in our so-called Christian lands are deceived by equally perverse notions, only they apply to various "saints" instead of divers gods.

> Where high the heavenly temple stands,
> The house of God not made with hands,
> A great High Priest our nature wears,
> The Guardian of mankind appears.
>
> He who for men their surety stood,
> And poured on earth His precious blood,
> Pursues in heaven His mighty plan,
> The Saviour and the Friend of man.
>
> Though now ascended up on high,
> He bends on earth a brother's eye;
> Partaker of the human name,
> He knows the frailty of our frame.
>
> Our fellow-sufferer yet retains
> A fellow-feeling of our pains;
> And still remembers in the skies
> His tears, His agonies, and cries.

Priests and saints and altars and shrines may not be your temptation. But you need someplace to go with your sins and your needs, your burdens, and your difficulties. They are too much for you to bear. Bring them to Jesus. Bring them to the throne of grace.

Come boldly, come quickly! For He has said, "Him that cometh to me I will in no wise cast out" (John 6:37).

10

THE VALIDATION OF CHRIST'S PRIESTHOOD

HEBREWS 5:1-10

In this passage we see a threefold vindication of our Lord's priestly office:

1. The vindication of superior appointment
2. The vindication of divine approval
3. The vindication of glorious attainment

"HE IS NOT A MAN, as I am, that I should answer him, and we should come together in judgment. Neither is there any daysman betwixt us, that might lay his hand upon us both" (Job 9:32-33). It was from a sense of complete frustration that Job uttered that painful cry, and he spoke for the human race. Here was a man plunged into the depths of grief, stripped of every earthly covering—wealth, position, honor, family, health, and all. One who had walked in conscious strength, security, and rightness now sat in the dust—bewildered, awed, afraid. Desperately clinging to his integrity, he still felt that God had become his enemy and was pressing him on all sides. He could argue his own righteousness before men, but sensed that in the presence of God his boasted uprightness would turn to mire and filth: "If I wash myself with snow water, and make my hands never so clean; yet shalt thou plunge me in the ditch, and mine own clothes shall abhor me" (Job 9:30-31). He could not meet God on equal terms. He could not offer human integrity against the demands of divine holiness. If only, then, he might find one who could touch him on the human level and touch God on the divine level, one to whom he could speak as a fellow, and yet who could approach God as an equal, there would be hope! But he knew of none who met the requirements or had the qualifications. "Neither is there any daysman betwixt us, that might lay his hand upon us both."

Job's "elemental cry," as Dr. G. Campbell Morgan designates it, was in the heart of man long before the patriarch uttered it. And as God heard it arising from a race as yet uncreated, He appointed the Daysman, the Arbiter, the Mediator, the Priest by a decree of infinite love and mercy. He did not immediately reveal Him, however, but over a long period taught man, through chosen means, what was the nature of the mediation and the character of the Mediator by whom they must be brought back to God. Notably, for this purpose, He established the Levitical order of priesthood in Israel. In this system the principle of divine appointment was constantly emphasized and demonstrated. "No man taketh this honour unto himself, but he that is called of God, as was Aaron" (Heb 5:4). It was a sin of sacrilege and presumption for any to intrude into the priest's office. Korah and his brethren presumed, and were destroyed in the presence of all the people. Saul presumed, and lost his kingdom. Uzziah presumed, and was smitten with leprosy. One of the chief factors in the apostasy and degradation of the Northern Kingdom was the elevation of non-Levites to the priesthood.

Now the great vindication of the priesthood of Jesus is His divine appointment. "So also Christ glorified not himself to be made an high priest; but he that said unto him, Thou art my Son, to day have I begotten thee. As he saith also in another place, Thou art a priest for ever after the order of Melchisedec" (Heb 5:5-6). Our Lord's priesthood is as firmly and divinely established as His sonship. As the one is made a matter of eternal decree, so the other is confirmed by divine oath. The statement "I will declare the decree: the LORD hath said unto me, Thou art my Son; this day have I begotten thee" (Psalm 2:7) is balanced by "The LORD hath sworn, and will not repent, Thou art a priest for ever after the order of Melchizedek" (110:4). If, then, the high priest of the Levitical order, temporary and preparatory as it was, commanded recognition and reverence, how much more the final and eternal appointment of the Son!

See how Jesus meets the demands of human need, as suggested in Job's plaintive cry. He can lay His hand upon me; He can meet me on my level; He is a man among men. "He took on him the seed of Abraham" (Heb 2:16), was made "in all points . . . like unto his brethren" (v. 17, author's trans.), was "in all points tempted like as we are, yet without sin" (4:15). Far more perfectly than any Levitical priest, He fulfills that basic requirement of the Levitical priesthood: compassion. That is what the children of Israel looked for and supremely valued in their high priest. Did not the breastplate and the shoulder pieces represent that very virtue, commanding the high priests to bear the people upon their hearts and their shoulders? But neither Aaron nor Samuel nor Jehoiada nor the later Joshua came within leagues of the compassion of Jesus. When Jesus looked upon the multitude as sheep scattered, having no shepherd, when He beheld the throngs of suffering men and women, when He contemplated Jerusalem and its approaching doom, His compassion was so deep that it became a veritable convulsion, an inward paroxysm, a soul anguish. Still He is touched with the feeling of our infirmities, and the compassion which He exhibited on earth moves Him in heaven.

There is no place where earth's sorrows
Are more felt than up in heaven:
There is no place where earth's failings,
Have such kindly judgment given.

We have found One who can lay His hand on us. But can He lay His hand on God? Can He meet God as a fellow, on terms of equality of being? Can He command God; has He authority with God; is He wholly acceptable to God? We remember the decree: "The LORD hath said unto me, Thou art my Son; this day have I begotten thee." And we remember the summons: "Awake, O sword, against my shepherd, and against the man that is my fellow (Zech 13:7). And we remember the majestic statement of the apostle John: "In the beginning was the Word, and the Word was with God, and the Word was God" (John 1:1). And the opening words of the great Kenosis passage: "Who, being in the form of God, thought it not a thing to be tightly held to be on an equality with God" (Phil 2:6, author's trans.). Aye, and many others, too! He is the Beloved of the Father, in the bosom of the Father, altogether and eternally acceptable. He can lay His hand on God.

Rejoice, then, Job, and every other troubled, burdened, sinful soul! A Daysman has been found! God has found Him and appointed Him, His own Son, very God of very God, Son of Mary, Son of man, who can "lay his hand upon us both." "There is one God, and one mediator between God and men, the man Christ Jesus" (1 Tim 2:5). Hallelujah!

Here, surely, is an appointment superior to that of Aaron or his sons, who could indeed touch the sinner on his level, and manifest such compassion as a fellow mortal might know, but who could come to God only on the ground of gracious allowance, not on any basis of equality or authority.

What is the significance of such a divine appointment? Let us suppose an alien is seeking to obtain citizenship in the United States, but his case is found to be full of legal obstructions. After some failures the would-be citizen appeals personally to the President. If the President, through the secretarial force of the White House, simply referred him to the usual channels of application, it would indicate no great interest in this alien's acceptance into the citizenry of the country. If, on the other hand, the President appointed the secretary of state, or the secretary of the interior, to clear the legal obstructions, that would signify a great desire on the part of the President to have this man a member of the commonwealth. If, then, God had stopped at the appointment of the Levitical priesthood, it would have evidenced no divine purpose to bring men into fellowship with Himself, for there was no putting away of sin, no perfecting of the worshiper, no real drawing nigh to God in that whole system. But if that was but preparatory to a greater appointment, intended to teach the principles upon which the better thing was based; and if God has fulfilled the promise of that preparation in giving us His own Son, made in our likeness, as the great Mediator, it can only mean that God's desire is toward us, His compassions are moved for us, and He is determined to remove every obstacle in the way of our coming and acceptance. Such an appointment, with all that it involves, spells out, in letters as big as the universe, the great, great love of God for poor sinners. The appointment of Jesus as our great High Priest means

For the love of God is broader
 Than the measure of man's mind;

And the heart of the Eternal
Is most wonderfully kind.

This blessed and divinely appointed High Priest of ours has won and received signal tokens of the divine approval, and in this present passage we have that approval stated with regard to His submissive praying and His suffering obedience.

"Who in the days of his flesh offered prayers and supplications with strong crying and tears to him who was able to save him from death, and was heard for his piety" (Heb 5:7, author's trans.). All the days of His flesh our Lord was a man of prayer. All the days of His flesh He was a man of tears. Prayers and tears, tears and prayers—thus the streams mingled and reddened until they demanded new channels of exit, and became "as it were great drops of blood falling down to the ground" (Luke 22:44). His days on earth were days of pouring out, days of self-giving. Living was costly to Him, for it was all part of His dying. Gethsemane and Calvary were not sudden experiences. They were the climax and consummation of a Gethsemane life and a Calvary life. Follow that radiant Man into whose arms the children have run and whose presence has brought life and light and joy to the burdened and heavy laden—follow Him in the shades of eventide up that hillside till He throws His weary length upon the grassy slope under some ledge of rock. Do you hear that groan? Do you hear that wail? Do you hear that cry? The weight of a world's sorrow is bearing down upon His soul, the darkness of a world's sin is wrapping Him around, the horror of a world's damnation is gripping Him. "Father, if it be . . ." (Matt 26:39*a*); but it is not time to finish that sentence. It is just being formed. "My God, my God, why . . . ?" (Matt 27:46). But that, too, must wait yet a season. Nevertheless, He will carry these in His heart and in His soul all the days of His flesh, and at the same time He will practice putting over against them these—"Not as I will, but as thou wilt" (Matt 26:39*b*) and, "Into thy hands I commend my spirit" (Luke 23:46). This is redemptive praying; these are redemptive tears. They rise, they flow, not to save Himself, but to save us. He is praying and weeping Himself on to the garden, on to the cross, on to the tomb, and on to the throne!

He "was heard for his piety." For all the dread that Calvary held for Him who knew what it meant, there was shrinking, but no rebellion. His prayers never once savored of unwillingness to see through to the end all that the Father's saving purposes imposed on Him. Such reverence, such piety, such godly fear, assured a hearing from "him that was able to save him from death" (Heb 5:7*b*), and that great third day, that glorious "first day of the week" (Matt 28:1), that glad Easter morn, brought the answer.

> Him from the dead Thou brought'st again,
> When by His sacred blood
> Confirmed and sealed forevermore
> Th' eternal covenant stood.

That was the divine approval upon the sacrificial praying of our sacrificing High Priest.

There is yet more. The prayers and tears led on to the sufferings and sustained Him in them. That was the school of obedience. There are human parents who regularly exempt their children from any obedience that means suffering, and they generally live to rue their folly. The philosophy of "progressive education" has already demanded a terrible toll in criminal sons and disillusioned parents. In all too many homes obedience is neither required nor expected beyond the whim and pleasure of the child. That, of course, is no obedience at all, and the child, no more subdued, learns no reverence for the law of the land nor for the Law of God. Over against such tragic folly, here is the divine order: "Though being a son, he learned the obedience from what he suffered, and was perfected" (Heb 5:8-9*a*, author's trans.). Our Lord had no propensity to disobedience, so this was not a case of being made obedient, as the children of men must be made. Rather, our Lord learned the true, complete, perfect obedience by obeying when it cost, when it meant suffering. After all, an invitation to have a candy bar does not teach obedience, but a call to some duty which requires missing a long-expected pleasure does teach the true meaning of obedience. The first rule of the soldier is obedience. Parade ground obedience may be good discipline, but only when obedience means possible, probable, or certain death has it been made perfect. God did not spare His Son the suffering involved in perfect obedience, for one who is to represent us and lead us in the way of obedience must Himself know the cost. This was the perfecting of the Son of God. Sharing all the perfections of the divine character, He stooped to our flesh and submitted to a course of obedience more rigorous than what all others have known. Thus, as man, He attained that perfection which fully approves Him as our great High Priest.

"And being made perfect, he became the author of eternal salvation unto all them that obey him" (5:9). That is the final validation of our Lord's priesthood. In the business world, the man who can produce secures the position. Produce the goods, and you stand accredited; fail to produce, and nothing can save you from being discredited in your field. By this test, Jesus stands approved. All His prayers and tears and sufferings and obediences and perfectings were bent to the one purpose—to obtain redemption for men. Here indeed is a rare commodity which none of the great founders of religions could produce. But where Zoroaster, Lao-tze, Gautama, Confucius, and Muhammad failed, the master Craftsman succeeded. None of them had the "raw material" out of which salvation is manufactured. Christ alone had all the resources—the union of the divine nature with the human, absolute sinlessness joined with infinite compassion for the sinner, universal sovereignty stooping to complete submission, perfect holiness bowing to the load of a world's sin. These were cast into the furnace with all the tears and sweat and blood of the Son of God, and came out a salvation, complete, eternal, for all who hearken to His voice.

Only He who brought forth salvation is worthy to mediate it. For Him is reserved the Pontifical throne. He only is Pontifex Maximus, "declared by God an High Priest after the order of Melchisedek" (5:10, author's trans.). Our salvation does not rest on our submission to earthly priests, fellow sinners as much in need of pardon as ourselves; but it is ours through faith in Him who redeemed us with His precious blood.

His death is my plea;
My Advocate see,
And hear the blood speak that hath answered for me:
He purchased the grace
Which now I embrace;
O Father, Thou know'st He hath died in my place.

11

ON TO PERFECTION!

HEBREWS 5:11–6:6

Three arguments are here presented for a life of progress:

1. The tragedy of a retarded growth
2. The splendor of a finished structure
3. The peril of a backslidden state.

WE THOUGHT we were at last properly launched into the main topic of our epistle—Jesus, our High Priest after the order of Melchisedec. But the writer suddenly breaks off again, this time telling us frankly that he is having considerable difficulty: "Of whom we have many things to say, and hard of interpretation" (Heb 5:11*a*, ASV). Yet it is not that the topic itself is so abstruse, but rather he feels that his readers are in no state to follow him. "My tongue is the pen of a ready writer," he says in effect, "but I am held in leash by your sluggishness—seeing ye are become dull in hearing." Their first going after Christ had been marked by a keenness which, had it been sustained, would have made teaching them a constant exhilaration and delight. But that sharpness of appetite, and ready grasp of the things of the Lord, had gone, and such inertia had taken them that even the elementary things taxed them. Once they were on the way to becoming teachers, but they stopped short, became satisfied with their attainment, lost the progress they had made, and returned to babyhood.

Now a baby is the most delightful and fascinating thing on earth. He brings with him sunshine and laughter. All his baby ways are wonderful. See the little fellow in his bed, laughing and cooing and humming and kicking and working—working as hard as he can to grow, as if impatient of babyhood and determined to become a man in a day! One day Mother says, "I just hate to see him grow up; he is losing his baby ways so fast!" We all understand that little bit of sentimental falsehood! Suppose he did not grow so many ounces per week, and did not develop his faculties of perception and understanding? Would not that mother weep her eyes out, and spend her last penny on medical care to coax normal growth? Very dear friends of ours had twin girls born to them. One of them grew normally, and was keen and bright. The other was retarded in her development, and was still practically helpless when her sister was really making the world go round! More abundant love was heaped upon the subnormal child, but it was love with a heartache. There is a difference between the laughing comedy of normal babyhood and the doleful tragedy of retarded growth.

So it is in the spiritual realm. A newborn babe in Christ is a joy, but protracted babyhood, or a return to spiritual babyhood, as in the case of the Hebrew Christians here addressed, is an unmitigated sorrow.

You can know the spiritual babe and the spiritual adult by the food they are able to receive and digest. "Every one that partaketh of milk is without experience of the word of righteousness; for he is a babe. But solid food is for fullgrown men, even those who by reason of use have their senses exercised to discern good and evil" (Heb 5:13-14, ASV). Milk is the proper food for infants; and while adults may never entirely strike it from their diet, the stronger foods bulk more largely. In the Word of God there is milk for babes and strong meat for full-grown men.

While on a hike in Smoky Mountains National Park, we came upon a yellow birch. It looked as if it were standing on stilts. The guide of our party, a professor of botany in one of our state universities, explained to us that the yellow birch takes root first in a dead log. It lives on the crumbling wood while it grows arms to embrace the log and digs down into the soil beneath. When the log is all decayed, the mature tree has established its contact with the new source of nourishment, and draws from the great deeps of earth. So there are the first principles, the elements, to nourish the life of the new believer, but he is expected to root himself deep in the Word until he is nourishing his soul on the strong meat.

Now we are given a sample of the milk, the first principles, which, to change the metaphor, form the foundation of the new life. The category consists of six items, which look like three pairs: the first pair indicates the new attitude of the soul—repentance from dead works, and faith toward God; the second pair has to do with initial rites—baptisms and the laying on of hands; the third pair, remarkably enough, looks to the end—resurrection and judgment. It is not our purpose to deal with these individually. The first pair seems normal enough. The second two, however, startle us. Among the great unities the apostle Paul lists "one baptism" (Eph 4:5), but here we have baptisms. We must remember that the Jews had many washings and baptisms, and the Christian Jew must come to discern the one baptism from among the many. The laying on of hands was certainly an apostolic custom, with more than one signification. Sometimes it was connected with the bestowal of the Holy Spirit, and again it marked certain men as set apart for particular ministries. Our first surprise at seeing resurrection and judgment listed among the first principles vanishes as we remember that these eschatological truths loomed large in our own earliest experiences of Christ, if indeed they did not strongly determine our decision to receive the Saviour.

These all are foundation matters. We can never discard them, any more than we can discard the axioms as we advance in geometry, but we must push beyond them if we would come to maturity. Other truths call for our contemplation, truths that will lift us to new heights, open new vistas, and make all life grander, fuller, nobler. Chief among these is the truth which the sacred writer seeks to set before us, but which is "hard of interpretation" (Heb 5:11, ASV) because of our dullness and immaturity and sluggishness. But so bent is he on helping us out of our rut and up to the hills of vision that he decides to pursue his course as God may enable him, and present to us the living portrait of Jesus, the Son of God, our great High Priest after the order of Melchisedec.

Foundations are vital, but they are not the whole house. A roofed-over foundation may serve an emergency, but it will not give the comfort and freedom and largeness of the completed building. "Wherefore let us cease to speak of the first principles of Christ, and press on unto perfection, not laying again a foundation" (6:1*a*, author's trans.), which is already laid, once and for all.

An unfinished building has something of the appearance of a ruin. To this day I remember the sense of tragedy which thrilled me when as a boy I looked for the first time upon "Edinburgh's disgrace," that partly built Grecian structure on the Calton Hill. The foundation was laid, but the architect's vision was not realized. "Why don't they start building again and finish it?" I asked in my boyhood enthusiasm. And why do not we, who have laid the foundation of "repentance toward God, and faith toward our Lord Jesus Christ" (Acts 20:21), carry up the walls and press the completion of the structure? Your life, my life, is a building planned as part of one magnificent structure, a holy temple, a habitation of God. Let us catch the vision of a completed life fitting in to the eternal cathedral of God, and "press on unto perfection."

> Build thee more stately mansions, O my soul,
> As the swift seasons roll!
> Leave thy low-vaulted past!
> Let each new temple, nobler than the last,
> Shut thee from heaven with a dome more vast,
> Till thou at length art free,
> Leaving thine outgrown shell by life's unresting sea!

Two reasons have been presented for going on: the tragedy of arrested development, and the lure of the completed building. Now a third argument is brought forward: the peril of standing still. Actually the peril of standing still is that we do not stand still, but go back. The unfinished building is not only akin to the ruin in appearance, but it quickly becomes a ruin. So a Christian who is not a building Christian is a crumbling Christian.

As the apostolic writer looked upon these Hebrew Christians, at first advancing, then static, then backsliding, he was impelled to warn them that in that direction lay grave danger. Some of them had already reached the danger point, and were standing on the brink of the precipice, playing with the thought of renouncing the Lord who bought them. Seeing this, he was the more urgent to hail them on to a life of progress, the surest safeguard against apostasy. The terms in which he couches his warning require separate consideration.

12

APOSTASY!

HEBREWS 6:4-9

In wrestling with this thorny passage we seek:

1. Clarification of the text
2. Consistency in the doctrine
3. Consolation for the saints

THE APOSTOLIC WRITER enforces his exhortations with strong reasons in a passage bristling with difficulties, and over which there have been endless disputes. It is a solemn statement from any view: "For as touching those who were once enlightened and tasted of the heavenly gift, and were made partakers of the Holy Spirit, and tasted the good word of God, and the powers of the age to come, and then fell away, it is impossible to renew them again unto repentance; seeing they crucify to themselves the Son of God afresh, and put him to an open shame" (Heb 6:4-6, ASV).

Some have sought to solve the problem of this heavy declaration by confining its application to the Jews of the first century, to the time of the destruction of the Temple and the sweeping away of the Mosaic system of sacrifice and priesthood. Some, fearing to jeopardize the doctrine of the perseverance of the saints, have considered those described as having fallen short of regeneration, and therefore no true believers. Others have concluded that the sin of apostasy is here put into a class by itself, as different from backsliding, and alone capable of annulling one's salvation.

As to the first of these suggestions, many will be unable to discern a difference in principle between a first-century Jew turning back from Christ to the Temple services, and a converted Hindu repudiating the Saviour to return to his idols. That the one rejects Christ in favor of a divinely appointed but now abandoned (because fulfilled) system can scarcely make his apostasy of an altogether different kind, more damnable and hopeless than any other apostasy.

The attempt to show that those here contemplated have fallen short of true Christian experience also has its difficulties.

The enlightenment spoken of is decisive and final in its nature—a "once for all" enlightenment. To argue that "tasting" of the heavenly gift is something less than "receiving" it would require our paring down Christ's *tasting* "death for every man" (Heb 2:9) to an experience short of actual death, for it is the same verb that is used. Again, if the phrase "were made partakers of the Holy Spirit" means only "going along with" the Holy Spirit up to the point of crisis, but not beyond it, what shall we make of the earlier verse, "For we are become partakers of Christ, if we hold fast the beginning of our confidence firm unto the end" (3:14, ASV)? The vocabulary does not help the weakened interpretation. Indeed, Dr. Dale says, "I know not how he could have chosen expressions which more forcefully describe the possession of a real and genuine Christian life."

Are we then shut up to the possible apostatizing of a true believer? This teaching is thorny, unpalatable, and involved in apparent contradiction. If one may apostatize after being in Christ, that looks like a breakdown in the doctrine of perseverance and security.

But is this the only place where seeming irreconcilables meet in the divine arrangement? The sovereignty of God and the freedom of the human will are so contrary that extreme positions have been taken on one side and the other; yet a balanced view takes account of both. In such a Scripture as "He hath chosen us in him before the foundation of the world" (Eph 1:4) we hear the voice of divine sovereignty; but the note of human responsibility rings through our Lord's cry, "Ye will not come to me, that ye might have life" (John 5:40). May we not similarly discern the sovereign election realized in perseverance, and at the same time human responsibility reflected in the exhortations to persevere and the warnings against apostasy?

A noted Calvinistic writer, Dr. Loraine Boettner, has suggested a sixfold purpose for these dark warnings:

> The primary purpose . . . is to induce men to co-operate willingly

> with God for the accomplishment of His purposes. . . . Secondly, God's exhortations to duty are perfectly consistent with His purpose to give sufficient grace for the performance of these duties. . . . Thirdly, these warnings are, even for believers, incitements to greater faith and prayer. Fourthly, they are designed to show man his duty rather than his ability, and his weakness rather than his strength. Fifthly, they convince men of their want of holiness and of their dependence upon God. And sixthly, they serve as restraints on unbelievers, and leave them without excuse.

One does not require to be an Arminian, or a near-Arminian, to accept the applications of these grave warnings to believers, on the human level. I like the frank courage of Dale of Birmingham, already quoted, when he says: "I would rather be charged by a whole council of theologians with introducing scientific inconsistency into a theological system, than dare to lessen the terror of a divinely-inspired warning, the undiminished awfulness of which may be needed to save some soul from death."

Let us, then, try to approach this difficult passage, not in the spirit of defending a doctrine, but to understand it in its setting. The sacred writer is concerned about the state of certain Hebrew Christians who, from all outward seeming, had embraced the faith of the Lord Jesus. Their early sincerity had been demonstrated by faithfulness to their profession, through persecution, spoiling of their goods, excommunication, and ostracism. With the passing of time, however, some wavering had been noticeable. Instead of pressing on, as formerly, they were losing ground, and there were indications that some were contemplating a return to Judaism. This treatise was written primarily to demonstrate the vast superiority of Jesus over the old economy and its ministers, and to recall the fainting ones to their former zeal. Here, then, to enforce the exhortation to "go on unto perfection" (Heb 6:1), this warning is sounded. It is based upon their experience. Men who had been so enlightened, who had tasted the love of Christ as they had, who had been made partakers of the Holy Spirit, to whom the Word of God had become sweet and the powers of the age to come made real—such men could not without grave consequences turn away from Christ. It would be crucifying the Son of God on their own behalf; it would be holding Him up to contempt.

I have no doubt that this is how the first recipients would read this paragraph; not stopping to argue its bearing on the doctrine of perseverance, or to limit its application to those who were wavering on the point of primary decision. Every one in that Hebrew Christian community would feel the weight of the words for himself, while those among them who had been inclined to yield to the pull of synagogue and Temple, Law and priesthood, would be deeply solemnized.

Dr. David Smith of Belfast, Ireland, believed that such apostasy as is here described was exemplified in the "dreadful story of that miserable mortal Francis Spira." Here is the story as he related it in the *British Weekly* some years ago:

> Spira was a lawyer of Northern Italy at the time of the Reformation. He had attained fame and wealth, but largely, as he confessed, by dishonourable devices, especially the taking of rich men's bribes for the oppression of the poor and the selling of innocent blood. The Gospel which Luther was preaching in Germany travelled across the Alps and reached the ears of Spira, and it touched his heart and changed his life. He professed the evangelical faith and preached it in Milan, Padua, and Venice with conviction and eloquence, and with such success that it seemed as though Italy would go the way of Northern Europe. The papal authorities took alarm, and Spira was arraigned before them. Intimidated by the threat of martyrdom, he abjured the Gospel, recanted his preaching, and made his peace with Rome by the payment of a heavy fine to be devoted to the adornment of Popish chapels. As he took the pen into his hand to write his recantation, the Holy Spirit pleaded within him: "Spira, lay down the pen!" but he persisted. And when he came to the signing of it, "Spira," said the voice within, "put not thy name hereto!" yet he did it.
>
> It was the sealing of his doom. He escaped martyrdom, but the cruellest death would have been far preferable to what he suffered. "Man," said he afterwards, "knows the beginning of sin, but who bounds the issues thereof? I felt a wound in my will which I have never got over. My will has never been itself since that fatal morning; it is paralysed at the heart." And so he died, an outcast from grace, his soul within him withered, cankered with remorse, no longer capable of repentance, faith, and new obedience.

I would hesitate to join Professor Smith in passing judgment on wretched Spira. God is the Judge. But the incident is not without its value in enforcing such a warning as we have before us.

A word of caution may be necessary here. Backsliding is not apostasy. Too many have thought themselves involved in the fearful condemnation of the apostate because they were guilty of some disobedience or neglect, perhaps long-continued. But, however serious such defections may be, they are quite different from a deliberate renunciation of Christ, which is the essence of apostasy. For the backslider there is mercy, remission, restoration; and although the great adversary would seek to despoil the penitent soul by persuading him that he had committed the sin that has no forgiveness, it is our privilege to press the pardoning grace of Jesus, and encourage full trust in the cleansing power of His precious blood. "He delighteth in mercy" (Mic 7:18).

I am glad this section of the epistle, so solemn and heavy, does not end on the minor note. After drawing this terrible picture of the apostate, and liking him to the desolation of a burned over wilderness, the writer suddenly breaks off into this: "But, beloved, we are persuaded better things of you, and things that accompany salvation, though we thus speak" (Heb 6:9). Now that word "persuaded" is the same word that Paul uses when he declares, "I know whom I have believed, and am persuaded that he is able to keep that which I have committed unto him against that day" (2 Tim 1:12). It is the persuasion of the gospel, the persuasion of Christ, the persuasion of blessed, divine certainty. While for the slothful there is warning lest they find themselves apostates at last, this glad persuasion appears for the comfort of God's people, that "he which hath begun a good work in you will perform it until the day of Jesus Christ" (Phil 1:6). That is our assurance as we press on unto perfection.

13

THE SOUL'S ANCHOR

HEBREWS 6:17-20

In this chapter we study:

1. The anchor of hope and the two immutable things
2. The anchorage of hope—within the veil

SAID BRIDGET after Pat's death, "I hope to meet Pat in heaven, but I don't expect to." Which saying not only revealed her opinion about Pat, but also indicated the true nature of natural hope.

Hope is a quivering, nervous creature, trying to be bright and cheerful, but alas, very frequently sick abed with nervous prostration and heart failure. Robert Louis Stevenson in his *Virginibus Puerisque* gives us this little word on hope and faith: "Hope is a boy, a blind, headlong, pleasant fellow, good to chase swallows with salt; Faith is the grave, experienced, yet smiling man. . . . Hope lives on ignorance; open-eyed Faith is built upon knowledge. . . . Hope is a kind old pagan; but Faith grew up in Christian days, and early learnt humility."

Christian hope is different, and its relationships are different. For what do we read? "But now abideth faith, hope, love, these three; and the greatest of these is love" (1 Cor 13:13, ASV). Faith is the first thing, hope is the consequent thing, and love the final thing. In the Christian sphere, hope springs from faith.

Natural hope is the next door neighbor to despair, but they are on bad terms. Christian hope is poles apart from despair, has no fellowship with it. Even in the days of calamity, Christian hope has nothing to despair of. While the man in the flesh is apt to say with Jacob, "All these things are against me" (Gen 42:36), Christian hope teaches us to say, "For our light affliction, which is but for a moment, worketh for us a far more exceeding and eternal weight of glory" (2 Cor 4:17).

Natural hope is the anemic invalid that it is because it has nothing solid to feed on. It feeds on dreams, "insubstantial aery things" that it can never be sure of, bubbles that are hard to get hold of, and that burst with the catching. That does not make for robustness or good health. But Christian hope is strong and virile because it is well nourished. "Blessed be the God and Father of our Lord Jesus Christ, who . . . begat us again unto a living hope by the resurrection of Jesus Christ from the dead" (1 Pet 1:3, ASV). Christian hope is living, because it is based on victory over death. Moreover, Christian hope feeds on something set before us which is as sure as God's throne. We are begotten again "to an inheritance incorruptible, and undefiled, and that fadeth not away, reserved in heaven for you, who are kept by the power of God through faith unto salvation ready to be revealed in the last time" (1 Pet 1:4-5). We have "the earnest of our inheritance" (Eph 1:14) right now in the person of the indwelling Holy Spirit. He in us and Christ on the throne constitute our twofold guarantee. Hope so nourished is certainly a strong hope.

God would have this hope of ours doubly sure; He would have our anchor doubly strong. How has He done it? By supporting the revelation of His counsel with an oath, "that by two immutable things, in which it was impossible for God to lie, we might have a strong consolation" (Heb 6:18). Having laid hold of the hope in Christ, we are given the strengthening of this double assurance—God's counsel and God's oath.

Our text tells us how God gave His counsel and His oath to Abraham. First of all, God came with a call and a promise. When that promise seemed impossible of fulfillment, Abraham "believed God, and it was counted unto him for righteousness" (Rom 4:3). Then God renewed the promise in the form of a solemn covenant. Sometime later, God put the faith of His friend to the test, commanding him to offer his own son Isaac. The faith and obedience of Abraham stood the test, and God stayed the hand of His servant. God did not seek the death of Isaac; He wanted the heart of Abraham. When, therefore, Abraham demonstrated his complete trust in God, God committed Himself completely to Abraham, saying: "By myself have

I sworn . . . for because thou hast done this thing, and hast not withheld thy son, thine only son: that in blessing I will bless thee, and in multiplying I will multiply thy seed as the stars of the heaven" (Gen 22:16-17). So He gave Abraham His oath. God cannot resist faith. Faith so intrigues God, so completely captivates Him, that He binds Himself over to an Abraham, a Paul, or a George Mueller.

But why should God go on His oath at all: Is not His word enough? Can God's oath make His word any stronger? Charles Lamb in his essay, *Imperfect Sympathies,* has this to say about the oath:

> The custom of resorting to an oath in extreme cases, sanctified as it is by all religious antiquity, is apt (it must be confessed) to introduce into the laxer sort of minds the notion of two kinds of truth—the one applicable to the solemn affairs of justice, and the other to the common proceedings of daily intercourse. . . . A Quaker knows none of this distinction. His simple affirmation being received upon the most sacred occasions, without any further test, stamps a value upon the words which he is to use upon the most indifferent topics of life.

If, then, there are men among us whose simple word is everywhere regarded as just as binding as any oath, why does God have to resort to an oath? Not at all to make His word more sure, but to make you and me more assured. It is God's great condescension. "For he knoweth our frame; he remembereth that we are dust" (Psalm 103:14). For our sakes He will resort to that which is utterly unnecessary to Himself.

"By myself have I sworn." We are told in our text that He used this form of oath because no other would have been appropriate. If He had sworn by anything else or anybody else, He would have been swearing by something or someone less than Himself, so dishonoring Himself and His word. Hebrew literature offers this imaginative passage in *Treatise Berachoth.* In answer to the question, "What meaneth 'by Myself'?" Rabbi Eliezer answers: "Moses spake thus to the Lord (Blessed be He!): 'If Thou hadst sworn by heaven and earth, I should say, since heaven and earth shall perish, so too Thine oath. Now Thou hast sworn by Thy great name: as Thy name lives and lasts for ever and ever, Thy oath also shall last for ever and ever.' " The stamp of eternity is upon that which God sware to Abraham.

This oath has come down upon Christ, the seed of whom He spoke. In Christ it passes over to us. The oath was to Abraham and to his seed. Since we are of the faith of Abraham, we are the seed of Abraham, so this oath of God is ours as it was his, but with this difference: Abraham received the oath as a reward of his faith, while we inherit it. It becomes ours from the very beginning, and to strengthen faith from more to more.

Outside the Peabody Maritime Museum in Salem, Massachusetts, there is an old anchor, whose original weight was 4,004 pounds. It doubtless served its ship well, but in a great gale its shaft was twisted. Our anchor of hope, reinforced by the oath of God, is proof against all tides and tempests.

> His oath, His covenant, His blood,
> Support me in the whelming flood.
> When all around my soul gives way,
> He then is all my hope and stay.

Where do we cast anchor? "Which hope we have as an anchor of the soul, both sure and stedfast, and which entereth into that within the veil; whither the forerunner is for us entered, even Jesus, made an high priest for ever after the order of Melchisedec" (Heb 6:19-20). Our anchorage is within the veil.

That means, in the first place, that we do not cast our anchor on anything within ourselves. For instance, we are not seeking our security in our own feelings. We had better not, for feelings are exceedingly changeable things. What you eat before you go to bed at night may determine your feelings when you rise next morning! Whether your coffee is hot or cold may have something to do with your feelings the rest of the day! This may sound trivial, but it is "more truth than poetry."

We shall not cast anchor in our experience, so dependent on temperament, so easily misinterpreted; nor in ever varying circumstances; nor in human judgment, never wholly trustworthy; nor in any ecclesiastical system, with its admixture of truth and error. The best anchor may "drag" in any of these unsafe anchorages.

A few years ago the Roman Catholic archbishop of Ottawa, Canada, discovered that many of the "faithful" were sending their children to the public schools in preference to the church schools, and having themselves assessed for the public schools. He was thoroughly aroused, and in an episcopal message declared his purpose to make a personal call on all Roman Catholics in his diocese who were behaving so scandalously. If any refused to have their assessment transferred to the separate schools, he would give orders to the parish priests to deny them the sacraments and refuse them absolution. This was serious business for devotees of the Roman faith, for it was tantamount to decreeing their eternal damnation, or at least lengthening indefinitely their purgatorial pains, if they did not yield to the episcopal demand. Thus have multitudes, wittingly or unwittingly, cast the anchor of their hope into the hands of a man whose arbitrary decree can cut them adrift.

Our hope is not so insecurely cast.

> We have an anchor that keeps the soul,
> Stedfast and sure while the billows roll,
> Fastened to the Rock which cannot move,
> Grounded firm and deep in the Saviour's love.

"Within the veil," says our text. On the day John Knox, the "great apostle of the Scots," passed from the conflict of this life, he called to his wife, "Go, read where I cast my first anchor." She understood, and read the seventeenth chapter of John's gospel, which commentators have entitled the "High-Priestly Prayer." We are "within the veil" there, in the Holy of Holies.

"Within the veil." The figure is, of course, drawn from the Temple. The great veil hung before the Holy of Holies, the inner sanctuary, where the Shekinah glory wrapped the Mercy Seat of the Ark of the Covenant. Within the veil came the high priest one day in the year, on the great Day of Atonement, to sprinkle the blood of atonement before and upon the Mercy Seat. Solemn and joyful was the annual event, yet it was marked by two imperfections. The high priest could not abide in the Holy of Holies, for he had no offering adequate to the demands of a perfect, lasting atonement. The service must be repeated again and again, yet could not take away sin. As a consequence, the high priest could not secure the right of entrance for others. He was not a forerunner, but came forth to leave the holy place as inaccessible as before to the people.

Our Lord corrected all that. Not into an earthly sanctuary, but into heaven itself He went: not with the blood of bulls and goats, but with His own blood. The service of atonement is now perfect. It needs no repeating. Therefore, He passed through the heavens into the presence of God for us, not for a moment, but to sit down on the right hand of the throne of the Majesty on high, "from henceforth expecting till his enemies be made his footstool" (Heb 10:13).

Moreover, when He passed through the heavens, He opened the way for believing sinners to press into the presence of God. The rending of the veil of the Temple in the moment of our Lord's great sacrifice betokened the taking away of the barrier, and the opening of the "new and living way, which he hath consecrated for us, through the veil, that is to say, his flesh" (10:20). Jesus entered as a Forerunner, Pioneer of the way to God, and we sinners, cleansed from our sins by His precious blood, have access with boldness into the holiest. And not only access now, but entrance at last: for "He'll not be in heaven, and leave me behind!"

Our anchor ground is the Holy of Holies, "within the veil" (6:19), where Jesus our High Priest ministers the blessings of His blood-bought salvation to all who come unto God by Him.

Philip Mauro has suggested that the picture here is that of the *anchoria* which was used in olden days in the harbors of inland seas, to assist vessels which could not make port under their own sail. In such case, a "forerunner" went from the ship into the harbor and fastened a strong rope to the anchoria, a great rock imbedded immovably close to shore. By means of a winch on board, the vessel, thus fastened, was brought in. It is a helpful thought. Because my anchor is cast within the veil, because I am fastened to the Rock, because I am joined to Him who is gone before, I shall make port at last.

Let us therefore look to our anchor, and see to our moorings. Then let the breakers roll and the floods swell and the tides lift and the gales sweep; let our sails be torn to shreds and our masts and tackle carried off as driftwood; let our timbers creak and the old ship rock and reel in the storm: we may still enjoy the quiet of the presence of God, and smile at the sea and the wind, for with our anchor fast "within the veil," we are safe, and drawing every day nearer to heaven and home.

14

A ROYAL PRIEST

Hebrews 7:1-3

In this and the following chapters we see how Melchisedec is a witness to Christ's superior priesthood:

1. The witness of the title—royalty and equity
2. The witness of the origin—independence and perpetuity
3. The witness of the tithe—superiority in prerogative
4. The witness of the benediction—superiority in beneficence

THREE TIMES the writer of this letter-treatise has introduced that strange designation from Psalm 110:4, "a priest . . . after the order of Melchisedec." Twice he has left us without a word of explanation, till at the third time we are ready to stop him and demand that he enlighten us on the meaning of that so remarkable reference to so mysterious a character, which he is applying with such assurance to our Lord Jesus. On first mention, he quoted the psalmist to show that Christ did not assume the office of priest unbidden, but by appointment of God; but he did not even hint that there was any particular meaning to "the order of Melchisedec." When again he introduces the phrase, a few verses later, the ground seems all prepared for explanation, but instead he breaks off to tell us that we are not ready for what he has to say. This, then—Jesus Christ a great High Priest after the order of Melchisedec—is the advanced teaching, the "strong meat" (Heb 5:14), that the writer desires to impart to us, and he decides at last to proceed, in the hope that the exhortation has stirred in us a desire to "go on unto perfection" (6:1). When, therefore, he for the third time mentions "Jesus, made an high priest for ever after the order of Melchisedec" (6:20), he is ready to develop his theme.

But who is this Melchisedec, who established the order of priesthood into which our Lord entered? The only historical reference to him is in the fourteenth chapter of Genesis. There Abram the man of peace goes forth as a man of war to rescue his nephew Lot from the army of the confederate kings who have come against the king of Sodom and his allies. By the blessing of God, Abram's little handful of braves wins a notable triumph, bringing back both captives and booty. The king of Sodom, hearing of the victory, goes on his way to meet the victor and to bestow upon him appropriate honors. At this juncture Melchisedec enters, forestalling the king of Sodom. This mysterious person is described as "king of Salem, priest of the most high God" (Heb 7:1). Three actions are attributed to him: he "brought forth bread and wine" (Gen 14:18); he pronounced a blessing upon Abram in the name of "God Most High, possessor of heaven and earth" (v. 19, ASV), and upon God Most High, who had wrought for His servants; and he received the tithe of the spoil which Abram freely offered. That is all. Yet that brief visit, marked by so simple a ceremony, inspired, or at least fortified, Abram's decision to refuse the king of Sodom's offer: "I have lifted up mine hand unto Jehovah, God Most High, possessor of heaven and earth, that I will not take a thread nor a shoe-latchet . . . lest thou shouldest say, I have made Abram rich" (Gen 14:23-24, ASV).

This apparently inconspicuous incident took place about two millennia before Christ. About midway down that long span the voice of inspiration lifted the name of that unknown person from its obscurity and revealed its place in the decrees of God, the psalmist declaring that the priesthood exercised so simply was an eternal order, into which the Son of God Himself was ordained. "The LORD hath sworn, and will not repent, Thou art a priest for ever after the order of Melchizedek" (Psalm 110:4).

That is the only break in the silence until our Lord had accomplished all His atoning work and entered into the holy place not made with hands. Then the God-breathed word was sent to a group of Hebrew believers, and through them to us all, giving the witness of "this Melchisedec" to the priestly ministry of our risen Lord.

Not that every question is answered for us. In some respects, indeed, what is written in our Hebrews passage deepens the mystery surrounding Melchisedec. If the seventh chapter of Hebrews had not been written, we should have no difficulty as to whether Melchisedec were a local king-priest in Canaan, or a Christophany, an appearing of Christ beforehand; but such phrases as, "without father, without mother, without genealogy, having neither beginning of days nor end of life" (Heb 7:3*a*, ASV), create a problem for us. If we take these as applying literally and directly to the person of Melchisedec, we shall doubtless accept Dr. G. Campbell Morgan's position: "Amid the varying interpretations to which I have referred, I would now say that I am personally convinced that this is the story of a Christophany; that here, as upon other occasions, there was granted to a man the appearing and ministry of none other than the Son of God, the One who is King of righteousness, and therefore King of peace." If, however, we think of these same remarkable phrases as applying rather to the priestly office, we may conclude with Spurgeon that "it is enough for us to believe that he was one who worshipped God after the primitive fashion, a believer in God such as Job was in the land of Uz, one of the world's grey fathers who had kept faithful to the Most High God." Other conjectures are not important enough to detain us.

Our chief interest is not in the identity of the person of Melchisedec, but in his witness to the priesthood of Christ. We are told that he was "made like unto the Son of God" (7:3*b*). Whether we take the natural or the supernatural view of his person, it is clear enough that God so ordered his life and the exercise of his priesthood as to present the true character of our great High Priest, Jesus.

His title is itself most suggestive, "being by interpretation King of righteousness, and after that also King of Salem, which is, King of peace" (7:2). The order of Melchisedec unites priesthood and kingship, in striking contrast to the Levitical order, in which these two offices were kept strictly separate. There were times, indeed, when the priesthood exerted great influence in the state, as in the days of Jehoiada, who brought about the overthrow and death of the usurping Queen Athaliah, established the young prince Joash on the throne, and dominated the policies of the king. But Jehoiada did not wear the crown. Moreover, the priestly office was strongly barred against the king. When Uzziah the king intruded, he was smitten with leprosy. Ordained into the earlier order, our Lord combines both offices in His person. He is a "priest upon his throne" (Zech 6:13).

Philip Mauro has written a book entitled *God's Apostle and High Priest* in which he proposes to show that our Lord fulfilled His apostolate in the days of His flesh; that He "is now appearing in the presence of God for us, fulfilling, as Minister of the heavenly tabernacle, the type of the Aaronic priesthood"; and that He is yet to be "the High Priest of the world to come, when He will, in fulfilment of the Melchisedec type, unite in His own Person the office and authority of King, with that of Priest." Thus our Lord's priesthood "after the order of Melchisedec" is thrown into a future age, in an apparent attempt to escape the present kingship. To me it is a glorious thought that Jesus is King, as well as Priest; that all the authority of universal sovereignty is engaged in His priestly work on our behalf; that He is ordering the ages in keeping with His eternal purpose concerning the church. He is not exercising a precarious priesthood in face of an order over which He has no control, or only some ultimate overruling. He is "gone into heaven, and is on the right hand of God; angels and authorities and powers being made subject unto him" (1 Pet 3:22). To fulfill His headship over all things to the church He was set "far above all principality, and power, and might, and dominion, and every name that is named, not only in this world, but also in that which is to come" (Eph 1:21).

Rejoice, the Lord is King!
  Your Lord and King adore;
Ye saints, give thanks and sing
  And triumph evermore:
Lift up your heart, lift up your voice;
Rejoice, again I say, rejoice.

Jesus, the Saviour, reigns,
  The God of truth and love;
When He had purged our stains,
  He took His seat above:
Lift up your heart, lift up your voice;
Rejoice, again I say, rejoice.

George F. Handel

Now look more particularly at the royal title: "first being by interpretation King of righteousness, and after that also King of Salem, which is, King of peace" (Heb 7:2). First, king of righteousness; after that, king of peace. The order is vital. The kingship of Jesus is exercised first in righteousness, and after that in peace. Only where He has established His reign of righteousness does He bestow His peace. We make a mistake when we think of Him first as the Prince of peace. He is a Man of war, in endless conflict with evil. He will have righteousness at any price, not peace at any price; but where His righteousness prevails, His peace follows. It is only "being justified by faith" that "we have peace with God through our Lord Jesus Christ" (Rom 5:1). Otherwise "there is no peace, saith my God, to the wicked" (Isa 57:21).

How pitifully men attempt to build peace on expediency rather than on righteousness, with the result that peace eludes them. We had our war slogan, "Remember Pearl Harbor!" I think the nations of the world, at least those nations which seek peace, had better "Remember Munich!" Already too much expediency had been followed, but there righteousness was sold for a peace which only gave the aggressor more advantage, till not only did the world pay in the cataclysm of war, but the shakings have not yet ceased, nor given promise of ceasing.

Melchisedec tells us that the priesthood of Christ is, above all else, ethical. As King of righteousness, He has not only laid a foundation of righteousness for all the exercise of His priesthood, so that He can justly minister the blessings of salvation to believing sinners; but all His priestly activity is to ethical ends, to produce in redeemed sinners a new character, likeness to Himself, and to establish at last "new heavens and a new earth, wherein dwelleth righteousness" (2 Pet 3:13).

"After that also . . . King of peace" (Heb 7:2*b*). Having fulfilled all righteousness, He made peace "through the blood of his cross" (Col 1:20), and so became the great Reconciler. Notice the cosmic scope of the reconciliation so effected. "It pleased the Father that in him should all fulness dwell; and, having made peace through the blood of his cross, by him to reconcile all things unto himself; by him, I say whether they be things in earth, or things in heaven"

(Heb 1:19-20). This is the basis of that "regeneration of all things" which will culminate the whole work of redemption, and the basis of the plea to sinners, "Be ye reconciled to God" (2 Cor 5:20). We are called to accept a reconciliation whose terms have been fulfilled.

The work of our High Priest aims at peace through righteousness, and what wonderful peace He brings to those who submit to His righteousness! To them He says, "Peace I leave with you, my peace I give unto you: not as the world giveth, give I unto you. Let not your heart be troubled, neither let it be afraid" (John 14:27). Indeed, the measure of our obedience to His reign of righteousness is the measure of His peace in our hearts, till, every controversy settled, all resistance broken, and the King of peace ruling in our hearts with undisputed sway, we pursue our journey with the song:

> Like a river, glorious is God's perfect peace,
> Over all victorious in its bright increase;
> Perfect, yet it floweth fuller every day,
> Perfect, yet it groweth deeper all the way.
>
> FRANCES HAVERGAL

If only men would receive the King of righteousness! They would find in Him the King of peace. How would the conflicting forces in men's lives be adjusted, the restlessness quieted, the anxiety cease! If only He were given place in the counsels of the nations! Then would "wars and rumours of wars" (Matt 24:6) be but echoes of the past. But fools that we are, we refuse His righteousness, and we lose His peace, sowing more and more the seeds of strife, to reap bloody destruction. Yet we despair not. We "look for that blessed hope, even the glorious appearing of the great God and our Saviour Jesus Christ" (Titus 2:13). We can almost hear the tinkling of the golden bells on the border of our High Priest's robe as He rises from His seat to come again and receive us unto Himself, to purge the earth with His judgments, and to make known His righteousness and peace in a Kingdom which shall have no end.

The Levitical priesthood leaned heavily on genealogy. None but a son of Aaron might be high priest, while even the lesser priestly offices were confined to the tribe of Levi. It was a mark of complete apostasy and a sign of utter degeneracy when the sacred offices were opened to others in the rebel tribes. On the return from Babylon, those who could not give documentary evidence of their lineage were barred, as polluted, from the priesthood, although one might have expected some degree of leniency after so long a disruption of the national life.

The order of Melchisedec is, in striking contrast to all this, independent of lineage. The priesthood of Christ is underived from ancestry, untransmitted to posterity. It belongs to Him by a higher right than generation, and none can claim it after Him.

There are values in the hereditary system which we of the democratic West do not always appreciate; but however it may be defended, it has its own dangers and abuses. One man may lift the office to dignity and strength, while another may sorely degrade it. The priesthood was subject to much fluctuation in Israel, and the people rose and fell with their leaders. Over its long history only a few great names appear, as Aaron, Eliezer, Jehoiada, Joshua, and none of these was perfect. Even Aaron failed at a critical moment and sanctioned the people's return to idolatry. Too much of the time it was a matter of "like people, like priest," resulting in the reverse, "like priest, like people."

The perfect priesthood, then, is one which finds the perfect priest, and keeps him. Such a priesthood is found in the timeless order of Melchisedec, and in the person of Jesus Christ, whose qualifications have been fully established. He has no equal for this high office of universal priesthood, and He has received His appointment in perpetuity, underived and untransmissible. We can be sure that our High Priest will not fail in the duties of His office, and we do not live in the fear that a successor, hereditary or appointed, will follow and fall down. There can be no fluctuations here.

Vilhjalmur Stefansson, in his *Great Adventures and Explorations,* has brought together the story of the lost European settlement in Greenland. This land was settled in 986 by Erik the Red, and grew to be a prosperous colony of ten thousand Scandinavians. Roman Christianity was introduced about the year 1000, the first local priest being established in 1056, and the first bishop of Greenland consecrated in 1126. The bishop, however, became nonresident after 1385, and the diocese lapsed in 1537 after a century and a half of silence.

Greenland was rediscovered by John Davis in 1585, but the European colony had vanished, absorbed into the race of aborigines. Not a Christian was to be found. The Eskimo paganism had claimed them. This submergence of a "Christian" community spells the failure of the Roman priesthood. I shall not commit the care of my soul to a priesthood that has even one such blot against it. It might fail me, too. The same applies to the Greek priesthood and the Jewish priesthood. Whether the order be Franciscan or Levitical, it cannot bear the weight of one soul, let alone a world of sinners. But I believe my great High Priest of the order of Melchisedec when He says, "I will never leave thee, nor forsake thee" (Heb 13:5).

He cannot fail, for He is God;
He cannot fail—He's pledged His word.
He cannot fail, He'll see you through;
He cannot fail, He'll answer you.

15

MELCHISEDEC WITNESSES TO JESUS

Hebrews 7:4-10

In this chapter we pursue the thoughts outlined at the head of chapter 14.

TITHING PRECEDED the giving of the Law. Here it is practiced four hundred years before that great transaction at Sinai, and it is the circumstances of the case, not the practice itself, that are considered unusual. It would not seem, therefore, that any objection can be raised against the principle of tithing on the ground of its being "of the law" (Heb 7:12). Too many chafe against any sort of regularity in the Christian life as being "legalistic." One is enjoying his "liberty in Christ" in measure as he disregards all law and order and lives according to the mood of the hour! Not so the spiritual giants of the ages. These have been men of discipline, men who have applied great and godly principles to their lives with relentless rigor, triumphing over the lax tendencies of the flesh. If Abraham was "free from the law" (Rom 8:2), he was not without law. He recognized God's right in him and in all his substance, and acted accordingly in the dedication of the tenth part of all. The covenant of grace does not abrogate God's rights in His children.

But he must be great indeed who will be God's representative to receive the tithes from Abraham! For who is this Abraham? He is the patriarch, as the Greek text emphasizes by separating the word from the rest of the sentence and giving it place at the end. The patriarch—think of the place he holds in the economy of God. When the primal light was well-nigh extinguished from the earth, God took this man out of darkness to make him the bearer of a light that should shine down through all the ages with increasing intensity to the consummation. His seed was to be as the stars of the heaven for multitude, and as the sand by the seashore. Nations and kings were to come of him. Of those nations should be the one that must be God's witness in the earth, the priestly nation; and of those kings should be the divine King, King of kings and Lord of lords, born after the flesh "of the seed of Abraham" (Heb 2:16). "And in thy seed shall all families of the earth be blessed" (Gen 28:14) was the promise to Abraham.

From the close, intimate relations which existed between Abraham and God (till "he was called the Friend of God," James 2:23) one should think that none would rival him as God's representative in the earth, to receive the tokens of men's submission to the Most High. But here this "Friend of God" brings the tokens of his own submission to the feet of another, Melchisedec. This was itself an acknowledgment of Melchisedec's superiority, if not in personal character, at least in office and ministry. To Abraham the essence of the recognized superiority was doubtless indefinable, but it is put down for us in the chapter we are now studying: Melchisedec was "made like unto the Son of God" (Heb 7:3), in a priesthood which transcended tribal distinctions, racial differences, and time itself.

Many years later, the offspring of Abraham was divided into tribes, according to the sons of Jacob. One of these, Levi, was appointed the priestly tribe, the sons of Aaron being the priests, and their fellow tribesmen the assistants. Now the sons of Levi were nothing superior to the other sons of Israel. They did not even have the dignity of the firstborn. They had therefore no natural right to levy tithes of their brethren, but a special commandment of God was given to establish a sanction for their doing so. It was, we might say, an arbitrary sanction, to meet a somewhat artificial situation. Apart from such a special enactment, the sons of Reuben might well demur at bringing tithes to the children of a younger brother. It was not so in the case of Melchisedec, to whom Abraham gave his tithes in recognition of a superiority which was native, and not established by law.

There is yet another consideration. The principle of federal representation comes in here. "As I may so say, Levi also, who receiveth tithes, payed tithes in Abraham. For he was yet in the loins of his father, when Melchisedec met him" (7:9-10). We are well enough acquainted with the principle of representation, but we have so lost the patriarchal conception that federal representation is rather foreign to us. A political question may help us here. Back in 1917, the Balfour Declaration committed the British government to support a Jewish homeland in Palestine, and the mandate which Britain accepted over that territory after World War I obligated her to implement the terms of that declaration. We shall all agree that the task was more difficult than was anticipated. The white paper of the Labor government was more or less a repudiation of the undertaking, and was regarded by many as a betrayal of trust. It is recognized that the action of the government in 1917 and 1919 involved all subsequent governments until the undertaking was realized or the mandate withdrawn. Commitments of this kind rise above party and changes of personnel.

Federal representation is still more binding, for it not merely commits the unborn generation to carry out a policy established by the father, but it makes the act of the father that of the unborn child. Now it is true that in His great mercy God does not inflict the toll of this principle without modification. He allows every man to answer for himself, to accept or repudiate the actions of his father. To this effect is the great eighteenth chapter of Ezekiel, summed up in the opening verses: "What mean ye, that ye use this proverb concerning the land of Israel, saying, The fathers have eaten sour grapes, and the children's teeth are set on edge? As I live, saith the Lord Jehovah, ye shall not have occasion any more to use this proverb in Israel. Behold, all souls are mine; as the soul of the father, so also the soul of the son is mine: the soul that sinneth, it shall die" (vv. 2-4, ASV). Nevertheless, the principle abides, and we have it exemplified in such a representative man as Abraham. He occupied a federal place, a patriarchal place, and his act of submission was reckoned to all his posterity. The Levitical order of priests, in the person of their father Abraham, acknowledged the superiority of the order of Melchisedec, calling the whole Aaronic line to witness that the final Mediator between God and man is a Priest of another order than their own, a

Priest who, in the language of John the Baptist, takes precedence over them, for He was before them, a Priest who can say, "Before Abraham was, I am" (John 8:58).

Before allowing this law of entail to slip from mind, a parenthesis is in order to show its wider application in two directions. In that profound latter portion of the fifth chapter of Romans, the Spirit of God reminds us through His inspired apostle that the first sin of Adam fell upon the whole human race, "that mankind inherits from primal Man, tried and fallen, not only taint but guilt, not only moral hurt but legal fault." I confess that it took me a long time to accept the straightforward, rugged teaching of the chapter on that point. It seemed a big enough responsibility for our first father to have transmitted to the whole race a bent to sin without involving us in the guilt of his sin; and it seemed enough that we should inherit a sinful nature without having to partake of his guilt too. That meant two strikes against us to begin with, and it appeared too much. Then I saw that unless this were a true principle, the other and glorious side of the case, of which the dark picture is used only as an illustration, was greatly weakened. For the apostle makes the entail of guilt in Adam not an end in itself, but a picture, and even the basis, of the entail of righteousness in Christ. As Adam has passed on to all his posterity a legacy of guilt and condemnation, so Christ has bestowed on all His seed an inheritance of justification. Now as Adam's seed is by generation, Christ's seed is by regeneration. We are "in Adam" by nature, we are "in Christ" by faith; and as Adam's sin was reckoned to us, so the perfect righteousness of Christ is put to our account in the new relation. "For as by one man's disobedience many were made sinners, so by the obedience of one shall many be made righteous" (Rom 5:19).

It is this same law, then, that commits the Aaronic priesthood to an acknowledgment of the higher order, and calls upon all who ever entered the holy place of the earthly tabernacle to bow down before Jesus, "made an high priest . . . after the order of Melchisedec" (Heb 5:5-7). Ordained of God for temporary uses, the Aaronic priesthood was forcibly swept away when it refused the submission due to God's great and perpetual High Priest. All need for an earthly order of priests came to an end when Jesus, by His own blood, entered once for all into the heavenly sanctuary.

A further witness to the superiority of Melchisedec was the blessing which he pronounced upon Abraham. He "blessed him that had the promises. And without all contradiction the less is blessed of the better" (7:6*b*-7). We remember how, when the seed of Abraham was just widening out into the twelve branches, the patriarch Jacob went down into Egypt to his long-lost son, Joseph. Now the promises given to Abraham had fallen upon Jacob. He stood in the place of Abraham as the channel of the covenant. Taken before Pharaoh, despot of a great empire, and not just a local kinglet as Melchisedec is reckoned to have been, a very different scene took place. Jacob blessed Pharaoh. For all his pomp and power, Pharaoh was the less in the economy of God, and Jacob the better, despite the years of cunning and deceit that marred his youth. Yet the Jacob who acted the part of the better in the presence of this powerful ruler, bowed, in the person of his grandfather, Abraham, to receive the blessing at the hand of Melchisedec, king of righteousness, king of peace.

Jesus is the supreme Blesser. The priests of the Aaronic order were instructed to bless the people of Israel with these words: "The LORD bless thee, and keep thee: the LORD make his face shine upon thee, and be gracious unto thee: the LORD lift up his countenance upon thee, and give thee peace" (Num 6:24-26). As for our great High Priest, He not only invokes blessing, but bestows it. Listen to His version: "Peace I leave with you, my peace I give unto you: not as the world giveth, give I unto you. Let not your heart be troubled, neither let it be afraid" (John 14:27). See Him ascending to the right hand of God, His passion fulfilled, His triumph complete! He is stretching out His hands in the attitude of benediction over His assembled disciples—and over you and me. "And it came to pass, while he blessed them, he was parted from them, and carried up into heaven" (Luke 24:51). That parting benediction is translated into endless benefaction, for we are "blessed . . . with all spiritual blessings in heavenly places in Christ" (Eph 1:3). He "daily loadeth us with benefits" (Psalm 68:19), and these will continue until the blessing of "peace on earth" merges into the rapture of heaven, and His high-priestly benefactions find their consummation in presenting us "faultless before the presence of his glory with exceeding joy" (Jude 24).

16

A CHANGE OF PRIESTHOOD

Hebrews 7:11-28

We consider this remarkable topic from three angles:

1. Why the change was needed
2. How the change was effected
3. What the change accomplished

"Changes are lightsome, and fools like them." Thus runs one of our Scottish proverbs, reflecting the canny, conservative disposition of my forebears. But in this world of "change and decay," frequently the only way to avoid decay is to effect a change. Arrangements serve their purpose until new conditions call for new arrangements; and when that time comes, failure to change spells disaster. A business concern will prosper with a modicum of organization until the increase in operation demands more careful planning. The great chain of stores reaching all parts of the country will not operate quite like the corner grocery store! A like need of change appears in a growing church, or a growing college. What is efficient at one point in the development of an institution would be the sum of inefficiency at a later stage.

God does not change. With Him there is "no variableness, neither shadow of turning" (James 1:17*b*), because He is infinitely and eternally perfect. That does not mean that He does not change His modus operandi. He did not make us all the same, and He does not treat us all the same. He has, indeed, one salvation for all, but His dealings with us in regard to that salvation are infinitely varied. As with contemporary individuals, so with the ages. God, looking down the years, decreed the unfolding of His great plan of redemption in keeping with the needs of the whole race, and of the successive generations. So in the wisdom of God the time came for the establishment of the priesthood in Israel, after the order of Aaron. He had already indicated in Melchisedec, however, that this Aaronic order was not the final one. It would serve its divinely ordained purpose, and then give place to the better order, in the person of the incarnate Son, who would bring priesthood to its perfection and realize the redemption determined before the foundation of the world.

It will be expected that each development in the divine plan will be perfect within its own limited purpose, but only the final operation will bring about the perfection in view. So, in regard to God's intention for it, the Levitical priesthood, as a system, was perfect; but with regard to the final purpose of God, it was decidedly imperfect. Its imperfection lay exactly in its inability to produce perfection. It could not bring men to the place of God's intention, namely, full communion on a basis completely satisfactory to the divine holiness. This is seen in a fact already noted, that the high priest of Israel, entering within the veil into the holiest of all, was in no sense a forerunner. His going in with the blood of the appointed sacrifice did not open the way for the people to press into the presence of God. The holy place stood as a constant testimony that "the way into the holiest . . . was not yet made manifest" (Heb 9:8).

Moreover, the Levitical priesthood was tied up to a Law which made nothing perfect. The Law of Moses was indeed an expression of the righteousness of God, declaring what the righteousness of God expected and demanded of men. To the disobedient heart the Law is but a goad to lawlessness. I suppose that is the reason that some advocate the abandonment of law in favor of free self-expression.

The story is told that a foremost champion of self-expression was once discovered in great perplexity. His little boy, dressed in brand-new clothes, was having a glorious time in a big, dirty puddle. Asked by his friend what he proposed to do, the philosopher replied: "I am trying to figure a way of getting him out of there without letting him know that I want him out." The heart of man is just like that—willful, rebellious, disobedient. However, until the requirements of God are clearly stated, the wickedness of man is not fully known. The Law does not make men wicked; it reveals their wickedness. By it men are shown to be transgressors, and sin becomes exceeding sinful, since it is a sinning against knowledge.

We shall not ignore the fact that the Law, backed by the sanctions of punishment, is in measure a deterrent to evil action, while those whose hearts have been turned to God will earnestly seek to obey His commandments. But at best the Law is "weak through the flesh" (Rom 8:3). It does not carry in itself the moral force to produce what it demands. Especially is this true in regard to the inner springs of life. The command "Thou shalt not steal" may secure a measure of obedience so far as avoidance of open theft is concerned, but the command "Thou shalt not covet" conveys no power to purge the heart of its evil desire. "The law made nothing perfect" (Heb 7:19). It found men out in their sin, and left them transgressors. The Levitical priesthood, tied up to this Law, did not provide a putting away of the sin which was thus discovered. Even the great yearly Day of Atonement was a yearly remembrance of sin.

That was "the weakness and unprofitableness" (7:18) of the Mosaic system which necessitated a change in the priesthood. Now we inquire from this passage how the change was effected.

The tie-up between the priesthood and the Law is so intimate that a change in the one involves a change in the other. The Aaronic order being basic to the whole system, a transference of the priesthood was revolutionary. When the ordinance governing the Aaronic monopoly of priestly functions was set aside, the entire economy of Moses was subjected to displacement. The priest of the new order "pertaineth to another tribe, of which no man gave attendance at the altar. For it is evident that our Lord sprang out of Juda; of which tribe Moses spake nothing concerning priesthood" (7:13-14). We shall not expect the new priesthood to function along the lines of the Mosaic economy, save as it will pick up threads of eternal principles and purposes which ran through the temporary appointments.

In the Mosaic arrangement, the priesthood supported the Law, and the Law supported the priesthood. The separation of the tribe of Levi to the priestly office was an item of Law. Having no natural right, they could be supported in their place of privilege only by "the law of a carnal commandment" (7:16). The new priest depends on no such arrangement. He holds His office by inherent right, "who is made, not after the law of a carnal commandment, but after the power of an endless life" (7:16). The Law established men in the priesthood by means of a fleshly ordinance, an ordinance which regarded men according to their natural descent from Aaron and according to their physical fitness. Such an arrangement could not maintain a priesthood at the highest point of spiritual effectiveness. Oliver Cromwell was the strong man of the English Commonwealth, but his son was a weakling who could not support the new order. David was a great king, but some of his sons who succeeded him were reprobates. So Eli was a good priest, but his sons were villains. A priesthood, then, which depends upon a law of the flesh, cannot lead men to holiness and perfect relation with God. The new priesthood, after the order of Melchisedec, is subject to no such fluctuations in spiritual power and worth. Our Lord is established in it on the basis of His own native fitness, and "the power of an indissoluble life" (7:16, ASV margin) is the guarantee of perpetual and uninterrupted efficacy. All this, says our writer, is "downright evident" (7:14, author's trans.).

At this point the inspired writer waxes very bold. Having shown that perfection was not secured by the Levitical priesthood, and that another order was to arise, necessitating a change of the Law, he now makes the amazing statement that this new priesthood demands a sweeping away of the former. The very commandment which established and secured the Aaronic order is canceled by the appointment of Christ. Now if the apostolic writer had said, "The priesthood of Christ does not, of course, interfere with the functions of our priests at Jerusalem. They will continue as the earthly representatives of the High Priest above, and their ministrations will symbolize His service for us in heaven"—if he had said that, he would have had the acclaim of all Jewry, but he would have been untrue to his message. However deep the affection of Hebrews for their ancient priesthood, they must be taught that, with the appointment of the new order, the old is abrogated. The commandment supporting it is withdrawn, and it must dissolve. "There is a disannulling of the commandment going before for the weakness and unprofitableness thereof" (7:18).

But that is counterbalanced by a further statement: "On the other hand, there is the bringing in of a better hope by which we draw nigh to God" (7:19, author's trans.). The very purpose of priesthood is to bring us to God, to give us access, to make us acceptable. That is exactly what the priestly office of Israel did not do, and offered no hope of doing. Therefore, whatever function it did perform in the purposes of God, it was impossible that it should persist when once that priesthood appeared which fulfilled its essential task. Christ, entered into the holy place, invites us to "draw near with a true heart in full assurance of faith, having our hearts sprinkled from an evil conscience, and our bodies washed with pure water" (10:22). That is the "better hope" of the gospel.

The change of priesthood was effected by turning from Levi to Judah, by basing the new order on essential worth instead of on hereditary appointment, by abrogating the laws governing the old order; and now a new sanction is introduced to put the new order beyond all dispute—the sanction of the divine oath. Here, as in the case of the oath to Abraham, it is not to strengthen the word of God, for that needs no strengthening, but it is for our sakes, that "we might have a strong consolation, who have fled for refuge to lay hold upon the hope set before us, which hope we have as an anchor of the soul, both sure and stedfast, and which entereth into that within the veil; whither the forerunner is for us entered, even Jesus, made an high priest for ever after the order of Melchisedec" (6:18-20).

Now what do we have as a result of all this change? First the priestly office is permanently in the hands of one Man, the God-man. "He hath an untransmissible priesthood" (7:24, author's trans.). There is no possibility of deterioration through the coming of an inferior successor. You know how a church will grow to great strength under an able pastor, and unless a most suitable successor is found, very trying days follow the death or departure of the one around whom it was built. I think of a work in Scotland whose founder was the active leader for sixty-four years! It became a great evangelical and missionary center. After a long vacancy a young man was called to the pastorate, but the relation was short-lived, and again the church had several pastorless years. The office of Christ will never be vacant, and will never fall into inferior hands.

Again, the One who fills the post of High Priest is eminently and perfectly fitted. "For such an high priest became us, who is holy, harmless, undefiled, separate from sinners, and made higher than the heavens" (7:26). For character and dignity there is not His equal. He has no need to offer sacrifice for Himself, being the sinless One; and in offering Himself, He has offered the one sufficient sacrifice for all. He does not require to be ever laying again the foundation of His intercessions in ever repeated offerings.

His mighty blood did once atone,
And now it pleads before the throne.

With an untransmissible priesthood in the hands of an all-perfect Priest, whose ministrations on our behalf find their all-efficient basis in the one all-sufficient sacrifice of Calvary, we shall not be disappointed in the service rendered. "Wherefore he is able also to save them to the uttermost that come unto God by him, seeing he ever liveth to make intercession for them" (7:25).

Now I should like to start all over again and dwell on that "able . . . to save . . . to the uttermost." For I see there the picture of our great High Priest taking hold of an uttermost sinner like Saul of Tarsus or Augustine or me, and giving him the cleansing of His precious blood, and refining him through the fires of His disciplines, and renewing him daily by His Holy Spirit, and making him walk in the light of God's countenance, till at last He presents that redeemed sinner faultless before the presence of His glory with exceeding joy, while the hosts of heaven lift their shout of wonder and praise to the God of all grace, who out of a bit of broken earthenware brought a son to glory, a radiant image and reflection of the Saviour Himself. Only let Jesus be your High Priest, and He will not rest till He has you among the uttermost sinners who have attained the uttermost and eternal holiness of heaven.

But I must not forget that, amid all the blessed aspects of full salvation hinted at here, the one perfection specially in mind is the perfection of communion with God. The test of all priesthood is its ability to give access to God, and the perfection of Christ's priesthood is that the uttermost sinner may come by Him to God and find full acceptance, a glad welcome, as a beloved son. This, He gives us now, so mighty and effective are His intercessions, based on that once for all sacrifice of infinite merit: till you and I, sinners that we are, unworthy as we are, can draw near to the everlasting throne of the divine majesty and address its occupant as "my dear heavenly Father." Now you cannot so approach God by any other than Jesus. No other priest, no other name, can give you this access. God will hide Himself from you, He will shut His ears to you, if you presume to come otherwise than by this great High Priest after the order of Melchisedec; and in that great day of appearing before God, if you stand without the advocacy of Jesus, the awful words of divine repudiation will thrust you into the outer darkness, a lost soul, lost to the uttermost. I beseech you, therefore, commit yourself to the care of the only Priest who can bring you to God. Let not the multitude of your sins deter you. He will save from the uttermost, to the uttermost, and none will have more right to the loving intimacies of the throne of grace than you, and I.

17

THE CROWNING POINT

HEBREWS 8:1-2

Here we view our Lord as:

1. The Occupier of the eternal throne
2. The Minister of the heavenly sanctuary

"WE HAVE *such* AN HIGH PRIEST" (Heb 8:1, italics added). Now, that so ordinary word "such" assumes great dignity here, for it gathers up into itself all that has been said in the epistle about our glorious Lord—His rank, His titles, His honors, His humiliation, His sympathy, His holiness, His triumphs, His office, His order, His ministry. Yes, our very common word is here carrying so great a weight of glory that we are baffled to define its content.

O could I speak the matchless worth,
O could I sound the glories forth
  Which in my Saviour shine!
I'd soar and touch the heavenly strings,
And vie with Gabriel while he sings
  In notes almost divine.

LOWELL MASON

And this is the crowning point of the whole epistle, that "we have such an high priest," so glorious in His person, so complete in His character, so able in His ministry. Line upon line His excellencies have been set before us, and now, before proceeding to the various aspects of His priestly work, we are asked to tarry at this point to allow the reality of it all to bear in upon our souls and to lift us up into living relation with our great High Priest.

In this moment of review and focus, two features are specially emphasized—His seat and His sanctuary.

"We have such a high priest, who sat down on the right hand of the throne of the Majesty in the heavens" (8:1, ASV).

> The highest seat that heaven affords
> Is His by sovereign right:
> The King of kings, and Lord of lords,
> He reigns in perfect light.

This place of honor is indeed His by sovereign, native right. It was His before the worlds were framed, before the ages began to roll. "Glorify thou me with thine own self with the glory which I had with thee before the world was" (John 17:5). So spoke He to the Father in the days of His humiliation, "Who in the beginning was the mighty Word" (1:1, author's trans.).

The throne of glory is His also by right of reward. A finished work has earned this seat of rest. Through much travail of soul He finished the work which the Father gave Him to do on earth. From the deep darkness of the place of a skull He cried with a loud voice, "It is finished" (19:30). And now the throne is the place of His rest.

A deep humiliation has earned the seat of exaltation. As He taught, He acted. "Whosoever exalteth himself shall be abased; and he that humbleth himself shall be exalted" (Luke 14:11). So He taught, and of the former statement He is Himself the noblest Example. Who has so humbled Himself as the Lord Jesus, "from the throne to the manger, from there to the cross"? He stooped to be made flesh, who was one in essence with the Father; to be made sin, who knew no sin; to be made a curse, who was the center of heaven's benedictions. "Christ Jesus . . . existing in the form of God, counted not the being on an equality with God a thing to be grasped, but emptied himself, taking the form of a servant, being made in the likeness of men; and, found in outward form as a man, he humbled himself, becoming obedient even unto death, the death of the cross; therefore God exalted him on high, and freely bestowed on him the name which is above every name, so that in the name of Jesus every knee should bow . . . and that every tongue should confess that Jesus Christ is Lord, to the glory of God the Father" (Phil 2:5-10, author's trans.).

It is infinitely comforting to remember that Jesus brought His divine nature into our human frame, and that He carried our human nature, which He took, into His divine exaltation. He is there "on the right hand of the throne of the Majesty in the heavens" (Heb 8:1*b*) not as God only, but as man. He did not "slough off" our humanity when He ascended to heaven: He is still a Member of our race—He is our race in its renewal. He is therefore no stranger to our needs, our temptations, our sorrows, our trials, our frailties.

> Though now ascended up on high,
> He bends on earth a Brother's eye;
> Partaker of the human name,
> He knows the frailty of our frame.
>
> Our Fellow-sufferer yet retains
> A fellow-feeling of our pains;
> And still remembers, in the skies,
> His tears, and agonies, and cries.
>
> In every pang that rends the heart
> The Man of Sorrows has a part;
> He sympathizes with our grief,
> And to the sufferer sends relief.

"We have such an high priest," so exalted, so compassionate. Surely we can commit our souls to Him without fear. Suppose a simple devotee of the Roman Catholic faith were to secure the personal services of the pope as his confessor and priest! He would certainly feel that he was receiving the utmost of priestly service, and all the benefits possible from it. But who would consider the priestly offices of a fellow sinner when the Lord Himself, the Man at God's right hand, brings all the resources of His exalted state, and all the love of His understanding heart, to the help of His people!

All this deals with the regal state of our great High Priest. The second thought has to do with the sphere of His ministry. He is "minister of the sanctuary, and of the true tabernacle, which the Lord pitched, and not man" (8:2). The contrast is, of course, with the tabernacle, or tent, which Moses pitched in the wilderness, and which, in its essential features, was the pattern of the Temple which Solomon afterward built. The contrast is not between false and true, but between shadow and substance, picture and reality. The tabernacle of Moses, in which Aaron ministered, was a faithful production "according to the pattern" (8:5) which God showed him, but it was earthly, carnal, making its appeal through the senses, and perishable. Such a sanctuary became Aaron, who was himself compassed with the infirmities of mortality, but He who only has immortality, who ministers after the power of an indissoluble life, must find the sphere of His service in a sanctuary as imperishable as Himself. His priesthood, therefore, is exercised in heaven, in the eternal sanctuary of the divine presence.

We of the nonconformist faith find the notion of a sanctuary somewhat foreign to our thinking. Sacred places have little appeal for us. I remember the days of my boyhood in Scotland, where the work of the ministry was held in high esteem. There the pulpit was a sacred place. It was hallowed by the preaching of the Word of God, and we were taught to hold it in reverence. We would not think of mounting the pulpit without special invitation, and then we felt that we were on holy ground. I confess that to this day I cannot shake off that old feeling of awe in entering a pulpit, my own or another, and I am still conscious of pain when its sanctity is violated by frivolous uses. But even that mild regard for a place, based simply on the use to which it is dedicated, and not on any sacramentarian idea, is largely disregarded, and sometimes even condemned. I am sure we gain immeasurably by a proper emancipation from localized sanctity, but we may also have lost a real help toward a heart appreciation of the biblical thought of a sanctuary. Every one of us will have to seek his own way back to this thought, that there is a hallowed place where the mysterious ministries of our great High Priest are exercised in the presence of God.

"A minister of the sanctuary." That word "minister" is significant. It translates a Greek word which indicates one who serves the state in a specified office. It is a civic term. The Holy Spirit, in teaching the inspired writers the vocabulary of the new covenant, set aside many of the religious captions of classical Greek because of their association with idolatry, and elevated other words from the secular sphere, pouring new content into them. This word before us is in the latter class, having its former sense enlarged till it includes the connotation of one who does service toward God in some stated office.

We derive our word *liturgy* from it. The verb form appears in the thirteenth chapter of Acts, where we read of the prophets and teachers of the church in Antioch *ministering to the Lord* (see Acts 13:2). It is definitely a word connected with the holy place.

We have a remarkable picture of Jesus as "minister of the sanctuary" in the eighth chapter of Revelation. I have no doubt that the angel there shown, standing over the altar, is our Lord in His priestly activity. The altar is the place of offering, and if we must identify the heavenly altar with the golden altar, the altar of incense, we shall remember that both the golden altar and the incense offered thereat, were sanctified by the blood which was placed upon the horns. Christ "through his own blood, entered in once for all into the holy place" (Heb 9:12, ASV). His blood has sanctified the altar for the exercise of His priestly work on behalf of redeemed sinners. As our prayers ascend to heaven, then, they are subjected to a twofold operation in the hands of our great High Priest. They are cleansed by the blood of the altar, cleansed from the selfishness and the grossness and the panic which we pour into them; and they are enriched with the "much incense" (Rev 8:3) of our blessed Lord's infinite graces. I declare we should not recognize our own prayers if we saw them as presented to the Father—so purified, so ornamented, so perfected. As they leave our hearts and lips, they are fit only for heaven's wastebasket, but as presented by Jesus at the altar, no wonder they are answered with mighty movements in the earth, the realization of God's purposes, the pouring out of God's judgments, the coming of the Kingdom of heaven!

Without such divine mediation, we should despair of any efficacy in our prayers, but what encouragement does our Lord's presence at the altar afford! Surely we can wax bold, and cut wide swathes in our prayers.

> Thou art coming to a King;
> Large petitions with thee bring;
> For His grace and power are such,
> None can ever ask too much.

He not only deals with our prayers, but our sins also, and our temptations, our burdens, our perplexities, our sorrows, our wants. The throne and the altar are His instruments on our behalf for pardon, cleansing, succor, strength, guidance, comfort, provision.

The throne and the altar mean exaltation and ministry, sovereignty and mediation, power and service. The Lord is my Minister! I bow in adoring wonder.

18

THE BETTER OFFERING

HEBREWS 8:3—10:14

This passage presents various aspects of our Lord's offering for sin:

1. The imperative of His offering (8:3)
2. The completeness of His offering (9:14)
3. The finality of His offering (9:25, 28)
4. The instrument of His offering (10:5)
5. The effectiveness of His offering (10:10, 14)

"IT IS NECESSARY for this man also to have something which he may offer" (Heb 8:3*b*, author's trans.), for offering is of the very genius of priesthood. "Every high priest is appointed to offer gifts and sacrifices" (8:3*a*, ASV). But whence arises this necessity, which imposes itself even upon the Son of God if He would fulfill His priesthood "after the order of Melchisedec" (7:21*b*)? It arises from the fact of sin. The offering that must be presented is an offering for sin, an offering that will cover sin, atone for sin, cancel sin, put away sin. It is conceivable that the Son of God might have represented man in a sinless economy, in which case no such necessity of having somewhat to offer would have rested upon Him, save as our thank offerings would have ascended by Him to the Father. That is in the realm of speculation, for we know nothing about a sinless economy. Even in the eternal Kingdom of heaven where no sin may enter, we shall be present as those who have been loosed from our sins, and whose acceptance with God rests upon the offering of our great High Priest.

This imperative of sacrifice is presented with the first entering of sin into our race. "So soon as, and so long as, sin is in the world, there is a saving activity of God." That saving activity begins with and rests on the provision of an offering for expiation. We remember how our first parents, stung to shame and fear by their sin, clothed themselves with fig leaves sewn together. This represented human efforts at recovery, but was rejected by God, who clothed them with coats of skin, necessitating sacrifice in the shedding of blood. This is the first picture given us in the Bible of God's method of restoring men—by means of an offering for sin. Franz Delitzsch truly declares that "the whole work of salvation was herein prefigured." Later, in connection with the giving of the Law, which was designed and destined to manifest the utter sinfulness of men in their transgressions of the commandments, God instituted the elaborate priestly system of Aaron, in which offerings for sin were multiplied almost without number, all to emphasize the necessity of expiation through appropriate sacrifice. Our sin, then, has imposed this requirement upon our great High Priest—He must have an offering to present on our behalf, sufficient to make adjustment, to make reconciliation, to restore us to divine favor.

Now the offerings whose blood the high priests of old brought into the Holy of Holies did not cost them anything. They were chosen to bring the offerings of the people themselves to God. Not so is the offering of Jesus. When David was commanded to build an altar on the threshing floor of Ornan the Jebusite, and to present an offering to God for the staying of the judgment upon Jerusalem which the presumptuous sin of the king had incurred, the good and loyal owner of the site desired to donate all the requisites for the sacrifice, including the animals. David, however, was of a different mind, saying to his generous subject: "Nay; but I will verily buy it for the full price: for I will not take that which is thine for the LORD, nor offer burnt offerings without cost" (1 Chron 21:24). Even so our great High Priest, although the sin for which He offered was ours, not His, would not, could not, offer "without cost." For one thing, He assumed the burden of our sin which was too heavy for us, and made Himself liable for the offering; and in addition, no offering was found in our hands sufficient to cover our sin. It was for that very reason that our Lord undertook the tremendous task. Listen to this remarkable statement of our helplessness from the psalmist:

> They that trust in their wealth,
> And boast themselves in the multitude of their riches;
> None of them can by any means redeem his brother,
> Nor give to God a ransom for him: . . .
> That he should still live alway,
> That he should not see corruption.
>
> PSALM 49:6-9 (ASV)

But I have omitted a sentence which our translators have put in parenthesis, and it stands out as the explanation of the whole: "For the redemption of their soul is costly, and must be let alone for ever" (49:8, author's trans.). Many things we can do for ourselves and for one another. Wealth will come to our aid in many matters, but when it comes to redemption, we have to give up. That is something beyond human help, beyond the power of riches to purchase.

But listen again as a voice still more ancient, by a flash of spiritual illumination, declares the hope of hopeless man.

> If there be with him an angel,
> An interpreter, one among a thousand,
> To show unto man what is right for him;
> Then God is gracious unto him, and saith,
> Deliver him from going down to the pit,
> I have found a ransom.
>
> JOB 33:23-24 (ASV)

Blessed be God, that angel, interpreter, mediator, that "one in a thousand," has appeared, crying, "Deliver him from going down to the pit, I have found a ransom." And what is that ransom, costlier, more precious, than all the wealth of this world? It is Himself! That is what our second text says: "Christ . . . through the eternal Spirit offered himself without blemish unto God" (Heb 9:14, ASV). No less an offering could cover our sin. He offered Himself in all the infinite glories of His divine nature, in all the absolute perfections of His human character, in all the perfect obedience of His humiliation, in all the exquisite sufferings of His cross. From that amazing moment in the councils of God when the eternal Word, "being in the form of God, counted it not a prize to be on an equality with God, but emptied himself, taking the form of a servant" (Phil 2:6-7*a*, author's trans.), right on to the moment in history when "being found in fashion as a man, he humbled himself, becoming obedient even unto death, yea, the death of the cross" (2:7*b*-8, ASV), He was engaged in one grand offering of Himself for us; and when He ascended on high, it was Himself, in all His obedience and abasement and sin bearing, in all His living and dying and living again for us, that He presented Himself before the throne of God. That was not the offering of a moment, but an offering that fills time and eternity, an enduring offering, eternally acceptable, eternally sufficient, eternally efficacious. Tell me only that "the Son of God . . . loved me, and gave himself for me" (Gal 2:20*b*), and my heart rests in the undisturbed assurance that "It is well, it is well with my soul."

Right here appears the great difference between the offerings of the priests of the Aaronic order and the offering of our High Priest, Jesus. Year by year those high priests carried the blood of their offerings into the Holy of Holies. Why the repetition? Because theirs was the offering of a moment, an offering which could not take away sin, but ordained only to sustain a temporary arrangement until the final offering should be made manifest. The offering of Jesus is that final offering. Being complete, it allows no complement or supplement. Being final, it permits no repetition. "For Christ entered not into a holy place made with hands, like in pattern to the true; but into heaven itself, now to appear before the face of God for us: nor yet that he should suffer himself often, as the high priest entereth into the holy place year by year with blood not his own; else must he often have suffered since the foundation of the world" (Heb 9:24-26, ASV). See how the offering of Christ is linked to the sufferings of the cross, as necessary to it, so that a repetition of the offering would mean a repetition of the sufferings, and all Scripture, and with special force this one, is dead against that thought. "Christ was once [for all] offered to bear the sins of many" (9:28).

With such emphasis on the finality of the offering of Christ, what a blasphemy, what a monstrosity, is the perpetual sacrifice of the Roman mass! It is the boast of the Roman hierarchy that Christ is offered four times per second on their altars! That the Son of God, obedient to the word of their priests, humbles Himself to be immolated on their altars four times for every tick of the clock! And to think that they make the efficacy of our Lord's complete and final offering depend upon this childish repetition! As I understand the Scriptures, the benefits of our Lord's sacrifice are mediated to us by the operation of the Holy Spirit, not by sacramental rites.

The finality of the offering of Christ has also this solemn word for us: "If we sin wilfully after that we have received the knowledge of the truth, there remaineth no more a sacrifice for sins, but a certain fearful expectation of judgment, and a fierceness of fire which shall devour the adversaries" (10:26-27, ASV). What does that mean? What is the willful sin after enlightenment? It is the willful, constant, unrepentant refusal of the truth, in which one has had adequate knowledge imparted to him. He may have inclined to it with some favor for a time, but at last has settled into adamant rejection. Lest any should so act, and thereby lose his soul, the reminder is solemnly given: "Remember, the offering of Christ is final. The rejection of Him is therefore the sealing of one's doom. For no further sacrifice for sin is provided" (10:26, author's trans.). Will a man refuse the only open exit from a burning building? Will a drowning man despise the only rope thrown to him from land? He is infinitely more foolish who will refuse Jesus, who has made the offering for sin which stands alone and final.

Now I want you to notice from our text that this one, final offering of our Lord, which is the foundation of His priestly ministry, necessitated the incarnation, His coming into our flesh. "For it is impossible that the blood of bulls and goats should take away sins. Wherefore when he cometh into the world, he saith, Sacrifice and offering thou wouldest not, but a body didst thou prepare for me" (10:4-5, ASV).

We have already in this epistle seen reasons for the incarnation, especially this: "It behoved him in all things to be made like unto his brethren" (2:17, ASV). But here is a further reason. The giving of Himself was more than the consecration of Himself to a particular task: it was also the laying down of His life. That meant entering into a state of being in which that was possible. He took our flesh, that He might die for us. He received a body as the instrument of the offering. "Who his own self bare our sins *in his own body* on the tree" (1 Pet 2:24, italics added). "For Christ also hath once suffered for sins, the just for the unjust, that he might bring us to God, being put to death *in the flesh*" (3:18, italics added). So the memorial of His offering runs thus: "This is my body, for you. . . . This is my blood" (Matt 26:26-28, author's trans.). And in a glorified body, in which nevertheless the marks of the sacrifice remain, He exercises His priestly ministries on our behalf.

And now let two verses tell us of the amazing efficacy of our Lord's offering. "We have been sanctified through the offering of the body of Jesus Christ once for all. . . . For by one offering he hath perfected for ever them that are sanctified" (Heb 10:10-14, ASV). Two thoughts already stressed reappear here—the instrument of the offering ("the body of Jesus Christ"), and its finality ("once for all"). But it is the added thought of the *effects* of the offering that is paramount in these verses. The offering of the body of Jesus Christ has effected our sanctification. The periphrastic perfect form of the passive in the former of these verses tells us that something has been done for us and in us with abiding results, all through the offering of Jesus. What is that something? "We have been sanctified." James Denney offers a thought here: "He came to be a great High Priest, and the body was prepared for him, that by the offering of it he might put sinful man for ever into the perfect religious relation to God." Dr. Denney could have left out the word "religious" without hurt to his definition. The offering of Jesus brings us to God, and establishes us permanently in right relation to Him, for fellowship, for service, for obedience.

But now, in the latter of our two verses, we who have been thus permanently settled in holy relation to God are spoken of as *being* sanctified. Here the present participle is used, indicating that we are objects of a process. We are entering experimentally into the realization of our perfect relation with God, and are all the time being led to new heights and depths and lengths and breadths of divine communion as the cleansing, renewing work of the Holy Spirit is wrought in us. So we are being made what we have been made. We have been sanctified; therefore we are being sanctified.

Still another perfect enters here; however, this time it is the perfect form of the verb *to perfect*. This amazing, once for all offering of our Lord is the instrument by which "he hath perfected for ever those who are being sanctified" (10:14, author's trans.). This sounds very paradoxical, very contradictory, and yet, as I think the more of it, it seems very necessary. With God there is only clean and unclean, no partly clean and partly unclean. There are no grays in God's color scheme. We are either fit for God's presence or we are not fit for God's presence. If we are clean, we are fit; if we are unclean, we are unfit. Perfection is just cleanness. The end of our being is to be fit for God's presence, to be clean, to be perfect. Now we cannot realize *any degree* of communion with God without fitness, without cleanness, without perfection. So, because we cannot attain to that estate, God provides it for us. The offering of Christ has secured it for us. "The blood of Jesus Christ his Son cleanseth us from all sin" (1 John 1:7*b*). On our first coming to Jesus we obtained that putting away of sin which gave us access to God. We were given a perfection not our own, and by virtue of which we might draw nigh unto God. This is something permanent, and holds good all the while the process of experiential sanctification is going on, bringing us in practical character ever nearer to that perfection in which we stand in Christ. And when at last we appear before God, accepted in the presence of men and angels, it will not be on the ground of any *degree* of sanctification to which we have attained, but on the ground of that *absolute perfection* which is ours through Christ, who offered Himself for us. What a powerful offering is this! By it we have been sanctified, we have been perfected, and experientially we are being sanctified.

Not what these hands have done
  Can save this guilty soul;
Not what this toiling flesh has borne
  Can make my spirit whole.

Not what I feel or do
  Can give me peace with God;
Not all my prayers, and sighs and tears,
  Can bear my awful load.

Thy work alone, O Christ,
  Can ease this weight of sin;
Thy blood alone, O Lamb of God,
  Can give me peace within.

I bless the Christ of God,
  I rest on love divine;
And, with unfaltering lip and heart,
  I call this Saviour mine.

19

THE NEW COVENANT

HEBREWS 8:6-13

Here we find that the defects of the old covenant give way to the blessings of the new:

1. A new inscription
2. A new relation
3. A new communion
4. A new absolution

THE MINISTRY of our Lord Jesus draws its superiority from His own excellence, from the higher value of His offering, from the heavenly sanctuary in which He engages His priestly activities, and from the better covenant which is the framework of its exercise.

The faultiness of the earlier covenant, which was the basis of Aaron's ministry, is here frankly admitted. Was God then operating on the trial and error principle, testing out the Levitical covenant with a view to discovering the perfect system out of the defects which the experiment would reveal? By no means! The earlier covenant, with all connected, was faultless for the purpose for which it was given, but inadequate for the ultimate ends of God. Indeed, the fault of the old covenant was necessary for the immediate intention. Since it was designed to reveal the inefficiency of man, it laid a burden on man too heavy for him to bear, as Peter reminded the church at Jerusalem. When the covenant was first presented to Israel, they embraced it without hesitation, never stopping to question their ability to meet its demands. "All that the LORD hath said will we do, and be obedient" (Exod 24:7). It remained for all their history to discover their inability under that covenant of obedience, and there was nothing in the covenant itself to mend their fault. A faulty covenant can never mend a faulty people.

A priestly ministry exercised in connection with such a covenant of Law could not be entirely satisfying. It consisted of a ceaseless round of offerings that could not take away sin, could not make the worshiper perfect, could not give access to the holy presence of God. In itself, it was a continual reminder of sin. Had not the better covenant been in the mind of God from the beginning, so that its grace reached even to those who were under the inferior engagement, there would have been no meaning to all the service of the tabernacle.

But the new covenant was in the heart of God before the older was given, even before the foundation of the world. All during the days of failure, when the covenant of Law was being shown inadequate, and the covenanted people displaying their inability to keep the holy commandment, God progressively revealed the better thing to come, till, when the breach of the covenant had become complete, and the Lord's fierce anger was about to break upon the unfaithful nation, the terms of the new covenant were clearly given to the prophet Jeremiah. It was announced as a new covenant to the house of Israel and the house of Judah, but the apostolic writer, illumined by the Holy Spirit, reveals to us that it is none other than the eternal covenant, which is to extend to all the world, and under which the Son of God is to accomplish His ministry of redemption on a universal scale. It is "to the Jew first, and also to the Greek" (Rom 1:16*b*). Here indeed is one respect in which the new covenant is better than the old, because it is wider in its embrace. It is not confined to one nation, but reaches out in equal grace to all.

The fault of the old covenant is corrected in the new. The insupportable burden which the former laid upon the people is removed. What the Law demanded, grace undertakes. The terminology changes from "Thou shalt" to "I will." The inability of man having been demonstrated, God is now free to make full proof of His grace. "What the law could not do, in that it was weak through the flesh, God sending his own Son in the likeness of sinful flesh, and for sin, condemned sin in the flesh: that the righteousness of the law might be fulfilled in us, who walk not after the flesh, but after the Spirit" (Rom 8:3-4).

As soon as we begin to examine the terms of the new covenant, we discover that, although it is a covenant of grace, it is not a repudiation of Law. "This is the covenant . . . I will give my laws into their minds, and upon their hearts will I write them" (Heb 8:10*b*, author's trans.). His laws are a gracious gift to us, for the enlightening of our minds, and they are inscribed on the "fleshy tables of the heart" (2 Cor 3:3), not upon tablets of stone. Thus we receive the Law by an inward disposition rather than by an outward imposition. Andrew Murray suggests an interesting analogy: "Why does an acorn so spontaneously grow up into an oak? Because the law of the oak is written in the heart of the acorn." There is nothing forced, nothing legalistic, about that. Yet it is Law. As one of the old Puritans said: "All's law, yet all's grace."

By way of example, let us remember that the whole Law is comprehended in one word, "Thou shalt love." Now "the fruit of the Spirit is love" (Gal 5:22). We love, therefore, not by reason of a command to be obeyed, but by virtue of a divine life within. "The love of God is shed abroad in our hearts by the Holy Ghost" (Rom 5:5). If it be so for the sum of the Law, it will be likewise for its segments.

Such an inscribing of the Law upon our hearts marks an immutable union between the believer and God: "I will stand in the relation of God to them, and they will stand to me in the relation of a people." C. H. Spurgeon has told us of a costly gift that he received from John B. Gough. It was an ebony walking stick with a gold head studded with California quartz. One night the preacher's house was entered, and his famous walking stick taken. The thief hammered off the gold head and took it to a pawnbroker, who, on careful examination, deciphered the letters, S-P-U-R-G-E-O-N. He invited the thief to wait a minute, but the invitation was not accepted! The inscription, though marred, indicated ownership, and the gold was returned. The adversary may do all in his power to separate us from God, but His law inscribed in our hearts settles the relationship, and that stands forever. In our sorest need we have the privilege of looking to Him for divine assistance, and He has a right to expect of us such worship, love, and obedience as a redeemed people owe to their God.

This relationship carries with it an intimacy of acquaintance, or, in more biblical parlance, communion. "They shall not teach every one his fellow-citizen, and every one his brother, saying, Recognize the LORD: for all shall know me personally, intimately, deeply, from the least to the greatest of them" (Jer 31:34, author's trans.). This is the work of the indwelling Holy Spirit. The apostle John refers to this fullness of knowledge as the privilege of every believer: "Ye have an unction from the Holy One, and ye know all things" (1 John 2:20). And again: "The anointing which ye have received of him abideth in you, and ye need not that any man teach you: but as the same anointing teacheth you of all things, and is truth, and is no lie, and even as it hath taught you, ye shall abide in him" (2:27).

Where do "pastors and teachers" come in here? They are helpers together of our faith, but there is no room for the "infallible" interpreter, for the *vox ex cathedra.* The most unlettered believer may have as intimate a knowledge of God as the most learned doctor. This is the knowledge which comes from time spent in the secret place, and it is the privilege of all, the most obscure as well as the man of fame.

William Guthrie, one of the notables of Scotland's covenanting days, wrote a small book of divinity which marks him as a true scholar in the things of the soul. In the course of preparing this work, called *The Saving Interest,* he heard of an elderly farmer in the west country who had experienced much of the ways of God. The minister made the journey to the crude farm home, and sat in rapt conversation with the simple saint through the whole night and all the next day, as if he were sitting at the feet of a great master—and so he was! "They shall all know me, from the least of them unto the greatest of them" (Jer 31:34).

"The last shall be first" (Matt 19:30). What is the foundation of this new inscription and this new relationship and this new fellowship? It is a new absolution: "For I will be merciful to their unrighteousness, and their sins I will remember no more" (Heb 8:12). Very different from the word to Moses: "In the day when I visit I will visit their sin upon them" (Exod 32:34). And so it must ever have been had not God looked upon the blood of "the Lamb slain from the foundation of the world" (Rev 13:8). "The blood of Jesus Christ, his Son, cleanseth us from all sin" (1 John 1:7).

Others of the older economy besides Jeremiah caught glimpses of the grace about to be revealed. Micah's song is notable: "Who is a God like unto thee, that pardoneth iniquity, and passeth by the transgression of the remnant of his heritage? He retaineth not his anger for ever, because he delighteth in mercy. He will turn again, he will have compassion upon us; he will subdue our iniquities; and thou wilt cast all their sins into the depths of the sea" (Mic 7:18-19).

But of all the multiplied expressions used to describe the great absolution, none is more wonderful than this in our text: "Their sins I will remember no more." The old sacrifices could not give us that, "but in them was there a calling to mind of sins year by year" (Heb 10:3, author's trans.). Only the once for all sacrifice of the Holy Lamb could serve to erase our sins from the memory of God, and only when we know that this is done can our smitten conscience be at rest.

Great God of wonders, all Thy ways
  Are matchless, godlike, and divine,
But the fair glories of Thy grace
  More godlike and unrivaled shine!
Who is a pardoning God like Thee,
Or who has grace so rich and free?

This is the covenant, the new covenant, before which the former, ineffective and broken by a faulty and rebellious people, becomes old, decays, and vanishes away. This is the covenant promised to Israel, extended to the whole world, to be consummated in the golden city of God, whose sky will never be darkened with the remembrance of sin, where law is love and love is law, where God and His people dwell in perfect communion, where "we shall know fully, even as we are fully known" (see 1 Cor 13:12).

20

NOT WITHOUT BLOOD

Hebrews 9:6-22

In this chapter we draw three contrasts between the blood of the old covenant and the blood of the new covenant:

1. The blood of acceptation
2. The blood of purification
3. The blood of dedication

These three words, "not without blood" (Heb 9:7), well represent the prominence given to the blood throughout the Holy Scriptures, a prominence not confined to the typical ceremonies of the Old Testament, but extended to the ultimate teaching of the New. This has been a great offense to many, aggravated no doubt by the materialistic emphasis of some earnest but mistaken Christians. Only through a total misunderstanding of the biblical conception of the blood could any call the teaching of Scripture "a religion of the shambles," or "a slaughterhouse faith."

When our Lord spoke to the Jews about the necessity of eating His flesh and drinking His blood in order to have eternal life and enter into living union with Him, they received His words with a crass literalism which He corrected with the statement: "The flesh profiteth nothing: the words that I speak unto you, they are spirit, and they are life" (John 6:63). The application of that statement to the New Testament references to "the precious blood of Christ" (1 Pet 1:19) would save a great deal of misunderstanding. Theology and hymnody should both be permitted to use the biblical terms without being burdened with or accused of such literalism and materialism as cumbers, for instance, the Roman conception of transubstantiation. Dr.

W. H. Griffith Thomas, who certainly was no spiritualizer of Scripture, said in commenting on the verse, "Without shedding of blood is no remission" (Heb 9:22) : "Why is this? Is there any charm or virtue in that red fluid which we call blood, that it can put away sin? No, the material substance itself is nothing, it is what the blood represents and symbolizes, death and life."

God Himself has defined His terms for us in this very regard. In connection with the prohibition against making blood an item of diet, He said: "For the life of the flesh is in the blood: and I have given it to you upon the altar to make an atonement for your souls: for it is the blood that maketh an atonement for the soul. . . . For it is the life of all flesh; the blood of it is for the life thereof: therefore I said unto the children of Israel, Ye shall eat the blood of no manner of flesh: for the life of all flesh is the blood thereof" (Lev 17:11-14). Blood means life. Blood shed means life poured out. Sacrificial blood is life poured out, yielded up, for redemptive purposes. We did not think of the blood banks during the war in terms of ugliness, horror, and the slaughterhouse; we thought of them in terms of life—life poured out to give life. And if blood plasma, gathered from the veins of multitudes of the nation, carried high potency for life into the veins of our men wounded in battle, think you not that the sacrifice of the Son of God, His life poured out even to the bloodshedding of Calvary, will carry high life potency, in the spiritual realm, to men sick unto death with the wounds and poisons of sin?

Alas for those who are "squeamish" about the blood of Christ! There is no other cure for their ills. A British officer wrote me during the war concerning a German prisoner, the extent of whose wounds demanded a transfusion. Being a Nazi, and filled with bitter hatred for the Allies, he demanded to know what sort of blood they proposed to give him. On learning that it was British blood, he refused it, and died. Whosoever is offended at the blood of Christ is in the sad case of having no other cure. He will die in his sins.

With this background, then, let us consider the references to blood in this chapter. The first, which gives us our title, laying emphasis on the requirement of blood in the divine arrangement for salvation, speaks of the blood of access. "Now these things having been thus prepared, the priests go in continually into the first tabernacle, accomplishing the services; but into the second the high priest alone, once in the year, not without blood, which he offereth for himself, and for the errors of the people" (Heb 9:6-7, ASV).

Do you have in your mind a picture of the tabernacle with its three compartments? The court had the brazen altar, where the sacrifices were slain, and the laver, where the priests washed. The holy place could be entered only by the priests, where they daily trimmed the lamps on the seven-branched lampstand, attended to the shewbread on the golden table, and waved incense before the golden altar. Beyond that, behind the great veil, was the Holy of Holies, where was the Ark of the Covenant holding the tables of the Law, with the Mercy Seat overshadowed by the cherubim. This was symbolically the place of God's presence, hallowed by the Shekinah glory. To enter here was to come into the presence of God. Only the high priest had this sacred privilege, and that only on one day of the year, the great Day of Atonement. On that occasion, with great solemnity, he passed alone through the holy place, even the priests being barred from their sphere of daily ministry lest they should be tempted to look beyond the lifted veil. Entering the place of awful sanctity, he offered an atonement for the sins of the nation. But even he dared not enter without blood. For him the blood of atonement was the blood of access. Any attempt to enter the sacred precincts without the covering blood of atonement would have meant death to the intruder, high priest though he be. Even for himself, being a sinner, he must present the blood, and as representing sinners he must present the blood. So covered, he was received on his own behalf and on behalf of the people whom he represented.

But all that solemn service did not open the way into the holiest. So long as the "first tabernacle" stood, the place of daily ministration, it was the Holy Spirit's constant testimony that access to the Holy of Holies was not yet secured. The day after the Day of Atonement, the priests could not pull aside the inner veil and pass on into the presence of God. The entrance of the high priest had not secured that privilege for them. Much less could the people, on whose behalf the high priest had entered with the blood of atonement, claim right of entrance. The priests were still confined to the "first tabernacle," and the people still could not come beyond the outer court. For all this offering, and all this service, and all this solemn entering in, and all this sprinkling of blood—all were a parable for instruction. That endless round kept saying, "This is not the true provision. These are only 'carnal ordinances, imposed until a time of . . . [perfecting].' "

"But Christ having come a high priest of the good things to come, through the greater and more perfect tabernacle, not made with hands, that is to say, not of this creation, nor yet through the blood of goats and calves, but through his own blood, entered in once for all into the holy place, having obtained eternal redemption" (Heb 9:11-12, ASV). The perfect Priest, having made the great sacrifice, has been received into the true sanctuary of God as our Representative on the ground of "his own blood," His own life wholly poured out unto God on our behalf. Now there was never a moment when the Lord Jesus was not utterly acceptable to God for Himself. The testimony of the Father in the days of the incarnation was "This is my beloved Son, in whom I am well pleased" (Matt 17:5). For Himself, Jesus could have stepped right into heaven from the mount of transfiguration. He had no errors of His own for which to offer. But there could be no access to God, no return to the heavenly sanctuary, for Jesus *as our Representative,* without blood that fully answered for our sin. In the sacrifice of Himself, He discovered the eternal redemption, and with that, "through his own blood, entered in once for all into the holy place."

"Once for all!" Because by His entering in "through his own blood" He has opened the way for the sinner. One of the miracles of the day of the cross was that strange rending of the veil of the Temple from top to bottom, which itself should have spoken to the leaders of Israel, and all the people. It was God's symbolic way of saying that the barriers were now removed, that the way into the holiest was now made manifest. This is the "bringing in . . . of a better hope, through which we draw nigh unto God" (Heb 9:19, ASV). Is it not unspeakably wonderful that "ye that once were far off are made nigh in the blood of Christ" (Eph 2:13, ASV)? Surely you will not despise such holy privilege! "Having therefore, brethren, boldness to enter into the holy place by the blood of Jesus, by the way which he dedicated for us, a new and living way, through the veil, that is to say, his flesh; and having a great priest over the house of God; let us draw near with a true heart in fulness of faith" (Heb 10:19-22, ASV). Do you want the password for entrance into the very presence of God, the password for heaven? Here it is—*the blood of Jesus!*

The blood of access is also the blood of cleansing. Again we see the symbol in the ancient ritual of Israel, and the reality in the redemptive work of Christ. "For if the blood of goats and bulls, and the ashes of a heifer sprinkling them that have been defiled, sanctify unto the cleanness of the flesh: how much more shall the blood of Christ, who through the eternal Spirit offered himself without blemish unto God, cleanse your conscience from dead works to serve the living God?" (9:13-14, ASV). The special reference here is to a rite instituted to remove ceremonial defilement. In Israel, one who touched a dead body or a bone or a grave was reckoned defiled, and could not touch the holy things until he was cleansed. The means provided for the cleansing was the ashes of a sacrificial heifer, mingled with running water, and sprinkled on the defiled person on the third and seventh day after the polluting contact. This reminds one, indeed, of the holy water used so copiously in Romish churches, where it is forgotten that outward ablutions were abolished with the sacrifice of Christ. Moreover, the defilement involved in this case was not moral defilement, though it symbolized the pollution of sin.

Now, however the "holy water" of Israel could "sanctify unto the cleanness of the flesh" in a ceremonial and symbolic way, none of the sprinklings of the blood or ashes of slain beasts could cleanse the heart or the conscience of the defilement of sin. Yet they pointed to the effectual cleansing of the soul which was prepared in "the blood of Christ." In the redemptive sacrifice of our Lord there was such a complete and perfect atonement made that the vilest may be cleansed. Man's inability to cleanse himself from the stain of sin is well expressed by Jeremiah: "Though thou wash thee with nitre, and take thee much soap, yet thine iniquity is marked before me, saith the Lord God" (Jer 2:22). But the blood of Christ is the great eraser of the stain of sin. Professional cleaners apply tests to discover what produced the stains upon the garments which we send for cleaning, then they apply chemicals which are specifics for the various types of stains. Only one thing can stain the soul—sin! And only one remedy is effective—the blood of Jesus!

There is a fountain filled with blood
  Drawn from Immanuel's veins;
And sinners plunged beneath that flood,
  Lose all their guilty stains.

The dying thief rejoiced to see
  That fountain in his day;
And there may I, though vile as he,
  Wash all my sins away.

William Cowper

Some may not care for the vigorous figure of the fountain of blood, although it is suggested by the prophet Zechariah; but do not allow a figure to hold you back from the blessed realization of cleansing from sin and from uncleanness by God's own and only instrument of purification, the precious blood of Christ.

Canon Howitt has left on record an incident which took place at the Parliament of Religions held in Chicago during the Columbian Exposition in 1893. Dr. Hale was speaker for the Unitarians, Swami Viv Kananda for Hinduism, and that picturesque figure, Joseph Cook, for Christianity. Dr. Cook was the last to speak, after all the other representatives had expatiated on the glories of their several religions. Dramatically he moved to the front of the platform and announced, "I want to introduce Lady Macbeth." You remember the tragic scene to which he was referring. She had incited her husband to the murder of their king, Duncan, while he was guest in their castle. Now at last her guilt had caught up with her, and, despite her wakeful brazenness, her anguish was haunting her sleeping hours. Her physician had been called to her aid, and while he was present, the guilty queen walked and talked in her sleep. Her distraught mind was uttering its guilt: "Out, damned spot! out, I say! . . . Here's the smell of blood still: all the perfumes of Arabia will not sweeten this little hand. Oh, oh, oh!" That is the Lady Macbeth whom Joseph Cook introduced to that great audience in Chicago. Then he turned to Dr. Hale, the Unitarian, with this: "Have you, sir, anything in your religion that will wash away her sin?" A silent cloud on his face was Dr. Hale's only reply. The same question to the Hindu met with like silence. Then extending his great arms toward the audience, he cried passionately, "The blood of Jesus Christ, his Son, cleanseth us from all sin."

You cannot serve God with the dead works of sin defiling your conscience. To serve the holy God you must be free from the dread, haunting sense of guilt. No religious ceremonials, no penances, no new resolutions, will suffice, but resting in the finished work of the Saviour will give all the confidence of a heart at peace with God.

> Not all the blood of beasts,
> On Jewish altars slain,
> Could give the guilty conscience peace,
> Or wash away the stain.
>
> But Christ, the heavenly Lamb,
> Takes all our sins away,
> A sacrifice of nobler name
> And richer blood than they.

The blood next appears in this chapter in connection with the ratification of the covenant. The terms of the covenant having been made known to the people assembled in the shadow of Sinai, and accepted, Moses inaugurated it with the ceremony of blood, sprinkling all that was related to the new order and its services, including the people themselves, with the words, "This is the blood of the covenant which God commanded to you-ward" (Heb 9:20, ASV). With respect to the tabernacle and all the vessels of the ministry, this sprinkling of blood set them apart from all common objects, and hallowed them for sacred uses under the covenant. As to the people who were thus sprinkled with the blood of the covenant, it both committed them to the obligations of the covenant, and guaranteed the blessings promised to obedience.

The previous chapter of this epistle introduced us to the new covenant, enunciating its wonderful terms, all acts of grace on the part of God. This great new covenant of grace was also dedicated with blood. We remember our Lord's solemn act in what we call the Last Supper. "And he took a cup, and when he had given thanks, he gave it to them. . . . And he said unto them, This is my blood of the covenant, which is . . . [shed] for many" (Mark 14:23-24, ASV). Then He went out to inaugurate the covenant of grace in the shedding of His blood, the pouring out of His soul unto death. "For where a covenant is, there must of necessity be the death of him that made it. For a covenant is of force where there hath been death: for it doth never avail while he that made it liveth" (Heb 9:6, ASV, margin). All the rivers of blood under the former covenant were only writing this principle large for our understanding, and now it is come to pass, that by the blood of the Son of God the new covenant is sealed, and its blessings guaranteed to faith.

The vessels of ministry under the new covenant are not things of earth, "copies of the things in the heavens" (9:23*a*, ASV), but "the heavenly things themselves" (9:23*b*, ASV), and they are dedicated for the higher ministry, not by the ceremonial sprinklings of the blood of goats and calves, but by the redemptive sacrifice of Jesus. Everything in heaven has become an instrument of our Lord's high-priestly ministry.

By faith we, too, are sprinkled with His precious blood, and so brought within the operation of the new covenant. All the unconditional benefits of the covenant are guaranteed to us, from the forgiveness of our sins to the final perfection in the presence of His glory. If "without shedding of blood is no remission" (9:22) of sins, which is the first blessing realized under the covenant, we may know that all subsequent blessings are equally dependent upon the shed blood of our Lord Jesus Christ. How we should value His sacrifice, and adore Him who went to the uttermost of devotion, even to the death of the cross, in order to establish a covenant of grace in which redemptive blessings are multiplied to us without number!

But is there no responsibility resting upon us under the covenant of blood? Only the responsibility of recognizing an accomplished fact. The shed blood of Jesus Christ is terribly possessive. It claims everything that it touches and every soul that it touches. It redeems in order to own. It says to every soul, "I have redeemed thee . . . thou art mine" (Isa 43:1). Has the blood of Jesus touched you and redeemed you? Then own this divine fact: "Ye are not your own . . . ye are bought with a price" (1 Cor 6:19-20). All holy living and loving service will flow from that, not as a legal obligation, but as a blessed privilege.

Precious, precious blood of Jesus,
Shed on Calvary,

Shed for rebels, shed for sinners,
  Shed for me.

Precious blood that hath redeemed us!
  All the price is paid;
Perfect pardon now is offered,
  Peace is made.

Precious, precious blood of Jesus,
  Let it make thee whole;
Let it flow in mighty cleansing
  O'er thy soul.

21

THE THREE APPEARANCES OF THE SON OF GOD

HEBREWS 9:23-28

In this chapter we consider:

1. The appearing in flesh for sacrifice
2. The appearing before God for intercession
3. The appearing in glory for salvation

DESPITE THE NUMBER who have made the three appearings of our Lord, mentioned in this passage, a topic of discourse, the wine has not failed, nor its flavor been lost. Here we are at one of the lookout points of Holy Scripture, whence we view in panorama the marvelous works of God in His Son.

The appearings are past, present, and future, the first mentioned being the present, the heavenly one, which is the main theme of the epistle; but we shall follow the historical sequence.

"Now once in the termination of the ages, for the disannulling of sin through His sacrifice, He has appeared" (Heb 9:26*b*, author's trans.). It is quite evident that the appearing here referred to is the incarnation. This is an appearing in the midst of man, and presupposes a prior existence in a state beyond our ken. It is an appearing at a point of time which established enduring consequences. There is something final about this appearing, something terminal. Previous ages have been preparatory, but the age which witnesses His coming into the world takes on the character of finality. We remember that that note was struck in the opening words of the epistle, and carries through to the end. Finality, in the Bible, does not mean mere lastness in time. Does not Christ say, "The last shall be first, and the first last" (Matt 20:16)? The "ages to come" (Eph 2:7) will be no more final than this. Preparatory, provisional ages passed away with the appearing of Jesus. What a sense of urgency this ought to give to us who are privileged to live in this age!

The point of supreme interest regarding this appearing of our Lord is its purpose. "He [hath] appeared to put away sin" (Heb 9:26). Think for a moment of the immensity of that task. How can even one sin be put away? In this world of law, of cause and effect, of action and reaction, of sequence and consequence, how can one wrong be disannulled? If it is true, as Carlyle expresses it, that "the casting of a pebble from my hand alters the center of gravity of the whole universe," how can sin be recalled? Macbeth faced this very problem in contemplating the traitorous murder of Duncan:

> If it were done when 't is done, then 't were well
> It were done quickly: if th' assassination
> Could trammel up the consequence, and catch
> With his surcease success: that but this blow
> Might be the be-all and the end-all here,
> But here, upon this bank and shoal of time,
> We'd jump the life to come. But in these cases
> We still have judgment here, that we but teach
> Bloody instructions, which, being taught, return
> To plague th' inventor: this even-handed justice
> Commends th' ingredients of our poison'd chalice
> To our own lips.

No thought ends in itself, no word is its own terminus, no act its own goal. They are all irrevocable, and flow on in the inexorable stream of consequence, to ourselves, to our fellows, and to God. How, then, can sin be put away?

Yet unless sin is put away we are utterly lost. "Sin, when it is finished, bringeth forth death" (James 1:15). It works havoc enough in life, but it will not rest in its tireless revenge until it has demanded the supreme, ultimate, eternal consequence—death! "The wages of sin is death" (Rom 6:23). It pays many tokens in sorrow and shame, but these all are only the earnest of payday, when we draw death, the last, final, everlasting death.

To grapple with this desperate, impossible situation, the Lord of life stepped from behind the veil of His eternal glory and appeared in our flesh. He hath appeared to put away sin. A divine undertaking indeed! And how did he accomplish it? By the sacrifice of Himself! We immediately think of the cross, but let us remember that all "the days of his flesh" (Heb 5:7) were of a piece, and constituted the appearing to put away sin. His sacrifice reached its climax at Calvary, where it was all gathered up into one supreme act, but it was sacrifice all along the line, from the stoop to take our flesh to the last darkness of Golgotha.

Here we are handling supreme mysteries. To put away sin He must take it upon Himself, submit to having it laid on Him, and be "made . . . sin for us" (2 Cor 5:21). "Who his own self bare our sins in his own body up to the tree" (1 Pet 2:24, ASV margin), Peter tells us. There was a goal and an end to all this sin bearing. All that flows from sin to its uttermost consequence must be borne before sin could be disannulled, and that is what happened at Calvary. Whatever of curse, whatever of shame, whatever of sorrow, whatever of sting, whatever of judgment, attaches to sin, He had to endure, so that for those who seek refuge in Him the processes of sin are no more effective, but reversed and abolished.

This putting away of sin is costly business, but it is glorious business. Instead of guilt and degradation and bondage and condemnation and death, we have pardon and justification and exaltation and liberty and life everlasting! Just to think that all those ultimate outflowings of sin were accepted by our Lord and exhausted, till sin's dominion is broken and we are made God's free men! Sin's reign was ended at Calvary, its tyranny broken, its demands paid and the account cleared. There is nothing left of all our sin! It has been put away, removed "as far as the east is from the west" (Psalm 103:12); it can raise not one claim against us, whether to impose its consequences or to demand our submission. If we only half believed it, we would be shouting for joy all the day long!

Having so appeared among men and accomplished His great purpose to put away sin, our Lord now makes His second appearing, this one before God. "For not into holy places made with hands did Christ enter, the antitypes of the true, but into heaven itself, now to appear before the face of God on our behalf" (Heb 9:24, author's trans.). The sacrifice of the goat provided the blood of access for the high priest's entrance into the Holy of Holies in the Temple; but since the blood of goats could not put away sin, the high priest's access was only momentary, and even then not into the true holy place of the very presence of God. It was very little, therefore, that he could accomplish for the people in this annual ritual. Everything here is in contrast. Christ Jesus offered *Himself,* and entered by *His own blood* into the *true* sanctuary, heaven itself, not for a moment, but *in perpetual acceptance.* The thought of His appearing openly in the holy place contrasts remarkably with the cloud of incense which darkened the inner sanctuary when the high priest of Israel entered. It is "before the face of God" that our Lord appears, indicating the most intimate presence, while in the earthly sanctuary God granted only the mystic glory of the Shekinah over the Mercy Seat. The aorist form of the verb is not without its significance here, for while it does not in itself mark permanence, it does remind us that our Lord's appearing for us before God was not a repeated act, like that of the ancient priests.

The wonderful truth here defined for us is not that Christ, as a reward of His sacrifice, is given the privilege of beholding the face of God; but that, as reward of His sacrifice, He is made to stand before God's face as the accepted, beloved object of God's vision. He is there, not to look upon God, but to be looked upon by God. And wonder of wonders, He turns all this acceptance to our account. He appears before the face of God "for us." Clothed in our humanity, in which He is glorified with the glory which is His everlasting portion with the Father, He stands as our Representative.

What does all this mean for us? It means that we are "accepted in the beloved" (Eph 1:6); that "we have an advocate with the Father, Jesus Christ the righteous" (1 John 2:1); that the treasuries of heaven are accessible to us to meet our every need; that every moment of every day the supply of grace keeps flowing to us; that we are remembered before God in our temptations, in our conflicts, in our sorrows, in every situation of life; that nothing will be spared of all the infinite resources of God to perfect the work of grace which He has begun in us, and to "present [us] faultless before the presence of his glory with exceeding joy" (Jude 24).

Before Dr. Chapman, in company with Charles M. Alexander, left America for his British evangelistic tour, he had received ten thousand pledges of Christian people who committed themselves to pray for him every day. What a backing for any preacher! Nevertheless, in his farewell address he declared that if he had to choose between the intercessions of ten thousand and the advocacy of Christ, he would gladly renounce the support of his many fellow believers and rely on the unfailing help of His exalted Saviour and Advocate. Let us indeed pray one for another, but let our confidence rest in this glorious fact, that He who, in the sacrifice of Himself, put away our sins, now appears in the presence of God for us, securing the benefits of His redemptive sacrifice to all who believe, and assuring the abundance of grace to bring us to glory. He appears for us!

Now we come to the third appearing. "As it is appointed to men once to die, but after this, judgment, so also the Christ, having been once offered to bear the sins of many, a second time will appear, apart from sin, to those who are waiting expectantly for him, unto salvation" (Heb 9:27-28, author's trans.).

You see against what a dark background this glory is depicted. The course of unsaved men, unredeemed men, is death and judgment. Nothing could be darker. The appointment which men most try to forget is the appointment which none can avoid. A few may escape their appointment with the collector of internal revenue, and some may break their appointment with the dentist, but none has ever been able to cancel his engagement with death. All the advancement of the curative sciences has not prevailed to keep men from the grave. The other appointment here named is just as inescapable—"after this, judgment." This is a divine certainty. God "hath appointed a day, in the which he will judge the world in righteousness by that man whom he hath ordained; whereof he hath given assurance unto all men, in that he hath raised him from the dead" (Acts 17:31). Let those who deny a future judgment produce such an assurance to convince us! The "after" of the sinner's death is judgment. Woe to the man who dies in his sin and must stand in his sin before the great white throne of divine judgment! I would not be in that man's shoes for a million worlds.

But see how the picture changes in Christ. Christ met the appointment of death, by the grace of God tasting death for every man. His appointment with death was itself the appointment with judgment, not for Himself, but for us.

He will appear the second time. That is the second of the two great loci of Scripture, of history, of divine purpose. He came, He will come again. And when He comes, it will be to be seen. He will *appear* the second time. Every eye shall see Him. That is the "one [not so] far-off divine event to which the whole creation moves."

The apostle here speaks of the appearing of our Lord as it bears upon a particular group—those who look for Him; those who are crying, "How long, O Lord?" (Rev 6:10)—whose prayer is one with the Spirit, "Even so, come, Lord Jesus" (22:20). To these, His appearing will have an altogether different meaning from all others. The sin question will not be in view at all. Christ is not coming to make another sacrifice for sin. He will have something to say to the unrepentant and the unbelieving about their sin. His coming will very definitely have to do with sin in regard to all who have spurned His grace. To these He will appear for judgment. Not so for His redeemed ones. His one sacrifice for sin was the all-sufficient answer to the sin question for them. So effectually has He put away our sin that it could not be found although all heaven's intelligence service went scouring the universe for it. To us He will appear apart from sin.

Instead of death and judgment, therefore, there is an altogether new sequence for the Christian. His death has been accomplished, in all its totality as the wages of sin, in the death of the Saviour. The "afterward," then, is not judgment, but salvation. "Unto them that look for him shall he appear the second time without sin unto salvation" (Heb 9:28).

The salvation here in view is the "salvation ready to be revealed in the last time" (1 Pet 1:5), as Peter expresses it. We have already tasted salvation in the joy of forgiveness, in the thrill of the new life, in the emancipation from sin's tyranny, in the blessedness of communion with God, in the multiplied experiences of divine leading, preserving, providing and delivering. But there yet remains the divine perfecting. "Beloved, now are we the sons of God, and it doth not yet appear what we shall be; but we know that, when he shall appear, we shall be like him; for we shall see him as he is" (1 John 3:2). The perfection of moral likeness to Christ is part of that salvation that awaits His coming.

The redemption of the body also looks for that day. For He shall "change our vile body, that it may be fashioned like unto his glorious body, according to the working whereby he is able even to subdue all things unto himself" (Phil 3:21). The body will then be a fit habitation for a redeemed spirit: what largeness, what fullness, what glorious perfection! Yet a perfection capable of endless development. "His servants shall serve him: and they shall see his face; and his name shall be in their foreheads" (Rev 22:3-4). All the work of grace begun in us here will then be brought to its fullness in glory. "He which hath begun a good work in you will perform it until the day of Jesus Christ" (Phil 1:6). Then shall all the fruit of the appearing in humiliation, and all the fruit of the appearing in heaven, be brought forth and made manifest before God and all creatures.

When first He came, our blessed Lord and Christ
Stooped to our flesh, and in the common lot
Of Abram's seed partook, by suffering taught
The cost of true obedience, till the tryst
Of Calv'ry was fulfilled: Who knew no sin
Was there made sin for us, and sank beneath
The curse divine, that we might wear the wreath

Of life and blessing. When He comes again,
Not He to low estate will bow, but we
Shall heavenward rise to Him. Our mortal frame
Will shake the ties of its mortality
And bear His image, His all-glorious Name
Writ in our forehead, everlasting seal
Of oneness made complete, eternal, real.

O blessed hope! with this elate,
Let not our hearts be desolate,
But, strong in faith, in patience wait
Until He come!

22

NOBLESSE OBLIGE!

HEBREWS 10:19-25

In this chapter, after reviewing our high privilege in Christ, we examine three consequent obligations:

1. Obligation Godward—communion
2. Obligation manward—confession
3. Obligation churchward—consideration

THE DELIGHTFUL, old-fashioned French phrase which I have used as the title of this chapter is just about the most apt expression of the principle of grace that I know. Rank and privilege impose obligations and require standards of conduct, not set out in so many rules and definitions carrying the sanctions of this and that penalty, but by an inherent fitness. Noblesse oblige.

When the French revolutionaries tried to break the spirit of the young crown prince by setting him degrading tasks, he faced them with a defiant, "I am a prince!" We "are not under the law, but under grace" (Rom 6:14). Shall we therefore sin? Shall we therefore follow the low desires of nature because we are not under the Law? Perish the thought! Noblesse oblige! The place of dignity and honor and privilege to which the grace of God has lifted us has indeed emancipated us from the slavery of mere rule, but it calls us to standards of conduct far higher than those enunciated by the Law.

The epistle to the Hebrews has set forth the excellencies of Christ over all Old Testament ministers, and the exceeding blessings which fall to those who by faith in Him are brought within the new covenant. Now at this point the sacred writer recalls the chief privilege which the priestly ministry of Christ has secured for us and exhorts us to improve our opportunities, and adopt such life procedures as are wholly compatible with our new and glorious position.

"Having therefore, brethren, boldness to enter into the holiest by the blood of Jesus . . . let us draw near . . . let us hold fast . . . let us consider one another" (Heb 10:19-24).

Look first at the privilege. We have seen the high priests of Israel make their solemn entrance into the Holy of Holies of the earthly sanctuary through the appointed blood of atonement, only to go forth again and be as much barred from the sacred place as any of the lesser priests until another year rolled; repeating again and again a ritual which secured no access for the people, not even for the king. We have seen our Lord Jesus, "the full outshining of the glory of God and the exact image of His substance" (Heb 1:3, author's trans.), take upon Him the seed of Abraham, "in all things . . . made like unto his brethren" (2:17), "in all points tempted like as we are; yet without sin" (4:15); we have seen Him offer Himself without spot to God, sealing with His blood the new covenant with its better promises, and making effectual purification of sins in the sacrifice of Himself; we have seen Him enter into the holy place of heaven itself, "now to appear before the face of God for us" (9:24, ASV), "made an high priest for ever after the order of Melchisedec" (6:20), and sitting on the right hand of the throne of the Majesty on high. At last a Man has been found who is wholly acceptable to God, and through His all-covering sacrifice for sin appears, on our behalf, our great High Priest and Advocate.

Here, then, is the great difference between the work of Israel's high priests and the work of our High Priest: because they were sinful men, who had nothing to offer save the blood of bulls and goats, they could but enter into the holy place made with hands, once a year only, and could share even that small privilege with none; Jesus, our great High Priest, because He is the eternal Son, "holy, harmless, undefiled" (7:26), and has offered the one effectual sacrifice of Himself, has not only obtained access into the presence of God to act on our behalf there, but has secured like acceptance, like access into the holiest, for all who come by Him. We have "boldness to enter into the holiest by the blood of Jesus" (10:19). This "boldness" is not just official sanction, a decree of privilege; it is a liberty of spirit, a deliverance from timidity, in realization of the complete right of entrance which the blood of Jesus gives us.

> With confidence I now draw nigh,
> And, Father, Abba Father, cry.

It is not enough to know that we have access into the holiest; we must know the way, and the next verse tells us: "by a new and living way, which he hath consecrated for us, through the veil, that is to say, his flesh." The structure here presents many difficulties which would be fruitful study for the classroom. Here we shall be content to gather together the sense.

First, the way is a new one. The word translated "new" originally means "newly slain," and although it had already become weakened to mean simply "new" when the New Testament was written, we should like to think that the Holy Spirit may have had the older sense in mind when He breathed this particular word into the mind of the writer. Christ, newly come from the cross, is the way to God.

We are not here contrasting the new way to God with an older way to God. It is a new way inaugurated where there was no road. When we were in Gatlinburg, Tennessee, recently, we walked some of the trails on the lower elevations, the higher being still blocked with snow. On one of these foot trails we read a notice which informed us that prior to 1928 this was the only way across the mountains. Now there is the beautiful Chapman Highway winding up past the Chimney Tops, through Newfound Gap, and down the southern slopes toward Asheville. Jesus is not like Chapman Highway, a new and better road replacing an old and less commodious one. There is simply no way to God apart from Him.

Let us not miss the grand assertion that the way is also "living." Jesus lives. As He is the living foundation stone of the Temple, so He is the living way into the presence of God. "I am the way . . . no man cometh unto the Father, but by me" (John 14:6).

How was the way opened, or inaugurated? "Through the veil, that is to say, his flesh" (Heb 10:20). Only by the great stoop of the incarnation could the highway of redemption be made. The Son of God must, as Son of man, pioneer the way from earth to heaven, and only through His great sacrifice in the flesh could it be accomplished.

Not as a teacher, not as an example, not as a leader only, can He bring us to God, but as a sacrifice for sin. As the great veil hanging whole before the Holy of Holies in the Temple signified "no admittance," so the unbroken body of Christ but emphasizes the sinfulness of the sinner and aggravates his condemnation. But the miracle of the rent veil in the hour of our Lord's sacrifice was God's symbolic declaration that by the rent body of Jesus the way into the holiest was now made manifest. Millions of dollars were expended upon the Chapman Highway, to give easier travel across the mountains. The blood of Jesus was the unspeakable price paid to open this way to God for us. The veil must be rent, the blood must be shed. And now

> No more veil! God bids me enter
> By the new and living way—
> Not in trembling hope I venture,
> Boldly I His call obey;
> There, with Him, my God, I meet
> God upon the mercy-seat!
>
> In the robes of spotless whiteness,
> With the blood of priceless worth,
> He has gone into that brightness,
> Christ, rejected from the earth—
> Christ, accepted there on high,
> And in Him do I draw nigh!

And in coming, we have His support as "high priest over the house of God" (Heb 10:21). He has not opened the way, secured our access, and then withdrawn to other interests. He is there "before the face of God for us" (9:24, ASV), to bring us nigh, attend us in our approach, and plead our cause. What perfect provision! The King's Son takes us by the hand, conducts us to the throne of infinite majesty, presents us as His brethren, and secures our acceptance as Himself and in Himself.

That, then, is the place of honor into which we are brought in Christ. Noblesse oblige! What conduct befits those whom grace has elevated to such heavenly privilege?

First, "let us draw near" (10:22). In other words, embrace our high privilege. Draw near for communion with God, that lofty experience which alone truly satisfies the soul; draw near for worship, offering the sacrifice of praise to God continually; draw near for supplication, to obtain mercy, and find grace to help in time of need; draw near for intercession, fulfilling our own priestly ministry in union with our great High Priest above. Thus only shall we know the life abundant, thus only shall we grow into the measure of the stature of the fullness of Christ, thus only will the river of God be to us waters to swim in.

But how shall we draw near? What is the befitting manner of approach to God? Not by carefully practiced genuflections, prostrations, and intonations, but "with a true heart in fullness of faith, sprinkled as to our hearts from an evil conscience, and washed as to our bodies with pure water" (10:22, author's trans.). To come to God "with a true heart" means to come with "a heart as it ought to be," as one of the German commentators has it. Indeed, the phrase "putting your heart into it" would aptly express what is intended here. Sincerity, earnestness, and gladness all combine in this "hearty" worship, this drawing near "with a true heart." God's complaint about Israel of old was "This people honoureth [draw near to] me with their lips, but their heart is far from me" (Mark 7:6). Let not that be said of us whose privilege is so great, so holy.

Again, our drawing near is to be "in fulness of faith." "He that cometh to God must believe that he is, and that he is a rewarder of them that diligently seek him" (Heb 11:6). But our coming to Him is on such a high plane, in such a blessed relationship, with such complete acceptance, that our faith must be of an uncommon sort. Fullness of faith, freed from all admixtures or adulterations, is the only faith worthy of such approach as we have to the Father in the Son, our great High Priest.

Another double characteristic of our drawing near is given: "having our hearts sprinkled from an evil conscience, and our bodies washed with pure water" (10:22). The first of these is plain enough. It stands alongside of a previous verse: "If the blood of bulls and of goats, and the ashes of an heifer sprinkling the unclean, sanctifieth to the purifying of the flesh: how much more shall the blood of Christ, who through the eternal Spirit offered himself without spot to God, purge your conscience from dead works to serve the living God" (9:

13-14). Our communion with God must not be hindered and stifled by a defiled, accusing conscience, when "the blood of Jesus Christ his Son cleanseth us from all sin" (1 John 1:7).

The other phrase is not so easily understood: "our bodies washed with pure water." Does this call for ablutions such as the priests of Israel were obliged to practice before the exercise of their duties in the Temple? That would scarcely be in keeping with the spiritual emphasis of the New Testament, although cleanliness is certainly a Christian grace. Does it mean baptism? Many think so. But to Vaughan's statement, "The reference to baptism is clear," Professor A. B. Bruce replies: "Is it? It would have been if the writer had said, 'and your bodies washed with the pure water of baptism.' Wishes count for much in the interpretation of such texts. A reference to baptism in such a connection of thought would imply an importance assigned to sacraments which I should accept only on very clear evidence." I think Professor Bruce is right. We can take the washing of the body no more literally than the sprinkling of the heart. As the first phrase speaks of the inward cleansing, the second balances it by stressing the sanctification of the body for holy uses: "The body is . . . for the Lord" (1 Cor 6:13).

So the manner of our drawing near to God is: heartily, trustfully, cleansed within and without, the whole man "holiness unto the LORD" (Zech 14:21).

A second obligation is imposed upon us by our high privilege: "Let us hold fast [an unbending] . . . confession of our hope" (Heb 10:23, ASV). One who has experienced the blessings of the Holiest has been filled with a living and sure hope that calls for open confession. The beginnings of salvation have given him a vision of the ultimate of salvation. He owes it therefore to the honor of his God and Saviour and to the need of his fellowmen to declare openly His hope in Christ. Noblesse oblige! And if persecution attend his confession, if it be answered with unbelief, scorn, and all manner of evil treatment, if he find the world, yea, and his own people, against him, if he be cast into conflicts with principalities and powers and rulers of the darkness of this world, if his confession cost him his very life; he must still hold fast an unwavering, unbending confession of his hope in Christ. Loyalty demands it, the need of the world requires it, and besides all that, the faithfulness of God urges it. "He is faithful that promised" (Heb 10:23*b*). The oppositions of the world cannot affect our hope. Sometimes they affect our grasp of the hope, sometimes they diminish our confession of the hope, but the hope itself, that which God has laid up for us in Christ, is steadfast as the throne of God, "for he is faithful that promised."

His every word of grace is strong
As that which built the skies;
The voice that rolls the stars along
Speaks all the promises.

Since nothing that this world gives can add to our hope, and nothing that this world does can take from our hope, let no consideration of this world diminish our grasp of the hope set before us, nor bend, even slightly, our glad, eager confession of it. Secret discipleship is neither honorable nor safe. Failure in the confession of our hope soon means a weakening in the grasp of our hope, with resultant backsliding. At an after meeting in the Tent Hall of Glasgow, Scotland, a young man said to Mr. McRostie, the superintendent, "Look here, I've tried this for a fortnight and it doesn't work." Knowing what the young man meant, the kindly missionary asked, "Did you tell anybody what happened?" "No, of course not" was the answer. Then came this dialogue:

Missionary—Suppose I had lighted a candle and put a bowl on top of it, what would happen?

Inquirer—The candle would go out.

Missionary—Suppose I had a lighted gas mantle and a globe with no ventilation, what would happen?

Inquirer—It would burst.

Missionary—There's the electric bulb shining, yet I see no outlet or ventilation.

Inquirer—Oh, I can tell you about that. It has a positive wire and a negative wire.

Missionary—Thank you. Now I know what's wrong with you. You have no outlet, no ventilation, no negative wire. Go out and tell others, at home and in the factory, of your faith in Jesus. That will be your outlet, your negative wire to make you shine.

A week later the two met, and the young man's radiant face told without words that "it worked."

We come to the third and last of our obligations under grace. "Let us consider one another to provoke unto love and to good works: not forsaking the assembling of ourselves together, as the manner of some is; but exhorting one another: and so much the more, as ye see the day approaching" (Heb 10:24-25). Here the social aspect of the Christian faith is strongly accentuated. We are not so many isolated units, but "we are members one of another" (Eph 4:25). We are one body. Our own spiritual welfare, therefore, is not the sum of our concern. We have a responsibility for each other. No true Christian will ever ask, "Am I my brother's keeper?" (Gen 4:9). Striving after "love and good works" himself, he will seek to order his life in such a way as to stir others to love and good works. It is a strange, a startling expression that is used here: "Let us consider one another unto a paroxysm of love and good works." We have heard of a paroxysm of anger, but here is the divine conception of hearts almost beside themselves with a passion of holy love, issuing in works of excellence and moral beauty. And we are to consider how we may help one another along to such blessed attainment!

Two hints are given us as to how we may exert such influence. "Not forsaking the assembling of ourselves together, as the manner of some is; but exhorting one another: and so much the more, as ye see the day approaching."

The value to ourselves of regular attendance at the house of God, the assembling of God's people for worship and hearing of the Word, in incalculable, while its neglect is both a symptom and a virulent cause of backsliding. I have no doubt that God gives special grace and a special ministry of the Spirit to those of His children who are cut off from the assembly, by sickness or other cause beyond their control, but neglect will rather be allowed to reap its own harvest of loss and chastening. It may finally prove the indication that the neglecter was not a child of God at all.

But our passage exhorts us to faithful attendance in the place of meeting, not so much for its value to ourselves, as for the contribution it makes to the upbuilding of others. The minister may not always miss you if you are absent, but somebody will—somebody who looks to you as an example and influence in his life, somebody who is inclined to follow in your steps. Your absence will discourage him and incline him to careless ways. On the other hand, if you are always present, and always present with joy, and always showing pleasure to see him there, you will be stirring the love of Christ in his heart and establishing his ambition to follow the Lord fully. "Consider one another . . . not forsaking the assembling of yourselves together."

"But exhorting," encouraging, consoling, helping. Yes, it means all that. It certainly does not mean continually taking one another to task, lecturing one another. This is the verb form of the same word which is used of the Holy Spirit, the *Comforter,* and of the Lord Jesus, our *Advocate,* and of Barnabas, "son of *consolation.*" Is not that a beautiful relation to hold to each other? Who would not "grow in grace, and in the knowledge of our Lord and Saviour Jesus Christ" (2 Pet 3:18), surrounded by such tender, powerful influence?

"And so much the more, as ye see the day approaching" (Heb 10:25). The nearer we are to the coming of the Lord, the more urgently should these obligations of fitness compel us, that "when he shall appear, we . . . [shall] not be ashamed before him at his coming" (1 John 2:28), being ourselves ready, and having helped others to a state of readiness.

23

WARNING AND ENCOURAGEMENT

HEBREWS 10:26-39

In this difficult passage we discover:

1. A solemn warning against apostasy, strengthened by a triple argument
2. A strong defense against apostasy, fortified by a triple appeal

THE HIGHLAND RAILWAY of Scotland carried us through countrysides of rare loveliness and scenes of wild beauty. Suddenly our delight was interrupted as we plunged into the darkness of a tunnel, for we were not favored in those days with "lights on" for such dark minutes. The epistle to the Hebrews is something like that. It presents to us panoramas of grand truth, till our souls are lifted up in very rapture; but suddenly we are recalled from our exultation as a scene of dark terror lies before us, and the strident tones of the warning trumpet blare out.

No sooner have we caught a glimpse of the exalted glory of Jesus, the Son, above all angels, than we see a vessel drifting from its moorings and wrecked on the hidden rocks, while the admonition rings out, "Don't neglect."

Now in infinitely tender mood the writer shows us our Lord entering our flesh, "in all things . . . made like unto his brethren, that he might be a merciful and faithful high priest" (Heb 2:17) over the house of God; but momentarily we are looking back at rebellious, disobedient Israel barred from the rest of God, and the warning against unbelief resounds ominously.

Again we are just introduced to Jesus, our "high priest . . . after the order of Melchisedec" (6:5), and are beginning to exercise our hearts in contemplation of Him, when our thoughts are interrupted with dark visions of hopeless apostates, strengthening the urgent call, "Let us go on!"

Then follows a long series of lofty visions. The manifold excellencies of our great High Priest are presented. We see Him making the more excellent sacrifice, and with His more excellent blood entering into the more excellent sanctuary, sealing the more excellent covenant and securing the more excellent blessings for His people. The sustained glory is almost too much for us. But just as we are rising into our privileges we are reminded that there is a dark side to this picture. The greater glory and the higher privilege make the responsibility weightier, and rejection renders all the deeper and more certain the damnation which awaits.

As the visions are successively more exalted, the appended warnings are progressively solemn and awful. Having reached the climax of vision, then, we face now the climax of admonition.

"For if we sin wilfully after that we have received the knowledge of the truth, there remaineth no more a sacrifice for sins, but a certain fearful expectation of judgment, and a fierceness of fire which shall devour the adversaries" (10:26-27, ASV).

We must face the question, problematical and mildly controversial as it is, what is the willful sin referred to, and who are liable to commit it? In order to seek an answer, let us remember the situation which the epistle was primarily written to meet. It was penned for Hebrews who had embraced the faith of the Lord Jesus and had manifested their sincerity by enduring much suffering at the hands of their unbelieving brethren. But they had grown weary and faint in their minds by the continued pressure. They missed the awe-inspiring ritual of the Temple and the ministry of the priesthood, and, remembering that these had been ordained of God, wavered as to the rightness of abandoning them. Many voices called to them to leave Christ and return to their former estate, in good standing with their families, their nation, and the synagogue. They were in grave peril. For their sakes primarily was this letter written, to show them the glory of Christ as greatly exceeding that of the older economy, His work as the fulfillment of the types and shadows of the former day, and to warn them that abandoning Christ would involve them in a state of utter hopelessness. For with them it would not be simply a case of rejecting proffered light, serious as that is, but renouncing light already received, turning Christ out after having embraced Him, repudiating truth which they had fully known. It was no mere "backsliding," but a deliberate turning to be adversaries of Christ after being numbered among His friends.

The Hebrews of that early age are not alone in danger of such an act of apostasy. Conceivably a Hindu convert to the Christian faith might so abandon Christ to return to his heathen temple, a Muslim to his mosque, a Confucianist to his ancestor worship, a worldling to his temple of pleasure. The incidents may differ, but the sin is the same in essence—not merely a compromised backsliding, but a deliberate, willed abandonment of Christ to return to the former estate, made worse by such an apostasy. For such an one inevitably becomes a hot adversary, a bitter opponent, a fanatical enemy. He must drown the accusations of his own heart in an orgy of hate.

In so turning away from Christ, a man is deliberately rejecting the only sacrifice for sin. Calvary is final, and one who willfully refuses that all-covering provision for sin has forsaken his own mercy and leaves himself bereft of all hope. For him there is nothing left but a "fearful expectation of judgment, and a fierceness of fire which shall devour the adversaries" (Heb 10:27, ASV). And I pause to add, solemnly and earnestly, that that is the end of all who ultimately reject Christ, whether they have previously claimed Him or not.

A reference to conditions under the Law of Moses strengthens the solemn warning. Sin offerings and trespass offerings were provided to cover offenders under the Law in view of the true atonement which God was preparing in His Son, the Lord Jesus. One who set aside the Law, scorning its demands and despising its provision, exposed himself to double condemnation, for not only had he offended, but he had shut himself out from mercy. Sufficient testimony being forthcoming, there could be but one verdict and one issue, death.

The impression is very general that things are easier under grace than under Law, that grace has introduced a certain immunity which the Law did not allow. That is not the teaching of the New Testament. The blessings under grace are vastly greater than those under the Law, but the sufficiency of grace is to meet the severer demands of the life under grace. So also the judgments upon those who despise the blessings of grace are sterner than those meted out under the older economy. Listen to the solemn "how much more!"—"One who set aside Moses' law, custom was that he died without mercy upon (the testimony of) two or three witnesses. By how much think ye shall he be deemed worthy of greater punishment who trod underfoot the Son of God, and accounted common the blood of the covenant by which he was sanctified, and maligned the Spirit of grace" (Heb 10:28-29, author's trans.). God has given His Son. The Son has given His blood in the unspeakable sacrifice. The Spirit of grace has been sent forth to open men's hearts to God's wonderful provision. Could God do more to save men? What, then, if a man first receive, then turn adversary and trample upon the Saviour, despise His sacrifice, and treat insolently the blessed Holy Spirit of God who brought the grace of God to him! For such an one there can be no other expectation than "wrath . . . to the uttermost" (1 Thess 2:16).

For God's justice has not been drowned in the great tide of mercy which flows from the cross. He is still the God of recompense. He has not thrown away the balances and the sword. Therefore the man who rejects and despises the provision of divine mercy may expect only the full weight of divine justice. "For we know him that said, Vengeance belongeth unto me, I will recompense. And again, The Lord shall judge his people. It is a fearful thing to fall into the hands of the living God" (Heb 10:30, ASV).

All this seems to be a warning to Christians, and raises the question, "Can a true Christian so apostatize, so turn away from the Lord, and be lost?" It is our sensitiveness regarding, and our jealousy for, the blessed teaching of the security of the believer that brings the question to our minds. Actually it does not arise in the text. The writer is addressing the whole Christian community. He does not stop to differentiate between professors and possessors. It is not his prerogative to separate the sheep from the goats. He takes their confession of Christ at its face value. Many of those who seem now to be wavering have given evidence of sincere adherence to Christ sufficient to convince the most careful board of examiners. He does not care to question their standing, but he is concerned with their state, and, seeing their peril, issues these strong warnings to call them back from the precipice of apostasy. He is not content to let them drop over, then write over their grave: "They went out from us, but they were not of us" (1 John 2:19*a*). If that has to be written of any, his blood will not be in the writing. Rather, he will encourage perseverance, the final evidence of reality.

The terror of such solemn and dark warning needs the softening of some word of encouragement, lest some should sink into despair. And, indeed, many have lost hope, and imagined themselves numbered among the reprobate, just by stopping at this point. Some dear children of God have been brought into terrible bondage, and plunged into awful darkness by a wrong reading of this passage. Lighting on some sin which they had committed in a moment of willfulness, they have imagined themselves guilty of the sin mentioned here, and, failing to read on to the end of the chapter, have agonized in the despairing prospect of falling into the hands of an avenging God. How Satan has harrowed the souls of these perplexed ones!

But the encouragement is as strong as the warning, and as mighty a bulwark against apostatizing. See, for instance, how the apostle recalls the past faithfulness of these Hebrew Christians. "Call to remembrance the former days, in which, after ye were enlightened, ye endured a great conflict of sufferings; partly, being made a gazingstock both by reproaches and afflictions; and partly, becoming partakers with them that were so used. For ye both had compassion on them that were in bonds, and took joyfully the spoiling of your possessions, knowing that ye have for yourselves a better possession and an abiding one" (Heb 10:32-34, ASV).

These Hebrews had not lightly made profession of Christ. It had cost them something to join the company of His followers, and they had stood to the reproaching and reviling and despoiling without shame, even with joy, with the early apostles "rejoicing that they were counted worthy to suffer dishonor for the Name" (Acts 5:41, ASV). Now we know that the apostolic principle is "forgetting those things which are behind" (Phil 3:13), but in times when the spirit droops and the soul is cast down and the knees grow feeble, it is a good time to call to mind the days of vigorous faith and high accomplishment. Such remembrance rebukes our fallen spirit, and calls us to renewed consecration. Living over those days in memory lays an imperative upon us to live them again in reality. We feel that it would be a betrayal of ourselves to live on the lower plane. Yes, memory can be as the very torment of hell, but it can be the minister of God to hold us up and bear us along when strength fails, for it is not so much remembrance of what *we* have done as of what the grace of God has wrought for us and in us.

Again the encouragement is strengthened by an appeal to future hope. "Cast not away therefore your boldness, which hath great recompense of reward. For ye have need of patience, that, having done the will of God, ye may receive the promise. For yet a very little while, he that cometh shall come, and shall not tarry" (Heb 10:35-37, ASV).

We learned earlier that one thing we have through our great High Priest is "boldness [or confidence] to enter into the holiest (10:19). This we are exhorted not to cast from us, because it is freighted with rich reward, both now, and at the coming of the Lord. We all know that a confident coming to God is much richer in returns than a hesitant approach. God loves the bold challenge of faith, and delights to honor it. To cast away that confidence of approach, for any reason, is unutterable folly.

> It is His will that I should cast
> My care on Him each day;
> He also tells me *not* to cast
> My confidence away.
> But oh! how foolishly I act
> When taken unaware!
> I cast away my confidence,
> And carry all my care.

His order is better than that!

The will of God does not always pay off immediately. "Ye have need of patience, that, having done the will of God, ye may receive the promise" (10:36, ASV). Abraham did the will of God in leaving Ur of the Chaldees, but he did not obtain immediate possession of Canaan. The only plot of ground he ever owned there he bought for money from Ephron for a grave. But the promises were sure, and in the fullness of time Canaan was the possession of the people of God. The immediate return for doing the will of God may be scorn and misunderstanding and loss, but even out of these may come the richer reward. At any rate, if the wages are not immediate, they are sure.

W. Y. Fullerton reminds us that "It is only the casual worker that is paid by the day, the less efficient servant that gets a weekly wage. The higher you rise the more remote is the reckoning. When you become a partner in the business you will need to wait until the yearly stock-taking for your share of the profits." "Ye have need of patience."

For yet a little while—how little, how little!—
He that cometh shall come, and shall not tarry.

A little while; oh, rest in this, ye troubled,
And calm your every fear;
Look up, lift up your heads, for our redemption
Is drawing very near.
A little while and trials will be over
And suffering all past,
Our light affliction lost in endless glory,
And faith be sight at last.

A little while, and He that cometh will come,
And will not tarry more;
Blessed are we if He shall find us watching
Beside the open door.
A little while, so little, oh, so little!
He bids us patient be
Until the clouds shall part, the shadows vanish,
And we His face shall see.

Who would think of yielding to the pressure of the world, the flesh, and the devil, of friends and foes, to turn away from the Lord, when He is "at the door"?

And finally this: "The just shall live by faith" (10:38) ; not by ceremonies, works of the Law, or ancient ordinances, which all are passing, but "by the faith of the Son of God, who loved me, and gave himself for me" (Gal 2:20*b*) . No delight has God in any who shrink back from this boldness of faith. Such shrinking back dishonors Him, dishonors His Son, dishonors the cross, dishonors grace, and the end of it can only be—perdition!

But our writer is determined not to end on the minor key. He is bound that he will "lift up the hands which hang down, and the feeble knees" (Heb 12:12) , so he climaxes his encouragements with a great confidence, in which he includes those whom he has shaken to the heart with the terror of his warnings. "We are not of them that shrink back unto perdition; but of them that have faith unto the saving [possession] of the soul" (10:39, ASV). This perfectly parallels the cheerful note by which the writer enlightens his previous warning against falling away: "But, beloved, we are persuaded better things of you, and things that accompany salvation, though we thus speak" (6:9). This persuasion of better things, this expression of confidence, is a powerful stimulus to faith. The apostle Paul uses this wisdom frequently. To the Philippians he writes: "Being confident of this very thing, that he which hath begun a good work in you will perform it until the day of Jesus Christ" (Phil 1:6). See how he intrigues Philemon: "Having confidence in thine obedience I write unto thee, knowing that thou wilt do even beyond what I say" (Philem 21, ASV). And even the vacillating Galatians are helped by the same means. One moment Paul is weeping, "I stand in doubt of you" (Gal 4:20), but immediately he is reviving them with, "I have confidence to you-ward in the Lord" (5:10). How many a hesitant, timid, discouraged youth has been set on the way to brilliant success by the confidence of his teacher. "I know you can do it" has a subtle magic about it. So the writer uses it toward these wavering Hebrews, till, pulled back from the brink of apostasy, they are found among the "stedfast, unmoveable, always abounding in the work of the Lord" (1 Cor 15:58).

24

THE MEANING OF FAITH

HEBREWS 10:38; 11:1, 6

Three big thoughts emerge in this chapter:

1. The principle of faith
2. The province of faith
3. The product of faith

"THE JUST shall live by faith" (Heb 10:38). We know this pregnant little statement as the watchword of the Reformation. Luther the reformer got it from Paul the apostle, and Paul the apostle got it from Habakkuk the prophet. So W. Y. Fullerton of London quaintly calls the ancient prophet the great-grandfather of the Reformation: Luther the father, Paul the grandfather, and Habakkuk the great-grandfather.

"The just shall live by faith." It is more than a theological maxim; it is a principle of life. So it was in the heart of the prophet who first received it from God and wrote it down for Paul and Luther and you and me. He was living in dark and threatening days, but so well did he learn his own text that before he lays down his prophetic quill he is singing the triumph of faith over all adversity.

> For though the fig-tree shall not flourish,
> Neither shall fruit be in the vines;
> The labor of the olive shall fail,
> And the fields shall yield no food;
> The flock shall be cut off from the fold,
> And there shall be no herd in the stalls:
> Yet I will rejoice in Jehovah,
> I will joy in the God of my salvation.
>
> HABAKKUK 3:17-18

Cowper has arranged it for our Western type of singing:

> Though vine nor fig-tree neither
> Their wonted fruit should bear.
> Though all the field should wither,
> Nor flocks nor herds be there;
>
> Yet God the same abiding,
> His praise shall tune my voice,
> For, while in Him confiding,
> I cannot but rejoice.

In the letter to the Hebrews, our Reformation text is still a working principle of life. It is not simply telling us that a man enters into life by an act of faith. That is indeed the beginning, but the verse contemplates the righteous man, the "justified by faith" (Rom 5:1) man, going on to live on the faith principle, his conduct stemming out from his faith. Exactly this is what is illustrated by multiplied examples in the eleventh chapter. In Abel, Enoch, Noah, Abraham, Moses, and the rest, faith was not just a formula for getting into a right relation with God, but proceeded from that to be the determining factor in their manner of life. They practiced faith, satisfied to have no other provision than God.

Dr. W. Graham Scroggie once told us of an experience in his early ministry. He was faced with a situation in his church which was utterly contrary to his teachings. His officers steadfastly refused to do anything about it. At last the issue was drawn, and the church was forced to choose between their minister and this intolerable condition. Their decision went against the minister and the precepts of the New Testament. Thus, suddenly the young preacher found himself churchless and homeless, with a wife and two children to support. As he went about packing his books and other few belongings, several townspeople called on him, one being the editor of the local newspaper. After some conversation the latter inquired, "What do you plan to do now?" The minister replied, "The same as I have done heretofore—trust God." "Rather risky, isn't it?" exclaimed the amazed editor. Well, is it?

Many Christians, I fear, would so regard it. We are inclined to surround ourselves with safeguards against God's possible failure when we launch out in faith (!). So we would modify our text thus: "The just [I hope I am one of them] shall live [part of the time] by [a modicum of] faith [plus handy safeguards]."

Thomas Chalmers, that great champion of the Free Kirk of Scotland, was a heavy man. One day he went to visit in a home where the woman was having great difficulty in this matter of the life of faith. To reach the house he had to cross a burn by means of a bridge that did not look any too strong. The cautious Scot began tapping the timbers with his heavy walking cane to see if they would hold. The woman of the house, observing the minister's hesitation, called out to him, "Lippen the bridge, mister, it'll bear ye." Dr. Chalmers walked confidently over, and said very earnestly to the woman, "Lippen Jesus, woman, He'll bear ye!" That is not just the initial step; it is the practiced attitude of the heart in every circumstance of life.

The first verse of the eleventh chapter of Hebrews has been called the definition of faith. It is an unhappy term. The Bible is not given to definition. This verse is rather functional than definitive. "Now faith is the substance of things hoped for, the evidence of things not seen" (Heb 11:1).

Observe the sphere in which this working principle of faith operates—"things hoped for . . . things not seen." That is, the region in which faith works is beyond present experience. Once the thing hoped for is attained, once the invisible floats into sight, faith's task is done, to work on something else still unrealized, something else unseen. Such phrases as, "I'll believe it when it really happens," or, "I'll believe it when I see it with my own eyes," are the antithesis of faith. Faith has nothing to do with anything amenable to the demonstration of the senses. As soon as such demonstration is forthcoming, there is no further need of faith. It ceases to operate. I do not need faith to assure me that there were whales sporting about just off Nausset Beach, Cape Cod, on a certain August day in the year of grace, 1947. I saw them. You who were not there need faith to know it, for you have only my word for it.

Since this is so, one might think that the region of faith's operation would become more and more restricted as we attain to more and more of faith's goals. So long as we are in this flesh, at any rate, it is not so. Every advance in knowledge only opens up more and wider vistas of search. That is why our learned men are specialists. It is impossible for a scholar to pursue every avenue of knowledge, so it comes to pass that he knows more and more about less and less. Faith is something like that. Every exercise of faith calls to bigger activities of faith. When one hope of faith is realized, larger hopes call. As for the unseen: well, you know how astronomers used to count a few thousand stars. Then the faith of astronomers claimed more than could be seen. Next came the telescope, confirming their faith. Faith went out beyond the reach of the first telescope, till new telescopes caught up with faith. And always faith reached out beyond the limits of the most powerful instrument of sight. Faith is insatiable. Faith keeps crying, "More! More!" Faith champs at the bit. Faith refuses to stay by present attainment. There is always something beyond for faith, and its next bound is always bigger than its last one.

Faith is no visionary, imagining aery, insubstantial things. See what faith does in the region of the hoped for and the unseen. "Faith is the substance of things hoped for, the evidence of things not seen." The "substance" of things hoped for. That word "substance," or rather the word so translated here, is quite remarkable for its versatility. It seems to have been a legal term, used of the documents by which one might substantiate his claim to property. Then it embraced any strong confidence of assurance. It appears five times in the New Testament. Twice Paul uses it to describe the certainty of his boasting. In this letter it comes up three times, once to describe the essential being of God, once the confidence of faith, and finally this use in our text, "the substance of things hoped for." The basic thought is surely that of absolute certainty, a certainty which cannot possibly be frustrated or disappointed. Faith is the strong foundation upon which hope may rear her palace of desire. Without faith, hope could only build "castles in the air," but the great Christian hope is sure because based on the certainty of God.

"The evidence of things not seen." This is not something apart from "the substance of things hoped for," but an enlargement. Faith acts in the realm of the unseen as "a means of conviction or of proof." The Syrian hosts were continually frustrated in their military campaign against Israel because Elisha the man of God kept telling their top secrets to the king of Israel. They decided to stop this leak by getting rid of the prophet. They came by night and besieged Dothan, where Elisha dwelt. In the morning the prophet's servant was all in a panic, and ran to his master, crying, "Alas, my master! how shall we do?" (2 Kings 6:15*b*). The man of God was not in the least perturbed, but answered, "Fear not: for they that be with us are more than they that be with them" (v. 16). Apparently the youth did not take it in, but as he continued to fret and fume, Elisha prayed, "Lord, I pray thee, open his eyes, that he may see" (v. 17*a*). And his eyes were opened to the sight of the mountain "full of horses and chariots of fire round about Elisha" (v. 17*b*). Now, Elisha did not need to see them. He had the certainty of them by faith. Faith was to him the means of proof, "the evidence of things not seen." The young man, lacking faith, and therefore lacking the certainty of this evidence, had to be shown.

He was like a certain old farmer on the island of Jersey, with whom a brother-in-law of mine was acquainted. This worthy gentleman, having been persuaded to deposit his money in the newly opened bank in town, became fearful for his treasure, and returned in a few days with the demand that he be shown his money. The manager pacified him with a promise to show it to him one week from that day, but not till the exact amount deposited, in the exact denominations, was spread out before him was he at rest in his mind. "Blessed are they that have not seen, and yet have believed" (John 20:29). To those who depend on sight, certainty endures only so long as the outward evidence is in view, but the man of faith has the abiding evidence of things unseen. I suppose that Elisha's servant would have been as full of terror the next day had another company of Syrians surrounded them; Elisha would have been undisturbed. How much better is the evidence of faith than the evidence of sight! It is continuous, not spasmodic.

So on I go, not knowing—
  I would not if I might;
I'd rather walk in the dark with God
  Than go alone in the light.
I'd rather walk by faith with Him
  Than go alone by sight.

This faith is not only profitable, but indispensable. "Without faith it is impossible to please him" (Heb 11:6*a*), and the more we reckon on Him, the more we please Him. He is not requiring heroic deeds and polished speeches. He is just asking that we live our lives as those who count on Him. Donald Hankey, who was not always conventional in what he said or in the way he said it, gave us this striking statement: "Religion is betting your life there is a God." Whether we like the phraseology or not, he has packed a deal of truth into that sentence. It is a modern paraphrase of this: "For he that cometh to God must believe that he is, and that he is a rewarder of them that diligently seek him" (11:6*b*). Here is the principle of faith: always act in the certainty of God, and in the certainty that He will never mock our search nor fail our trust.

25

ABEL AND THE WORSHIP OF FAITH

HEBREWS 11:4

In this study we consider:

1. The basis of faith worship
2. The essence of faith worship
3. The witness to faith worship
4. The testimony of faith worship

HUSH! Tread softly and speak low. Two men are at worship, and in their acts of worship great issues are forming. The whole human race is being divided into two great streams, the one climbing up to God and glory, the other marching out to darkness and doom. For one is offering true worship, and the other, false; and while true worship is the noblest and the most ennobling occupation of the human soul, false worship is the most damning exercise in which man can engage.

"By faith Abel offered . . . a more excellent sacrifice than Cain" (Heb 11:4). That brief, modest statement tells the whole story. The essential difference between the offerings of these brothers was not that one brought a lamb and the other a basket of fruit. Rather, it was this: the worship of Abel stemmed from faith, that of Cain from self-will.

To understand the faith of Abel, we must see what lay behind it. Everything goes back to one's conception of God. Dr. J. H. Jowett gives us this little gem: "What are your primary thoughts about God? The prints of those thoughts will be found in your courtesies, in your intercourse, in the common relationships of life, in the government of commerce, in the control of the body, and in the affairs of home and market and field"—and we may certainly add, in our worship.

Now the primary thought of God ought to be His holiness. That is the primary thought of the angels that surround His throne, as Isaiah learned in the day of vision. And did it not affect their worship? Listen to Jowett again: "It was the vision of a throne, 'high and lifted up.' And those who stood about the throne were not moving in light and familiar liberty. 'Each one had six wings; with twain he covered his face, and with twain he covered his feet.' How solemn, and how reverent, and how worshipful! And the voices which he heard were not the jaunty songs and liltings which are sung by the fireside. 'And one cried unto another, and said, Holy, holy, holy, is the Lord of hosts.' "

Abel held that primary thought of God—His holiness; and, as in the case of Isaiah the prophet, it struck him with a consciousness of his own sinfulness. "Woe is me! for I am undone; because I am a man of unclean lips . . . for mine eyes have seen the King, the Lord of hosts" (Isa 6:5). So cried the prophet, and such a cry was in the heart of Abel as he contemplated approaching the holy God in worship. For was he not born in sin? He was not conceived in the time of his parents' innocency in the garden, but after sin had come and wrought its diabolical work in human nature. He had been born with the Fall in his blood. Sin was native to him, and he knew it all the more as he reached out for recovery and communion with God. The thought of drawing near to God in worship raised in his mind the question of acceptance. Thomas Binney has well expressed what must have troubled the heart of Abel:

> O how shall I, whose native sphere
> Is dark, whose mind is dim,
> Before th' Ineffable appear,
> And on my naked spirit bear
> The uncreated beam?

Not until we have arrived there are we ready to offer true worship.

God had already shown that there was a way of recovery, of restoration to divine favor and communion. He showed it in the garden, when He rejected the fig leaves by which the guilty pair sought to clothe themselves, and provided coats of skins—the purchase of blood. It was a primary and a basic lesson. God will receive the sinner, by the way of shed blood. He was pointing to "the Lamb slain from the foundation of the world" (Rev 13:8), who should in the fullness of time appear to "put away sin by the sacrifice of himself" (Heb 9:26). So it was established that the sinner, in his approach to God, must be covered by blood.

Abel, therefore, trembling at the thought of God's holiness and his own sinfulness, believed God in regard to the way of acceptance, and brought his slain lamb. "By faith Abel offered."

Cain, on the other hand, had an inadequate conception of God's holiness, therefore an inadequate sense of sin; consequently he felt no need of a covering, an atonement. He came offering the worship of self-will and self-sufficiency and self-righteousness.

Indeed, it was the worship of self rather than the worship of God. His concern was not to ascribe all worth to God (the true meaning of worship), but to draw God's attention to his worth. Cain is first ancestor to the Pharisee who "prayed . . . with himself, God, I thank thee that I am not as other men" (Luke 18:11), and of all who to this day are offering the works of their own hands to God. In every case the result is rejection.

"This man went down to his house justified" (18:14), said our Lord of the poor penitent in the corner of the Temple court. So it was with Abel. As he offered in faith "he had witness borne to him that he was righteous, God . . . [testifying] of his gifts" (Heb 11:4, ASV). I do not know how in those days the communication of the divine pleasure and displeasure was conveyed. Campbell Morgan offers the interesting suggestion that worship was offered at the gate of Eden, where the cherubim stood with their flaming sword to guard the way of the tree of life. One may imagine Abel and Cain building their altars on the sacred site. As Abel bows low by his sacrifice, seeking divine mercy, we can see the angel of the Lord touching his altar with the flaming sword, till wood and fat send up their flame and smoke. But Cain stands sullenly by his altar as no such touch marks the acceptance of his gifts.

Be all this as it may, we know how witness is borne to the believer today. "He that believeth . . . hath the witness in himself" (1 John 5:10). "There are three that bear witness in earth, the Spirit, and the water, and the blood" (5:8).

The Spirit answers to the blood,
And tells me I am born of God.

To know that one stands righteous before God is the ultimate answer to the sin question.

Did you ever hear a dead man speak? The first man who ever died is speaking from his altar today, and he cries to us, and especially to every son of Cain, "It is the blood that maketh an atonement for the soul" (Lev 17:11*b*) ; and again, "By grace are ye saved through faith; and that not of yourselves: it is the gift of God: not of works, lest any man should boast" (Eph 2:8-9) .

26

ENOCH AND THE WALK OF FAITH

HEBREWS 11:5-6

Concerning the walk of faith we study:

1. The faith that produced it
2. The witness that accompanied it
3. The issue that consummated it

ENOCH IS THE FIRST MAN of whom it is written that he walked with God. He stands therefore as the prototype of the walk of faith.

Our text refers first to the issue of Enoch's walk of faith, and ends with an analysis of the faith that brought him to that happy consummation. Suppose we reverse the order, and begin with the character and content of Enoch's faith.

"He that cometh to God must believe that he is, and that he is a rewarder of them that diligently seek him" (Heb 11:6). Such being the content of Enoch's faith, I gather that by the time he arrived on the scene, and perhaps for a long time before, God had withdrawn Himself from that immediate intercourse with man which marked the early days; till, as now, it required faith to perceive the existence of God. John Wesley doubted that "faith, even in the general sense of the word, had any place in paradise. It is highly probable," he says, "from that short and uncircumstantial account which we have in Holy Writ, that Adam, before he rebelled against God, walked with Him by sight and not by faith. . . . He was then able to talk with Him face to face, whose face we cannot now see and live; and consequently had no need of faith, whose office it is to supply the want of sight."

This "want of sight" did not cast the least uncertainty upon the existence of God for Enoch. That was rather the first of all certainties.

He would as soon have doubted his own identity as the being of God. To Enoch all creation about him was vocal with the testimony of God, and the witness of the fathers was too vital to be ignored. Enoch, therefore, set out on his search for God, not as one seeks for some hidden treasure in the uncertain hope that there may be such a cache, but with the certainty of an unquestioning faith. "He that cometh to God must believe that he is," must, to use Donald Hankey's phrase, "bet his life that there is a God."

And then, the faith of Enoch believes that God "is a rewarder of them that diligently seek him [out]" (Heb 11:6*b*). By what awards does God recompense those who search after Him? The reward of seeking God is just finding Him, not through our Sherlock Holmes skill in tracking Him down, but through His grace and faithfulness in revealing Himself. Faith is assured that, however dark the way, however long the search, at some point of the road God will come forth from the shadows, saying, Here I am! Many rich benefits accompany the find, but God Himself is the soul's reward. "Ye shall seek me, and find me, when ye shall search for me with all your heart" (Jer 29:13).

This does not refer only to a first meeting with God in salvation, but to a continual seeking and finding. Faith looks for God everywhere, in every circumstance. She knows that God is in the light and in the darkness, in the height and in the depth.

> He plants His footsteps in the sea,
> And rides upon the storm.

Faith, therefore, spurred by holy desire, takes no refusal. Every day must be a new adventure in finding God, in some new setting of experience.

Jacob awoke from his dream, exclaiming, "Surely the LORD is in this place; and I knew it not" (Gen 28:16). "And he called the name of that place Bethel: but the name of that city was called Luz at the first" (28:19). Now Jacob was only a babe in faith; and he was still not far advanced in the life of faith when his Jabbok became Peniel. Yet for faith even the desert of weariness is a house of God, and the brook of struggle becomes the place of vision, the place of the face of God. A revival meeting is not the only setting where faith can sing,

God is here, and that to bless us
With the Spirit's quickening power.

Faith looks for God in the wide spaces of prosperity and in the straitened paths of adversity; in the glad day of jubilation, and in the dark night of mourning. "Oh that I knew where I might find him!" (Job 23:3), cried Job; and he found Him right there, in the desolation of his losses and bereavements and humiliations and sufferings.

Enoch so acted on his belief "that . . . God . . . is, and that he is a rewarder of them that diligently seek him," that by the time his firstborn son, Methuselah, came into the world, the seeking and finding of God, morning, noon, and night, had become an unbreakable habit, he had settled to a constant walk with God. "And Enoch walked with God after he begat Methuselah three hundred years" (Gen 5:22). He had sought Him so assiduously, and so learned the secret of finding, that He finally found "for keeps," till God and Enoch were inseparable companions. Enoch had become God's "briestman," to use a Scottish word. What a triumph of faith!

Think of what benefits accrue from such walking with God! For one thing, there was divine assistance in the ordering of the home, now blessed with the firstborn son, and later with sons and daughters. Let all our family men get into step with God, and walk with Him, and see how suddenly the curve of juvenile delinquency will drop! Judging from his name, Methuselah (man of the javelin) might have been another Cain or Lamech, a man of violence and murder; but with a father who walked with God, the impetuous youth was tamed, and lived through a peaceful old age. One's heart aches for boys and girls so early thrust forth into the seething temptations of this world, lacking the restraining power of godly parentage. Or again, one grieves over the lonely vigils of godly mothers who are deprived of the backing of the father of the home in the Christian training of the children. The odds are against parents who do not walk with God.

Walking with God, Enoch did not need to worry about the way. He had an infallible Guide. My wife has often remarked that when she is driving alone, she pays close attention to direction and route, but when I am with her she does not think about that, reckoning that I know where we are going. The times that I have gone out of the way do not seem to shake her confidence! Walking with God means freedom from the care of the road, assurance that we shall be kept from going astray. Infinite wisdom has planned the course, and infinite grace will lead us on to the blessed destination.

Walking with God, we need not fear what may beset us on the journey, whether rough road, stormy weather, or enemy assault. He is a safe Guide and a trusty Champion. Robert Laws, the great pioneer missionary of Africa, went through many a terrifying storm on Lake Nyasa. His wife, though not a good sailor, never shrank from accompanying him on these hazardous voyages. One dark, stormy night, seeing his wife clinging to the rigging, the good missionary asked, "Afraid?" "No!" came the confident answer. "Why?" again queried her husband. "Because you are at the helm!" She knew his skill as a navigator, his acquaintance with the lake, and her confidence was unbounded. The man who walks with God has nothing to fear.

> I walk with Thee and all is light,
> At morn, at eve, at wakeful night;
>   The way I do not ask to see,
>   Thy presence is enough for me.
> Thou art my Guide, and fears take flight.
>
> Nor weal, nor woe, shall e'er excite
> My heart that owns Thy sov'reign right.
>   Whate'er befall it best shall be,
>   I wait to do Thy glad decree,
> Rejoiced if still on Beulah height
>   I walk with Thee.

But the greatest boon of walking with God is the witness that it brings to the heart. "Before his translation he hath had witness borne to him that he had been well-pleasing unto God" (Heb 11:5*b*, ASV margin).

We are usually quick enough to let people, especially our own folks, know when we are displeased. It would be a touch of grace and godlikeness to let them know when we are pleased with them. There is a sweet satisfaction in having such witness borne to us by those for whom we deeply care. When we were married, my wife received a book—a cookbook, as it happened—entitled *A Thousand Ways to*

Please a Husband. That title itself suggests that wives like to know that they please. A little more attention to one another's pleasing ways and actions, and a bit less emphasis on minor defects, would make many a home happier.

I rejoice to think of our heavenly Father's readiness to whisper His pleasure into our hearts, and I can think of nothing more completely satisfying than such witness, unless it be our contemplation of our blessed Lord's own incomparable perfections. Combine the two, and heaven is already come down to our hearts. "My beloved is mine, and his desire is toward me" (Song of Sol 7:10), is the ecstasy of the bride of the Song of Solomon. We, too, may know such delight. "We are ambitious," writes the apostle Paul, "to be well-pleasing unto Him." Do we share that ambition? Walking with Him will bring the assurance of His delight in us to our hearts.

Enoch's walk of faith culminated in a manner quite beyond his expectation. The death of Adam, fifty-seven years before Enoch's translation, was doubtless accepted as the pattern of common experience. There had been two murders in the history of the race, but these were abnormal. It was in the decease of the first man that death revealed itself as the master of the race. We hear the monotonous tolling of the death knell in the fifth chapter of Genesis, till we come to the sudden and startling change in the story of Enoch. God had something different for this man of faith who sought Him out every day to have His company. You know how the little Sunday school girl told the story: that God and Enoch went for a walk every day, and one day they walked so far from Enoch's house that it got dark before they knew it, and God said to Enoch, Don't bother going home tonight; it's nearer to My house, so just come home with Me. I reckon that is pretty close to the truth. "Enoch walked with God: and he was not; for God took him" (Gen 5:24).

Enoch's faith did not contemplate such exemption from the common lot, yet his translation is attributed to his faith. "By faith Enoch was translated that he should not see death" (Heb 11:5). I declare, you can never tell what "exceeding abundantly above all that we ask or think" (Eph 3:20) the Lord will do for the man who delights in His company, and whose faith seeks Him out continually.

And then, Enoch became the prototype of all who "should not see death." "Behold I shew you a mystery; We shall not all sleep, but we shall all be changed, in a moment, in the twinkling of an eye, at the last trump: for the trumpet shall sound, and the dead shall be raised incorruptible, and we shall be changed" (1 Cor 15:51-52). "Even so, come, Lord Jesus" (Rev 22:20).

27

NOAH AND THE WORK OF FAITH

Hebrews 11:7

In this brief chapter we observe:

1. The content of Noah's faith
2. The activity of Noah's faith
3. The effect of Noah's faith

"In Abel we see how faith makes death the path to life. In Enoch, how faith conquers death. In Noah, how faith saves others from death by the work it does for them." Thus excellently does Andrew Murray sum up the relation between these men of faith. The worship of faith blossoms into the walk of faith, and fructifies in the work of faith. "By faith Noah, being warned of God concerning things not seen as yet, moved with godly fear, prepared an ark to the saving of his house; through which he condemned the world, and became heir of the righteousness which is according to faith" (Heb 11:7, ASV).

Two elements are specially evident in the faith of Noah. He believed God concerning the coming of judgment; and he believed God concerning the provision for salvation. This judgment of a flood was something "not seen as yet," something outside and beyond the experience of men, utterly foreign even to the thinking of men. To the rationalist, therefore, it was the epitome of absurdity. But "faith is . . . the means of conviction of things not seen" (11:1, author's trans.), and Noah believed God without question. The judgment was as much a fact to him as if he were already viewing the carcasses of sinners floating on the dark waters.

While rationalists laughed, and unbelievers went on their undisturbed way, Noah's faith filled him with "godly fear" (v. 7, ASV).

There is a fear that paralyzes. The roar of the tiger transfixes its prey—freezes it to the spot. Godly fear has the opposite effect. It moves men to action. So it did Noah. It moved him to follow the divine instructions for salvation, as fully believing in the efficiency of the provision as in the certainty of the judgment. The ark was a work of faith. He had never seen a ship. He had no experience of huge hulks floating on water, rising and falling upon the billows. But he believed God. So godly fear and godly confidence combined to spur his work to its consummation.

From other Scriptures we learn that Noah preached while he built. One hundred and twenty years did this man of God spend in faith and fear, building and preaching. His work was not only to build the ark, but to people it. Perhaps you think he had rather a poor showing for a century and two decades of preaching! Well, he won his wife and his three sons and their wives. He gained his own family, and that speaks volumes for this preacher of righteousness. Just think of living with a preacher for a hundred and twenty years and then being ready to stand with him against the world! I take my hat off to that preacher! He "has the goods," and he shines all the brighter against a whole world's unbelief.

But was Noah so unsuccessful? Did only eight souls people the ark? Why, the human race was preserved in that ark. The billions of souls that have inhabited the earth since the Flood went into that ark. Noah went in a father and came out a patriarch, a second Adam. You and I owe our being, under God, to the faith of Noah, and to his work of faith. In like manner, all who ascend the steeps of light to the Holy City, the New Jerusalem, will do so because of the faith of Noah. He peopled heaven as well as this world.

We are not called upon to build an ark. It has been once for all prepared. Christ is the ark of salvation, of whom Noah's ark was a prophetic picture. But there is a work of faith for us, too. The peopling of the ark is the blessed task in which we are given a share. "Ye shall be witnesses unto me" (Acts 1:8*b*), said our Lord, establishing the duty of the whole church, "in Jerusalem, and in all Judea, and in Samaria, and unto the uttermost part of the earth" (Acts 1:8*c*). "Go ye into all the world, and preach the gospel to every creature" (Mark 16:15).

That is our work of faith, bringing souls to Jesus. To do this work, we must have the faith of Noah—the faith that believes God concerning the certainty of judgment, and the faith that believes God concerning the adequacy of salvation. The first will spur us to action, the second will give assurance to our labors. Our generation does not relish the message of judgment, and we preachers are too often guilty of suppressing or softening that part of our message, lest we offend. But how that weakens the call of the gospel, allowing men to slumber over the brink to irrevocable ruin! My brethren, we, the children of God, must catch anew the terrible reality of judgment to come, and the blessed sufficiency of Christ's redeeming grace. Stirred by that twofold faith, we shall rise from our sloth, "stedfast, unmoveable, always abounding in the work of the Lord" (1 Cor 15:58).

Set us afire, Lord,
  Stir us, we pray!
While the world perishes,
  We go our way,
Purposeless, passionless,
  Day after day.
Set us afire, Lord,
  Stir us, we pray!

28

PATRIARCHAL FAITH

HEBREWS 11:8-19

In this passage we see:

1. The faith of youth, daring
2. The faith of manhood, enduring
3. The faith of old age, triumphing

FAITH FIRES YOUTH to noble adventure. Faith sustains men in the long years of disillusionment and waiting. Faith steadies the aged in the day of shattering trials. And that is the story of Abraham, as told in this New Testament anthology of faith.

"Abraham, being called . . . obeyed" (Heb 11:8, author's trans.). How the call came to him we are not informed. Was it stirring in his heart for years, to break out at last in an imperious conviction? Or did it come suddenly, in visions of the night, with a compelling urgency? Did the prevailing idolatry, home training, study of God's dealings with his fathers, play any part in shaping Abraham's decision? Or was it wholly a sovereign breaking in of God upon the soul? I am inclined to the thought of long workings of the Spirit of God, culminating in the irresistible "now." Even the most unexpected call is but the climax of sustained preparation. The crisis explains the process.

"By faith Abraham . . . obeyed" (11:8). A master's faith in his servant determines the kind of orders he gives. A servant's faith in his master finds expression in obedience. Where faith is wanting, obedience is hesitant and incomplete, lacking heart. Saul's faith in God was only partial, so again and again we find him giving partial obedience, with disastrous results to himself and the nation. Abraham, notable for his faith, rendered notable obedience.

Obedience, in some situations, requires faith of a high caliber. So it was in the case of the patriarch. It was no Dogpatch that he was called to leave. Ur of the Chaldees was not a hovel of barbarism, but a center of culture and commerce. The archaeologist has discovered for us that the Chaldean youth of Abraham's time was struggling with the same mathematical problems as vex the college student of today! And from this place of learning, this hub of commerce, this paradise of opportunity for ambitious men, Abraham was called to go forth.

Moreover, he was asked to go out, "not knowing whither he went" (Heb 11:8*b*). He was given no map with destination and route marked. All the directions he had were, "unto the land that I will show thee" (Gen 12:1*a*, ASV) : just the promise of God for a guide. "That was enough for anybody," you say. But in practice, would you consider it enough for yourself? Most of us like to know where we are going, and it takes a heap of believing to go out from our settled place, not knowing what lies ahead.

So Abraham pioneered the way of the unknown for all who should receive a like call from God, and many have followed his faith. When William Booth resigned from the Methodist Connexion in 1861, because the consuming passion of the evangelist could not be satisfied in the ordinary rounds of a circuit minister, he followed in the steps of Abraham. A man in poor health, with a frail wife and four little children, stepped out of a settled appointment which many a man of talents might covet, as superintendent of the Newcastle-on-Tyne circuit, not knowing the future, save that he must reach the perishing multitudes. I think there is peculiar kinship between Abraham and Booth. Even the portrait of the aged "General" reminds one of the patriarch. "Who follows in their train?"

Faith in its venturesome stage has only begun. The long years of endurance mature and ripen it.

Abraham, after a stopover of some years in Haran, where he lost his aged father through death and secured a devoted servant, Eliezer of Damascus, finally came into "the land of promise" (Heb 11:9*a*). He was then seventy-five years old, still young considering that he had another hundred to go! It would be interesting to know what his thoughts were in those early days in Canaan. I am sure he wondered quite often just how this land would come into his possession. Would there be some strange sequence of events that would establish him king over the Amorites and the Canaanites? Instead of that, he found himself year after year a camper. Thirty-seven years after his arrival, when his wife, Sarah, died, he possessed not even enough ground in Canaan for a grave. The field of Ephron, which he purchased at that time, was, so far as we have record, all that Abraham owned of the land after a century of dwelling in it. He never even built a house, but lived "in tents with Isaac and Jacob, heirs with him of the same promise" (11:9*b*). He came as a prospective owner, and lived out a hundred years as a sojourner.

Now the question: how did Abraham come to a reconciliation with this situation? How did he surmount the disappointment of being without possession in the land promised to him? Why did he remain there, when he might have returned to the more settled, more cultured, more luxurious life of Ur?

The answer might be given: the promise was made to him as patriarch, to be fulfilled in the nation that should spring from him. This indeed was revealed to Abraham in that remarkable vision following his one recorded military campaign for the recovery of Lot. But another and deeper answer is given us in our great faith chapter. It was not just a matter of deferred possession—deferred for several generations. Abraham's faith rose higher and saw farther than an earthly possession, for himself or for his offspring, and laid hold of "the city which hath the foundations, whose architect and framer is God" (11:10, author's trans.).

He "became a sojourner" (11:9), says the Revised Version, following the ingressive aorist; which suggests to me that at some point, probably not without a struggle, he accepted his position as a sojourner in the land which he had entered in anticipation of ownership. Had he received personal possession, it is likely that his vision would have stopped there. As it was, he overleaped even the yet unborn nation's occupancy of the land, and fastened upon that "one far-off divine event to which the whole creation moves." Canaan became to him a parable of something better and more enduring, "the city which hath the foundations," and he believed that his presence in the land had something to do with that ultimate goal, the final economy of God, the perfect society of the redeemed.

"And I saw the holy city, new Jerusalem, coming down out of heaven from God, made ready as a bride adorned for her husband. And the wall of the city had twelve foundations, and on them twelve names of the twelve apostles of the Lamb. . . . The first foundation was jasper; the second, sapphire; the third, chalcedony; the fourth, emerald; the fifth, sardonyx; the sixth, sardius; the seventh, chrysolite; the eighth, beryl; the ninth, topaz; the tenth, chrysoprase; the eleventh, jacinth; the twelfth, amethyst" (Rev 21:2, 14-20, ASV). Let him that hath more wisdom, or more daring, than I, tell the meaning of the twelve foundations. Dimly, as in a parable, Abraham saw this city of the foundations afar off; nearer, but still in an apocalypse, the aged John beheld it. Are we of their company? Are we men of the far horizons? Do we live in the redeemed?

Some, like Cain, are building their own little cities here, only to leave them to the dust of the desert, the havoc of war, or the destruction of that great day of God, "wherein the heavens being on fire shall be dissolved, and the elements shall melt with fervent heat" (2 Pet 3:12). Others, seeking "the city which hath the foundations," are investing their lives in eternal values. David Livingstone lost from the civilized world in the deep jungles of Africa, Adoniram Judson languishing in filthy Burmese prisons, Zinzendorf turning his back on titles and wealth for the gospel's sake, Dober stooping to the status of a slave in the West Indies that he might more effectively witness to the slaves there: these are the true sons of Abraham.

Abraham was not alone in his vision, as a whole paragraph here tells us. The "these all" of verse thirteen may include the antediluvian saints mentioned earlier in the chapter, but verse fifteen points back to the exodus from Ur of the Chaldees, so I take the paragraph as referring principally to Abraham, Sarah, Isaac, and Jacob. At any rate, it is speaking of some who were recipients with Abraham of the promises of God, and who shared the far vision and the large faith of the patriarch. It says of these that they were "seeking after a country of their own" (Heb 11:14, ASV). Wherever they dwelt in this world, they were conscious of a lack of kinship. They were aliens in Chaldea, in Damascus, in Canaan, in Egypt. In none of these could they be more than sojourners. Their spirits rose in desire and search of "a better country, that is, a heavenly" (11:16, ASV). The heavenly country had entered their souls and they could be content with nothing short of its realization.

When the kingdom of heaven really takes root in our hearts, we too shall confess that we are "strangers and pilgrims on the earth" (11:13*b*). We shall no longer live as if all our inheritance were here, in houses and wealth and fame and rounds of pleasure. Our lives will be lifted up into the current of an eternal purpose, and we shall find home at last in the heavenly city, the New Jerusalem.

> I am far frae ma hame,
> An' I'm weary aftenwhiles
> For the langed-for hame-bringin',
> An' ma Faither's welcome smiles;
> An' I'll ne'er be fu' content
> Until ma een dae see
> The gowden gates o' heaven,
> An' ma ain countrie.

Now we are to see faith in the crucible, for testing and for perfecting. For God's testings are not just to see how good a man is, how strong his faith, how real his devotion; but to improve the man and perfect him in faith and holiness. Abraham's faith came to its crowning glory, not in its adventuresome expression when he "went out, not knowing whither he went" (11:8*b*); nor in the weary years when he struggled through to an abandonment of earthly ambition and a vision of the eternal city; but when the evening shadows were falling upon him, and he was asked to offer up the son of his love, the son of promise, the son of miracle, the son of hope.

The record says nothing about the Gethsemane through which Abraham passed that terrible night, save that the little phrase, "God did test Abraham" (Gen 22:1, author's trans.) opens the shutter and lays bare all the anguish that wrung the good old man's soul. Will human love bear the strain of offering that son of his old age, the pride and comfort of his declining years? The battle was fought on that field, till the sovereign rights of God were fully acknowledged, and Abraham bowed his hoary head, saying with Job, "The Lord gave, and the Lord hath taken away; blessed be the name of the Lord" (Job 1:21).

But what about this other side of the question? As far as the covenant of God was concerned, Ishmael did not exist. "In Isaac shall thy seed be called" (Gen 21:12*b*). That meant that all the promises of God to Abraham were wrapped up in Isaac. If the words of God had any meaning, there could be no seed as the stars of the heaven and as the sand by the seashore, apart from Isaac; there could be no outflow of blessing from Abraham to the ends of the earth, save through Isaac; there could be no city of God, no city of foundations, without Isaac. What, then, could Abraham do in face of the command, "Take now thy son, thine only son, whom thou lovest, even Isaac, and get thee into the land of Moriah; and offer him there for a burnt-offering" (22:2, ASV)?

Were all these God-inspired hopes to go for nought? Had God changed His mind? Had He turned back from His promises? Had He despised His own covenant? Had He altered His purposes? Faith was in the fiery furnace heated seven times over, till Abraham's Gethsemane was but little short of the bloody Gethsemane of his more illustrious seed. Then slowly the light broke. Did not Sarah conceive Isaac when she was past age, and when he himself was as good as dead? It was a miracle of God, to give life where there was no life. And was not the same God able to give back life when it was taken? Resurrection was as much a prerogative of El Shaddai as creation. The resources of God reached out beyond death.

Carry that twofold battle and victory far into that unspeakable night, and you have the explanation of the calm record, "Abraham rose early in the morning, and saddled his ass, and took . . . Isaac" (Gen 22:3, ASV). "By faith Abraham, being tried, offered up Isaac . . . accounting that God is able to raise up, even from the dead" (Heb 11:17-19, ASV). Faith, triumphant in its severest test, received its reward, and the old father, who had suffered all the pangs of giving his beloved son up in death, received him back in what the pen of inspiration boldly declares to be a parable of resurrection. Faith can not only remove mountains; it can defy death, and all the more, since Jesus died, and rose again. "O death, where is thy sting? O grave, where is thy victory? . . . Thanks be to God, which giveth us the victory through our Lord Jesus Christ" (1 Cor 15:55-57).

A man whose faith will go out with God into the unknown; whose faith will accept the status of a sojourner where he might be a possessor, for the sake of the city of God; whose faith will yield up life's choicest treasures without murmur: that man has qualified for the title, "the Friend of God" (James 2:23). We who believe are the sons of Abraham, but have we acquired his title?

29

THE PROCESSES OF FAITH IN THE SOUL

HEBREWS 11:23-27

In this search we trace back:

1. Faith's noble renunciation to
2. Faith's deliberate choice, to
3. Faith's long calculation

"AT LONG LAST I am permitted to speak for myself." I shall not soon forget the weird thrill which these opening words of Edward VIII's last speech as king of England inspired. The body of his address revolved around the phrase, "The woman I love." Then came the solemn statement, "I have therefore executed an instrument of abdication on behalf of myself and my heirs." It was something for the world to talk about. Some regarded it as a heroic renunciation. Here was the romance of dreams—he gave up an empire for the woman he loved! Others looked upon it as a base betrayal of high duty for selfish satisfaction. However we judge the act, and whether the motives were noble or ignoble, it was a great renunciation, one of the greatest in history.

But Edward is quite outclassed by Moses. Both in its moral worth, and in its far-reaching effects, Moses' renunciation towers like an Everest above the English monarch's romantic and tragic abdication. "By faith . . . Moses refused to be called the son of Pharaoh's daughter" (Heb 11:24, ASV). By faith—there is the secret of its grandeur. But we must go back a piece.

"By faith Moses, when he was born, was hid three months by his parents, because they perceived that he was an elegant child; and they did not fear the order of the king" (11:23, author's trans.). You know, of course, that the order of the king was that every male child should be thrown into the river. Had the king some thought of an offering to the sacred river, and perhaps to the sacred crocodile?

Now every mother thinks her babe is elegant. And what father is not supremely proud of his firstborn son? Yet we must believe that the baby Moses was a bit more elegant than the average. They "perceived," not just "imagined," that their child was exceptionally lovely, and this was God's way of stirring in them a determination to make every possible effort for his preservation.

The Scripture says, "They were not afraid of the king's commandment" (11:23*b*). Are we to take that in an absolute sense? Then why did they hide the baby? Why did they not openly defy the decree? The fact is, they *were* afraid, in a natural sense, but faith was greater than fear. It was a proper measure of fear that made them hide the child, but there was not the kind of fear to move them away from their resolve. Faith does not call for the neglect of reasonable precautions, but for steadfast adherence to a God-inspired purpose.

The faith of Amram and Jochebed secured the life of their child. But it did more. It goes far to explain the life of faith upon which Moses embarked after forty years in the Egyptian court. We may not say that faith is hereditary, but a parent's faith has a way of getting into a child and finding new expression in his life. I go to my biography shelves and pick out volume after volume on the men of great faith, only to discover that in most cases they were suckled and nurtured in faith. Augustine had the faith of his mother, Monica, faith not without tears. John McNeil had a father who began each morning with "I will go in the strength of the Lord God," recited on the doorstep as he set out for his day's work. David Livingstone had behind him that deep, reverential type of patriarchal piety so beautifully depicted in "The Cotter's Saturday Night." The Wesleys had Susannah for their mother, a pattern of maternal faith and devotion. It is not, then, without reason, that the story of Moses' faith is prefaced with a statement concerning the faith of his mother and father. What kind of preface are we writing to the life story of our children?

The first great expression of Moses' faith, then, was his act of renunciation. He "refused to be called the son of Pharaoh's daughter." When did he take this step? "When he was come to years" (Heb

11:24), says our King James Version. "When he was grown up," declare the revisers. "When he was grown to manhood" is Way's offering. Yet the Greek word is the common one for "great." It can mean great in size or bulk, or it can mean great in power and attainment. It is used sometimes, indeed, of age, especially when contrasting an older with a younger. The Septuagint of Exodus 2:11 uses the same word, translating a Hebrew expression of similar meaning, which can refer to greatness of age, greatness of stature, or greatness of accomplishment. So perhaps the translators are right, but I cannot forget that description of the lawgiver in Stephen's "defense," as we call it: "And Moses was instructed in all the wisdom of the Egyptians; and he was mighty in his words and works" (Acts 7:22, ASV). In the light of such a statement, it would be quite admissible to translate our verse, "By faith Moses, when he became great, refused to be called the son of Pharaoh's daughter." He was a scholar, he was a noted orator, and he was a man of action.

Perhaps his greatness as an orator will be disputed on the ground of his own statement, "Oh, Lord, I am not eloquent, neither heretofore, nor since thou hast spoken unto thy servant: for I am slow of speech, and of a slow tongue" (Exod 4:10, ASV). It will help us, however, if we remember that Moses spoke thus of himself forty years after the time when it was said of him that he was "mighty in his words," and those forty years he had spent in the wilderness with sheep or goats. A man of eighty, after forty years of silence, would hesitate to take up public speaking, especially before kings, whatever his early reputation had been!

Holy Scripture has not satisfied our curiosity about Moses' greatness prior to his call to lead Israel, nor have we much to go on in extrabiblical literature, but these few hints reveal a man great in rank, great in learning, great in public address, great in exploits; and now we see him greatest of all in the renunciation of all these. Whereto he might have grown by remaining in the Egyptian court is a matter of speculation. It has been suggested that he was in line for the throne itself. None of it could hold him when faith had wrought its processes in his heart. "By faith" he "refused to be called the son of Pharaoh's daughter" (Heb 11:24).

Is there a suggestion of ingratitude there? The Egyptian princess had taken pity on him when she found him in his little basket of bulrushes by the river's edge, and had spared no pains in caring for him as a son. Everything that royal wealth could command was his. And now, when he could have served Egypt well, he ditches the whole thing and opposes the authority of the imperial throne. Frankly, I hope they are right who think that by this time Moses' foster-mother was dead. I think it would have broken her heart. But whether or not, Moses had a prior loyalty, to God and to God's people, who were his own people, and that prior loyalty demanded the great renunciation. "He that loveth father or mother more than me is not worthy of me. . . . And he that taketh not his cross, and followeth after me, is not worthy of me" (Matt 10:37-38).

How did Moses arrive at this tremendous act of faith? It was a matter of choice, and his choice determined his action. Two courses lay before him—pleasure and suffering. The pleasure was the temporary enjoyment of sin. That is exactly what the pleasures of Egypt and its royal court had become to him—the short-lived enjoyment of sin. His early training at the hands of his own mother, Jochebed, had left him in no doubt about the sinfulness of so much that was accepted without question in his environment. Idolatry and gilded vice went hand in hand, and Moses found himself more and more an alien in the midst of it all. Pleasure there was, but he saw well what Robert Burns later expressed:

> But pleasures are like poppies spread,
> You seize the flower, its bloom is shed;
> Or like the snow falls on the river,
> A moment white, then melts for ever;
> Or like the Borealis race
> That flit e'er you can mark their place;
> Or like the rainbow's lovely form,
> Evanishing amid the storm.

Over against the scene of luxury and indulgence which the court life of Egypt presented was a picture of suffering—an oppressed and enslaved people, groaning beneath the lash of heartless taskmasters, sweating to approximate the impossible demands of the rulers, and broken with anguish by reason of the cruel decrees of the pharaohs. It is likely that the barbarous edict under which Moses almost perished had by this time been relaxed, but the lot of the children of Israel was still thoroughly miserable. Moses knew that these people were God's people, and his people. Could he continue to enjoy the privileges of an Egyptian prince, entering into all the pleasures of the court life, while God's people, his people, bowed the neck in cruel bondage? In such a case the most innocent enjoyment would be sin. He could no longer live with himself in such selfish exemption from the lot of his people. Very shame would cry out against him. To identify himself with God's people, who were his people, however he might have to share their evil treatment at the hands of the Egyptians, would alone satisfy the deep yearnings of his soul.

Back of faith's great renunciation is faith's determined choice. We must trace still farther. Back of faith's deliberate choice is faith's long calculation. Moses arrived at his choice of identification with God's people and their sufferings by "accounting the reproach of Christ greater riches than the treasures of Egypt" (Heb 11:26, ASV).

What did Moses know about "the reproach of Christ"? Manifestly this is a New Testament phrase imposed upon an Old Testament situation. We know that our Lord was exposed to ridicule, slander, blasphemy, and all manner of diabolical treatment at the hands of unbelieving men, culminating in all the suffering and shame of the cross. His few followers were called upon to share His reproach, which at first they were barely able to do. You remember how Peter winced when the servant girl said, perhaps sneeringly, "Thou also wast with Jesus of Galilee" (Matt 26:69*b*). His denial on that occasion was well reversed later when the reproach of Christ again caught up with him, and he stood firmly before the Sanhedrin and declared, "We cannot but speak the things which we have seen and heard" (Acts 4:20).

From the days of the apostles till our own day, no one has truly followed the Lord without knowing something of the reproach of Christ. Some have borne so much of it that they have made bold to use words belonging to the Lord Himself, "The reproaches of them that reproached thee fell on me" (Psalm 69:9*b*, author's trans.). The primitive church knew it, the Waldenses knew it, the Reformers knew it, the Scottish covenanters knew it, the early Wesleyans knew it; in our own day, converts from Judaism and Romanism know it, those who turn to Christ from Islam, from Buddhism, or from any ethnic or pagan religion, know it, and even in our officially "Christian nation," "all that will live godly . . . shall suffer persecution" (2 Tim 3:12). The reproach of Christ has not died out!

But just as Christ belongs to all ages, so the reproach of Christ is in the world ever since sin came in. However little revelation of the coming Saviour was given to the antediluvians, it was the reproach of Christ that Abel endured at the hands of Cain, and it was the reproach of Christ that Noah suffered when he flung his testimony of faith into the teeth of a world's wickedness and unbelief. Wherever you have the witness of God, you find the reproach of Christ. To espouse the cause of the downtrodden, groaning people of God was to invite the reproach of Christ. Moses did not use the phrase, nor even know it, but its application to Moses indicates Christ's union with His people in all ages, and the unity of God's people of all time.

We need not dwell on the treasures in Egypt. The modest language of the Bible is sufficient indication that they were vast, and any volume of Egyptian archaeology will confirm it. The vast wealth expended on the dead, of which the solid gold inner coffin of Tutankhamon is but one example, indicates the extent of the royal riches. It all lay at Moses' feet.

Then he made his calculation. On the one side was reproach, on the other, treasure. Which was more profitable? On the face of it, and by any worldly criterion, the treasure was the better bargain. But, then, it was not just a comparison of reproach and treasure. It was the reproach of Christ versus the treasure of Egypt. Even so, for the man of the world that would make the scale bear down still more heavily on the treasure side, for what treasure could be surer or more plentiful than that of Egypt? The man of faith had a different system of accounting. To him the treasure of Egypt was no different from the treasure of Babylonia or India or any place else. It was still exposed to the moth and the rust and the thief, and even the present enjoyment of it could not purchase the deeper satisfactions of life.

On the other hand, the reproach of Christ looked rugged for one who was accustomed to be held in honor as a royal prince. To identify himself with this submerged people, and share with them the disdain of the "superior race," would be bitter medicine. But in that direction lay riches, greater riches than all Egyptian wealth. There he would have God and right and truth and a good conscience. The reproach of Christ was rather to be endured than the reproach of his own heart. What if, in returning to his people, he became a victim of the taskmaster's rod? That would not sting like the scorpions of self-condemnation which he carried in his bosom so long as he preserved his sheltered, but false, position. So he "reckoned the reproach of Christ greater riches than the treasures in Egypt."

Faith's accountings are strange in the eyes of the world, but after all, they are sounder, because they are completer. The world's reckonings do not go beyond a few uncertain years. Faith's calculations bring into the sum the very end, the finalities. "He had respect," says our King James Version, "unto the recompense of the reward." The verb here has the thought of turning the eyes away from every distraction to fasten them upon one object. The compound word rendered "the recompense of the reward" suggests finality, the reward that comes ultimately. The New Testament usages of the word are confined to this epistle, and refer once to the reward of disobedience, once to the reward of Christian confidence, and in this place to the real results of two alternatives of conduct.

Moses, then, squarely asked of the way of renunciation, "What is the sure return from walking this way?" And he asked the same question of the way of indulgence. The eye of faith refused to be dazzled with intermediate promises or darkened by immediate perils. He would make no reckoning apart from the end. What he saw at the end of Egypt's road robbed that way of all its fascination; and what he saw at the end of the way of the cross canceled all its terror. Folly bases its calculations on beginnings, but faith reckons with endings. How do you do your figuring?

Here, then, are the processes of faith. It first determines ultimate rewards. In the light of these it calculates the true riches. On the basis of that calculation it makes a choice. In keeping with that choice it announces its renunciation of this world that it may stand with God and His Christ and His Kingdom and His people. Has faith wrought its great work in us? Have we given our irrevocable "Nay" to the world, the flesh, and the devil, and our everlasting "yea" to Christ and His calling?

30

FAITH THAT KINDLES FAITH

HEBREWS 11:27-28

Here we perceive in Moses:

1. Faith in its noble sacrifice
2. Faith in its heroic defiance
3. Faith in its redemptive ministry

WHEN GOD has a great movement to launch, He raises up a man; till that man and that movement are so intertwined that the one has no existence in thought without the other. The great and notable day of salvation was ushered in with the coming of a Man. "In the fulness of time God sent his Son, made of a woman, made under the law, to redeem them that were under the law" (Gal 4:4-5, author's trans.). In like manner that earlier salvation, lesser but nevertheless a parable of the greater, saw God's man ready.

This man of God's choosing, born into the general misery of the Hebrews, but by the providence of God brought up in the luxury of the Egyptian court, had come to look beyond immediates and intermediates to ultimates. These ultimates he made a factor, and, as it proved, a determining factor, in his calculations, till he reckoned "the reproach of Christ greater riches than the treasures in Egypt" (Heb 11:26). It was no mere laboratory calculation; he followed it through to logical choice, deciding to "suffer affliction with the people of God, rather than have the temporary enjoyment of sin" (11:25, author's trans.). This meant repudiating the false position in which he stood. So, after faith had wrought her work in his soul, Moses "refused to be called the son of Pharaoh's daughter" (11:24).

Such a step affected his standing in the nation. His repudiation of that royal adoption of forty years before required his surrender of all that Egypt held for him—its wealth, its power, its fame, its glory.

"By faith he forsook Egypt, not fearing the wrath of the king" (11:27*a*). Some say this refers to his flight from Egypt after his murder of the Egyptian; others, seeing how that conflicts with the actual story, refer it rather to the Exodus forty years later, which would break in on the orderliness of our chapter. I am inclined to think that what is in view is a moral forsaking of Egypt rather than a physical. I can see our princely prince, Moses, carrying his great decision up to Pharaoh, and, in face of the rising wrath of the highly offended monarch, renouncing in order his rank, his offices, his honors, his titles, till he had stripped himself of everything that spelled Egypt. All the reproaches, promises, persuasions, and threatenings of the king could not move him from his chosen path, and when he went out from the last stormy interview, he knew that he was under the royal displeasure, that he was a persona non grata in the eyes of the ruler; but this position he accepted fearlessly, because he had his eyes fixed on a higher throne: "he endured, as seeing him who is invisible" (11:27*b*). "Now faith is . . . the proof of things not seen" (11:1, author's trans.), and that assurance of the unseen made the glory of Egypt and the wrath of Pharaoh alike insignificant factors in the thoughts and actions of Moses. One whose vision is filled with God can despise the one and ignore the other.

Such are the men whom God calls to lead His great movements in the earth—men whose certainty of God makes them willing to forsake all and endure all. Such was Martin Luther for the Protestant Reformation; such was William Carey for the modern missionary movement; such was David Livingstone for the opening of Africa; such was Roger Williams for religious liberty. And God has a host of men of like faith, whose record is written above. You and I may not lead movements that will drastically turn the tide of history, but we can honor God and bless men by the faith that forsakes Egypt, fears not the face of man, and endures trial and temptation, "as seeing the unseen One" (11:27*b*, author's trans.).

The faith of one man will strike fire in the souls of others—not always immediately, but finally and inevitably. Carey's faith met only rebuffs at first from the Baptist leaders of England, but the one who so gruffly rebuked the young enthusiast when he suggested a discussion of the missionary question at a ministers' conference, was one of the most faithful in "holding the ropes" when Carey and his friends went down to explore India's gold mine of souls.

The faith of Moses did not find immediate response in the oppressed Hebrews. "He supposed his brethren would have understood how that God by his hand would deliver them" (Acts 7:25), but instead he met with resentment and suspicion: "Who made thee a ruler and a judge over us? Wilt thou kill me, as thou diddest the Egyptian yesterday?" (Acts 7:27-28).

For one thing, the faith of Moses needed some working over. There was too much of the grit of self-confidence mixed in with it, too much haste, too much heat. The "backside of the desert" (Exod 3:1) was God's appointed schooling ground for Moses and his faith, and when he came forth at God's bidding, it was with a refined, enlightened, humble faith, which drew instant response from a despairing people: "And the people believed: and when they heard that the LORD had visited the children of Israel, and that he had looked upon their affliction, then they bowed their heads and worshipped" (4:31). And I think that at this sight Moses took his shoes from off his feet, for he was on just as holy ground as when he stood before the burning, unconsumed bush: God was in the midst of His suffering but indestructible people.

Without this answer of faith to faith, the great redemptive movement would have stopped right there; but the disciplined faith of the man of God was irresistible, God's hour had struck, and His people were willing in the day of His power. With faith responding to faith, then, Moses "instituted the passover, and the sprinkling of the blood, [so] that he who was destroying the firstborn might not touch them" (Heb 11:28, author's trans.).

Do I have a faith so steadfast through all testings, so radiant despite discouragements, so triumphant in all conflicts, that others take courage to throw off their fetters and enter into the glorious liberty of the sons of God? Or is my faith so drooping that my fellows are disheartened, and confirmed in their bondage?

O for a faith that will not shrink,
Though pressed by many a foe,

That will not tremble on the brink
  Of poverty or woe,

That will not murmur nor complain
  Beneath the chastening rod,
But, in the hour of grief or pain,
  Can lean upon its God;

A faith that shines more bright and clear
  When tempests rage without,
That when in danger knows no fear,
  In darkness feels no doubt.

The only way to lead people out of bonds into freedom, out of darkness into light, out of death into life, is to bring them to "the passover, and the sprinkling of the blood." "Jesus Christ, and him crucified" (1 Cor 2:2) is the great message for sinners. The world today is full of gospels which are no gospels, panaceas which do not ease men's miseries, because they cannot take away men's sin. Culture, self-improvement, the new psychology—none of these can set the captives free; but Jesus, the Lamb of God, is the great Emancipator, His blood the great cleanser of sin. His salvation is a feast of security, a feast of deliverance, a feast of redemption. "Christ our passover is sacrificed for us; therefore let us keep the feast" (1 Cor 5:7-8).

31

OUT AND IN

HEBREWS 11:29-31

In this chapter we have a picture of:

1. Faith triumphant in flight
2. Faith triumphant in assault

IT WOULD SEEM that every great movement of faith must face an apparent impasse before it is well launched. Young faith is full of daring, ready for exploits, but it is inexperienced, and frequently mixed with much self-confidence. An early trial is, therefore, wholesome, having a sobering effect, and tending to cast the soul wholly on God. Being thus shut up to God, one discovers anew His faithfulness and learns to put no trust in the flesh.

Look at the children of Israel. They are exactly in the place of God's ordering, "before Pihahiroth, between Migdol and the sea, over against Baal-zephon" (Exod 14:12). Yet that place became a death-trap in their eyes, and in the eyes of their enemies. Here they were, a vast mob, shut in by mountains, desert, and sea, and the Egyptian army at their heels. "And the children of Israel cried out unto the LORD" (14:10*b*). Their chiding of Moses indicated that their faith was badly bruised, but their calling upon the Lord was evidence that it was still alive.

Difficulties are no proof that we are out of the will of God. More often they are the portals into a larger experience of His will. When we are led out by Him, let us expect seas and mountains and enemy forces. For "His paths are in the deep waters" (see Psalm 77:19), and "He maketh his mountains a way" (see Isa 49:11); and if we are beset by foes we take courage from the testimony of David, "For by thee I have run through a troop; and by my God have I leaped over a wall"

(Psalm 18:29). Our Lord's word concerning His church, "The gates of hell shall not prevail against it" (Matt 16:18*b*), was as much a promise of mortal combat as of glorious triumph.

What shall we do at "the Red Sea place"? Moses said, "Stand still" (Exod 14:13), and God said, "Go forward" (14:15*b*). Both were right. The "stand still" was the preparation for the "go forward." Moses, with his faith refined and matured in forty years of waiting, could quell the frenzy of the children of Israel with his reassuring "Fear ye not; stand still, and see the salvation of the LORD" (14:13). Yet for all his bold front before the people, Moses must have evidenced some panic in his crying to the Lord, for there was an element of reproof in the Lord's reply, "Wherefore criest thou unto me? Speak unto the children of Israel, that they go forward" (14:15), as much as to say, "Did I bring you to this point to deliver you into the hand of Pharaoh, and not to lead you out with a strong hand? Do not I plant My footsteps on the sea, and shall I not make this sea a way for My people?" Let us remember always that when the way is through, there is a way through.

Thus rebuked and reassured, "by faith they passed through the Red Sea as by dry land" (Heb 11:29*a*). It is amazing how easily things are done "bv faith." The impossible becomes the sublimely simple. Before faith's imperious tread the mountains become a highway, the seas dry land; the crooked places are made straight, and the rough places plain. The children of Israel did not swim over, nor build a fleet of barges; they walked. It was no great feat of human engineering that got them over the Red Sea. God sent His east wind, and God held up the walls of water, while His people went through dryshod.

"Which the Egyptians assaying to do were drowned" (11:29b). What was faith on Israel's part was folly on their part. Israel faced the rolling waters, and by faith went over on dry land. The Egyptians faced an open path, and by folly found a watery grave. The way that is safe to faith is perilous to unbelief. When Paul spoke the name of Jesus over the demon-possessed, the demons fled and souls were delivered; when the sons of Sceva attempted exorcism by the name of Jesus, they got wounds and shame for their trouble. So Moses led Israel "by faith" in a pageant of triumph, while Pharaoh took a long chance, and led his army to destruction.

When we cannot see our way,
Let us trust and still obey;
He who bids us forward go
Cannot fail the way to show.

Though the sea be deep and wide,
Though a passage seem denied.
Fearless let us still proceed,
Since the Lord vouchsafes to lead.

"He brought them out . . . that he might bring them in." The great and howling wilderness was not God's destination for His redeemed people, but the "land flowing with milk and honey" (Exod 3:8). Enough has been said in this epistle to the Hebrews about the generation whose faith failed, so that instead of entering into the rest of Canaan, they wandered in the desert until death removed them. So it was the children of those who came out of Egypt that entered the promised land. This great faith chapter says nothing about that break. It regards the chosen nation as a whole, omits the sad episode of failure, and leaps from the triumphant exit from Egypt to the victorious entrance into the land.

It will not be out of place, however, for us to remember Israel's forty years in the wilderness, for too many have exercised faith to leave the Egypt of their total bondage, but have not followed through to the Canaan of complete victory. Willing to accept the free offers of the gospel, they have drawn back from the price of full consecration. The day of challenge and opportunity found them unwilling, and from Kadesh-barnea they fell back to something less than mediocrity in Christian experience, "bound in shallows and in miseries." Let the faith that brought us out be exercised in the farther reaches of Christian experience, till we are proving "what is that good, and acceptable, and perfect, will of God" (Rom 12:2*b*).

As the Red Sea rolled its barricade against the exit of faith, so Jericho challenged faith's triumphant entry to the land of promise. But that frowning fortress was no more a barrier to faith than was the sea, for faith's God shakes both sea and dry land. The great walls of Jericho might withstand the assaults of armies, but the tramp of faith, the trump of faith, and the shout of faith are too much for them. "By an earthquake," says Professor Garstang. "By faith," declares the apostle by the Holy Spirit, looking behind and beyond secondary causes and instruments to the great spiritual reality, human impotence commanding God's omnipotence. The learned professor may be right; but even as God's use of the east wind made the crossing of the Red Sea no less a miracle, so the fall of Jericho was no less miraculous if God sent an earthquake to accomplish it. The fact remains, confirmed by the spade of the archaeologist, that the defensive walls of Jericho crashed outward, giving easy access to the soldiers of Israel.

What is that in your life which bars the way to consecration, victory, enlargement, usefulness, joy, peace, and power? What is that key decision which has to be made before you enter into the more abundant life? What is the pivotal point of controversy between you and the Lord, cutting you off from the rich blessings of Canaan? That is your Jericho. Lay siege to it by faith, sound the trumpet of faith against it, lift the shout of victory over it, and it too will crumble as did the Jericho of thirty-three centuries ago, and become the portal into an altogether new measure of life.

There was a harlot in Jericho, bound over to her sin. There she would have remained till her dying day, had not the hosts of God stormed that city. But the news of the coming of God's army was good news to her. It heralded the day of her deliverance, and her entrance into a life of honor instead of shame, freedom instead of bondage, blessing instead of cursing. She joined faith to faith, embraced the cause of the Lord, and in the day of Jericho's judgment found herself safe in the camp of Israel. "And Salmon begat Boaz of Rahab" Matt 1:5, ASV). Thus she became great-great-grandmother of David the king, the royal ancestor, after the flesh, of our Lord Jesus Christ. Israel's triumph of faith brought salvation to the sinner.

So is our victory bound up with someone's salvation. As long as we are in the wilderness of disobedience, compromise, and defeat, some poor sinner is held in his or her Jericho of sin; but let us move forward into the victory of Christ, and see what trophies will be won, to grace the triumph of our divine Captain.

32

FAITH IN THREE MOODS

HEBREWS 11:32-40

In this chapter we see faith expressing itself in three directions:

1. Faith in its heroic achievements
2. Faith in its noble endurance
3. Faith in its long patience

WHEN JOHN WROTE his gospel, he found himself handling a topic which, if treated exhaustively, would have required more library shelves than were available to house the volumes. "There are also many other things which Jesus did, the which, if they should be written every one, I suppose that even the world itself could not contain the books that should be written" (John 21:25)

When the writer to the Hebrews began giving examples of faith from sacred history, he soon became conscious of a similar dilemma. Only he viewed it in terms of time rather than of space. "The time will fail me," he says, "if I proceed to tell of all who might well take their places alongside those already referred to" (see Heb 11:32). Indeed, he has carried us along far enough, so that it is more helpful to allow us to pursue the course for ourselves; just as a teacher of mathematics works out a few examples in the new algebraic principle, then bids the students apply it for themselves in the problems presented.

By way of encouragement to follow through the line of thought developed, a brief list is given, without individual enlargement, and not in historical order. Five out of six mentioned by name are from the turbulent, violent period of the Judges, well described in the Scriptures: "In those days there was no king in Israel: every man did that which was right in his own eyes" (Judg 21:25). The book of Judges makes sorry reading for the most part. Yet that wild, lawless, apostate age was not without its galaxy of heroes of the faith, men who, though far from perfect in personal character, yet rose above their times to the vision of God, and wrought in God's name for God's people and God's cause. If we sometimes think that we are living in a dark age, let us remember Gideon and Barak and Samson and Jephthah and Samuel. We too may be "lights in a dark place."

Only David is mentioned among the kings, as if the writer would challenge us to find out for ourselves who might stand beside him in the royal line of faith. Of the northern kings, not one could qualify here, and only a few of the sons of David, such as Asa, Jehoshaphat, Hezekiah, and Josiah. When it comes to the prophets, however, they are all ranked with the nobility of faith. They could not be prophets otherwise. As for Samuel, he might be listed in all three categories. He was the last of the judges; he was almost a king; he was certainly a prophet. Above all, he was a man of faith!

What were the characteristic achievements of these and other stalwarts of faith? They are cataloged for us in two distinct divisions—the daring of faith, and the enduring of faith.

See what can be accomplished when faith goes forth in all its daring, shouting for the battle, hurling defiance at the foe! They grappled with kingdoms till those kingdoms licked the dust; they wrought righteousness, whether in personal action or in enforcement of judgment; they launched out on the promises of God and found them true; they "faced the lion's gory mane," and found a friendly pillow; they fell down bound into the flames of the seven times heated furnace and walked free and unscathed among them, communing with the Son of God; they moved among drawn swords that could not reach them, put on the strength of the unicorn, summoned irresistible power in battle, and put to flight great armies of foreign powers. Faith also entered the homes of sorrow, to give "beauty for ashes, the oil of joy for mourning, the garment of praise for the spirit of heaviness" (Isa 61:3). "Women received their dead by a resurrection" (Heb 11:35, ASV).

It would be a good exercise in Bible searching to match all these statements with the appropriate incidents of the Old Testament.

Space and time alike forbid it here. We pass on to an even more profitable exercise—application.

"Our wrestling is not against flesh and blood, but against the principalities, against the powers, against the world-rulers of this darkness, against the spiritual hosts of wickedness in the heavenly places" (Eph 6:12, ASV). The kingdom of darkness, "your adversary . . . as a roaring lion" (1 Pet 5:8), the fiery darts and still more fiery trials, alien armies of wickedness, all meet us on our way and seek to bar our progress. All around us there are men "dead in trespasses and sins" (Eph 2:1) who must be called to life in Christ Jesus, but the great enemy stands guard over their carcasses. Have we the faith that dares to challenge the hosts of evil, for our own salvation and the deliverance of others?

> Christian, dost thou see them
> On the holy ground,
> How the powers of darkness
> Compass thee around?
> Christian, up and smite them,
> Counting gain but loss;
> Smite them by the merit
> Of the holy cross.

"This is the victory that overcometh the world, even our faith" (1 John 5:4).

There are times when faith is called to endure rather than to dare, and while this may not be so heroic, it is quite as noble. "Others were tortured to death, not accepting the release which they might have had for yielding, that they might secure a better resurrection; others were tried with mockings and scourgings, and even with bonds and imprisonment; they were stoned, they were tempted, they were sawn in pieces, they died at the sword's point, they went about in sheepskins and goatskins, being in want, afflicted, ill treated—of whom the world was not worthy—wandering over deserts and hills, in dens and caves of the earth" (Heb 11:35*b*-38, author's trans.).

This all is most descriptive of the experiences of the prophets as a group. We remember that our Lord addressed Jerusalem as "thou that killest the prophets, and stonest them which are sent unto thee"

(Matt 23:37); while Stephen hurled the condemnation at his own generation: "As your fathers did, so do ye. Which of the prophets did not your fathers persecute?" (Acts 7:51*b*-52, ASV).

If enduring is as much the work of faith as daring, we conclude immediately, contrary to a very common notion which experience ought long ago to have dispelled, that faith is not a magic charm to avoid suffering. It is not an "escape mechanism" from the sterner disciplines of life. God does work remarkably for His people in times of general distress, but not in granting them complete exemption from the common lot. That would create an artificial situation, men seeking the Kingdom of God simply as a means of securing the kingdom of this world. It is good that young Christians learn to "think it not strange concerning the fiery trial which is to try" (1 Pet 4:12*a*) them, for many, encouraged in a false expectancy, have well-nigh slipped when affliction came, being dismayed, "as though some strange thing happened unto" (1 Pet 4:12*b*) them.

For one thing, faith is itself a cause of suffering. So it was with the prophets. So it has been with the martyrs, and we have been warned that "all that will live godly in Christ Jesus shall suffer persecution" (2 Tim 3:12). "This present world" (Titus 2:12) is a world at enmity with God. Its attitude to the Lord Jesus Christ is still, "Away with him, crucify him" (John 19:15). Such a world will not handle the followers of Christ with kid gloves. If they do not hang or burn us, it is perhaps because we are not worth it—we are not enough like our Lord to bother with.

All hell is arrayed against Christ, and His people may expect attacks from that quarter. Converts from heathenism frequently experience the assaults of spiritual forces. Death in the family, blight on crops, strange maladies, have often been traced to the curses of the witch doctor, the emissary of Satan. God has permitted these curses to operate in part for purposes of wisdom and grace, perhaps to teach faith that there is a foe to withstand. The "world-rulers of this darkness" (Eph 6:12*b*, ASV) are in America as well as in Africa.

Suffering is allowed as a means of proving and refining faith. "Ye greatly rejoice," says Peter, "though now for a little while, if need be, ye have been put to grief in manifold trials, that the proof of your faith, being more precious than gold that perisheth though it is proved by fire, might be found unto praise and glory and honor at the revelation of Jesus Christ" (1 Pet 1:6-7).

The proving ground reveals what is in an automobile, but God's proving ground puts something into a soul. That is the difference between the mechanical and the moral. All refinements of character come to maturity through discipline—discipline imposed, measured, and controlled by the grace of God. We sometimes think of grace in terms of a talisman, magically and instantaneously producing all the virtues in the soul. As a matter of fact, grace is a thorough disciplinarian. Paul has a startling word about grace in his letter to Titus: "The grace of God . . . hath appeared . . . teaching us" (Titus 2:11-12). That word "teaching" means child-training, the imposition of discipline. Saving and disciplining—that is the work of grace. If faith is to be perfected, it must be disciplined in the furnace of affliction.

> When through fiery trials thy pathway shall lie,
> My grace, all-sufficient, shall be thy supply.
> The flame shall not hurt thee; I only design
> Thy dross to consume, and thy gold to refine.
>
> JOHN RIPON

Faith brings suffering. Faith is perfected by suffering. And faith supports suffering. "Faith is . . . the proving of things not seen" (Heb 11:1, author's trans.). What should we ever do if we had no vision beyond what is seen, if our sufferings bounded our horizon? When we are hemmed in on every side, it is faith that sees a path through the sea. When our best efforts seem to bring only failure and we face nothing but wilderness, faith endures "as seeing the unseen One" (11:27*b*, author's trans.). When death leaps upon us before we have well begun our race, faith rejoices in the prospect of "a better resurrection" (11:35*b*). When the enemy seems to prevail, faith lifts the shout of ultimate triumph.

On the sixteenth of October, in the year 1555, when "bloody Mary" reigned in England, two bishops, Latimer and Ridley, were burned together at the stake in Oxford for their adherence to the Protestant faith. When the first lighted faggot was laid at Ridley's feet, his companion martyr said to him: "Be of good cheer, Mr. Ridley, and play the man; we shall this day light such a candle by God's grace in England, as I trust never shall be put out." It required another century for that candle of gospel truth and freedom to reach a steady flame, but it still burns after four hundred years. Faith saw the victory ahead, and sustained these men in their sufferings for Christ's sake.

"Of whom the world was not worthy" (Heb 11:38), says our text. That is quite the contrary of the world's judgment. The world considers the man of faith no fit company. Did it not lift its cry against the apostle Paul, "Away with such a fellow from the earth: for it is not fit that he should live"? (Acts 22:22). And its voice was the same for Paul's Master: "Away with him, crucify him" (John 19:15). "It is enough for the disciple that he be as his master, and the servant as his lord" (Matt 10:25). You are in royal company when the world excommunicates you, ostracizes you, cold-shoulders you, thrusts you out as unwelcome in its society; and the eternal reversal of the world's judgment stands written in the sacred page: "Of whom the world was not worthy."

This great chapter closes with a glimpse of yet another aspect of the faith life—faith waiting. Although "well attested by their faith," these "received not the promise" (Heb 11:39, author's trans.). We have already been told that one of the achievements of their faith was to receive promises, but there was one promise, or rather a whole set of promises, which they fondly cherished, but which they all died without realizing. They looked for a better country, a better rest, a better establishment, under a better King. They passed from this earthly scene, still expecting, assured that their faith was making its contribution to the bringing in of that better hope.

The better thing for which they looked has come upon us. That indeed is the whole message of the epistle. Let godly Andrew Murray sum up for us these blessings for which the saints of old looked, but which God had forseen for us.

> To them God spake in the prophets; to us in the Son. To them was offered the rest of Canaan; to us the rest of God. Their high priest was a man who died; ours is a Priest for ever, in the power of an endless life. Their sanctuary was on earth, and even that had its veil; ours is the true sanctuary, with the veil taken away. Theirs was the old covenant, in which there was no power to continue; ours is the new, with the heart made new by the Spirit. Theirs was

> the blood of bulls and of goats, ours is the blood of Jesus. Theirs was a sanctifying cleanness of the flesh; ours is thè cleansing of the heart from the evil conscience. Theirs a worship which made nothing perfect; in ours we are perfected for evermore. Their worship was a witness that the way into the Holiest was not yet open; ours is the blessed experience that in the new and living way we have living access into the very presence and love of the Father. God hath indeed provided *some better thing* for us.

Does this mean that they are robbed for our sakes, that they do the believing and we do the receiving? By no means. Their faith is fully rewarded in Christ. The cross is timeless. Its redemptive blessings stream out both ways, embracing the men of the old covenant along with us of the new. Its operation is, so to speak, retroactive. The fathers remained in the shadows, their full salvation waiting for the appearing of the Saviour, and the good thing which is ours in present possession. Now, not apart from us, they enter in and are made perfect. Here is the communion of the saints, the unity of the saints. They went before us, but they must wait for us. See, they are marking time, with their eyes straining forward and their hearts beating high; till the blood of the new testament throws open the gates of the city of God for us, and as we move up to claim our blood-bought heritage, the "forward march" rings out for them, and they spring into line, marching in step, shoulder to shoulder, our brethren and companions in the Kingdom of God. Our privileges *now* are far beyond their privileges *then;* but we are not a whit ahead of them in their present realization of the better thing. The shadows are as much past for them as for us. "We are not divided; all one body we."

The ultimate of the better thing is not yet. That still is in promise, and we wait. We wait for "the adoption, . . . the redemption of our body" (Rom 8:23*b*). We look for "that blessed hope, and the glorious appearing of the great God and our Saviour Jesus Christ" (Titus 2:13). We look for "new heavens and a new earth, wherein dwelleth righteousness" (2 Pet 3:13). From one generation to another the church has sustained and handed on this faith. In a very real sense, then, not apart from the last generation, and the last convert before the sound of the trumpet, shall we be made perfect. Then shall the hope of the fathers and the hope of the church be realized, their faith and ours justified, in the Holy City, the heavenly Jerusalem, "when the saints go marching in."

> Ten thousand times ten thousand
>   In sparkling raiment bright,
> The armies of the ransomed saints
>   Throng up the steeps of light:
> 'Tis finished, all is finished,
>   Their fight with death and sin:
> Fling open wide the golden gates,
>   And let the victors in.

33

RUN THE STRAIGHT RACE

HEBREWS 12:1-2

From these verses we glean:

1. Instruction for the race
2. Inspiration for the race
3. Imitation for the race
4. Incentive for the race

THERE IS NO INDICATION that any of the apostles ever contended in the Grecian or Roman games, but that they were not immune to their fascination is evident from several allusions to them, with application to the Christian life. Paul is so partial to the games that those who champion the Pauline authorship of the Hebrews epistle have a good friend in the present passage.

It is the track of faith which is presented to us here, for the twelfth chapter continues the subject of faith begun at the end of the tenth and expounded by a series of illustrations in the eleventh.

The instructions for the race include a reminder that we are not here dealing with a fifty-yard dash, but with a long grind. "Let us run with patience" (Heb 12:1*b*). It is a test of endurance, something that demands staying with, or "staying under," as the Greek has it. *Life* magazine did not throw any more bouquets than it had to when writing up Preacher Gil Dodds as "King of the Mile," but it made much of his "incredible stamina," his "grueling pace which kills off his rival milers in three quarters of a mile." Stamina: that is the word. Faith is not a momentary burst of emotion, but a settled habit of the soul which carries us round the first lap and the second and the third, and equally round the ninth and the tenth to the finishing line.

That patience, endurance, and stamina are required is emphasized by the word used here for "race." It is the origin of our word "agony." Primarily signifying a gathering for contests, it then was used of the contests themselves, and, since these were of the severest sort, the word took on the connotation of struggle, exertion, anguish. In this last sense we took it over into our language. The running, then, is not the slow double that we used to do round the parade ground in training days, but it is total effort.

The life of faith is so presented at times that a false impression of passivity is conveyed. I know that the way of salvation is "not try, but trust," and that the Christian life is "not I, but Christ" (Gal 2:20). This does not mean that we are carried dreamily to heaven on a sponge-rubber cushion. Faith is impelling, activating, urgent. It summons all there is of us to the conflict, the contest, the charge, all the time knowing that "our sufficiency is of God" (2 Cor 3:5). There is indeed the rest of faith, a blessed condition of the heart that lends poise and strength and calm to the uttermost exertions of faith. "Let us run with patience."

"Run light," exhorts our experienced coach, speaking in the Holy Ghost. "In running I put aside all weights. I take off excess poundage first. I see that my clothing is as light as possible—not tight and likely to bind me anywhere." So Gil Dodds informs his young admirers; and when he ran an exhibition cross-country from Wheaton ball field, I noticed that he stepped out of a grown-up snowsuit, and ran light. "Wherefore . . . let us lay aside every weight, and the sin which doth so easily beset us, and let us run . . . the race that is set before us" (Heb 12:1).

When this was written to the Hebrew believers of the first century, the apostle had a particular weight in mind, and a particular sin. The synagogue with its ritual, and the Temple with its priesthood, still held their appeal for those who had been brought up in the tradition. It was a dangerous appeal, for it held those Jewish Christians back from the full freedom of the gospel, and hindered their progress in Christ. Moreover, so long as they played with the now-abolished order, they were in peril of being drawn right back into it under pressure of persecution or persuasion. The synagogue and the Temple were the weight; the sin to which toying with them exposed these hesitating

Christians was apostasy from Christ. That was their "besetting sin," which does not mean the sin which they were most habitually committing, but the sin which stood around within easy striking distance so long as they failed to cast aside the weight.

Every weight carries an easily besetting sin. The rich young ruler had a weight—his riches. When he was challenged to lay it aside, he refused, and the besetting sin smote him—he rejected Christ. Is there something in this world upon which you have set your heart? That is your weight, and you cannot tell into what deplorable sin it will plunge you if you do not cast it from you. My Christian brother, if you are holding on to something—something in your business life, something in your social life, something in your family life—which puts a drag on your feet in following after Christ, beware! The offspring of that weight is a sin which is closer than you think, a sin which will shame you, and blight your testimony, and give the enemies of the gospel good cause for rejoicing.

"Lay aside every weight." William Guthrie, one of our Scottish preachers of the covenanting period, and author of that spiritual classic, *The Saving Interest,* was a born sportsman. He loved the rod and the gun. He was the eldest son of the laird of Pitforthy, and heir to the lands of Pitforthy and Easter Ogle, a paradise for fishing and hunting. After his conversion under Samuel Rutherford, and the dedication of his life to God for the preaching of the gospel, Guthrie realized that such an estate would be a weight to a man of his temperament, with the too great likelihood of the sin of neglect. He therefore made over the lairdship, with full possession of the lands, to a younger brother, that he might devote himself to the work of the gospel. Not that he never fished or hunted thereafter, but they never became a snare, and William Guthrie became one of the greatest preachers of that period of great preachers, a mighty winner of souls. Alexander Whyte says of him that "for handling broken bones and guiding an anxious enquirer no one could hold the candle to William Guthrie."

There is only one way to escape the besetting sin—lay aside the weight that gives it vantage ground. Run light!

We have here inspiration for the race. "We . . . are compassed about with so great a cloud of witnesses" (Heb 12:1). Here it is most inviting, even tempting, to think in terms of the great amphitheater, with tiers upon tiers of spectators looking down at the contestants in the arena. The thought could not have been wholly absent from the writer's mind, since he is speaking of a race, a contest. The verb, "compassed about," is quite in keeping with the idea, and the figure of the cloud is not opposed to it. It is the word "witnesses" that gives us pause. They are not spectators, looking on, but "martyrs," confessors giving testimony.

In his great hymn, Philip Doddridge thinks in terms of spectators:

> A cloud of witnesses around
> Hold thee in full survey;
> Forget the steps already trod,
> And onward urge thy way.

That may be part of the truth, but it is not the whole truth, nor the main part of it. We are surrounded with a cloud of men and women who have a testimony to bear to us regarding this race of faith. Who are they? Abel, Enoch, Noah, Abraham, Moses, Joshua, and all the other named and unnamed heroes of faith listed or not listed in the eleventh chapter of our epistle.

And what is their witness? Every one of them is saying to the Christian contender, "You are on the right track. It is true that 'the just shall live by faith.' God did not mock our trust and He will not mock yours. We saw the goal only afar off, yet we have arrived. God is faithful. 'Go on going on, Christian!' " So runs their unanimous testimony, while each one would have a little special word out of his own individual experience: Abel would say, "Without shedding of blood is no remission" (Heb 9:22). Enoch would say, "God's company far exceeds the society of sinners." Noah would add, "The ark holds!" Abraham would sing for us,

> I'd rather walk in the dark with God
> Than go alone in the light.

Moses would assure us, "I'd rather have Jesus than anything this world affords today." And Joshua would raise his battle cry, "Jehovah-Nissi!" So on and on, each one adding to the testimony of the other, all for our encouragement.

There is inspiration in a great crowd of spectators. But suppose every one of them is a champion, a winner, whose feet have in other days burned up these boards! And suppose they are infusing their crowned zeal into your heart, adding the wisdom of their combined experience to your knowledge. Would not the inspiration be tremendous? Gil Dodds would soon do a four-minute mile in such a situation! Here, then, in our race we have the hosts of winners backing us, encouraging us with their testimony of the reality of God, the faithfulness of God, and the rewards of God.

But for all the inspiration afforded by these heroes of faith, they are not our pattern. The imitation of great men is usually ludicrous. Frequently enough it is their idiosyncrasies that are copied. In the early days of my ministry a certain outstanding preacher in Canada had many youthful imitators. He was a tall, dignified gentleman, and a master in the pulpit. His miniatures were scattered all over the country. I came upon one of them in a tiny church in a small northern town. He was a little fellow, with little training and little experience, but he was quite sure he was ordained to be the great man's successor! To see him attempt to walk like his hero, throw himself into a big chair with the air of an autocrat, and assume a lofty manner as he conversed in pompous tones, was almost too much of a strain on one's good manners. Mannerisms which were natural to the great man, and not out of proportion to everything else about him, were unspeakably comical in the imitator.

It is good to learn from others. Their faith and their failures alike hold lessons for us. But if we make them our pattern, we shall get drunk with Noah; we shall lie like Abraham; we shall deceive like Jacob; we shall show temper like Moses; we shall commit adultery like David. So the Scriptures, while giving us the inspiration of their victory, call us to imitate none of them. "Let us run . . . the race . . . looking unto Jesus" (Heb 12:1-2). A medieval symbol of the church was the polestar, bearing the motto (in Latin), "He who does not look at me goes astray." How many have gone astray by looking to men, fellow sinners, rather than looking off to our polestar, the Lord Jesus!

Only in Jesus has faith had its full expression and its full fruition. He is "the file-leader and perfecter of faith" (Heb 12:2, author's trans.). At every step of our pilgrim journey, on every lap of our great race, He is the one who goes before, mapping out the way, all the way to the consummation at the throne of God. When faith is facing an impossible test, look off unto Jesus. When your human idol lies smashed at your feet, look away to Jesus. When you wonder if there is anybody you can trust, look to Jesus. There is no breakdown in Him. He pioneered the way of faith through temptation, through a world's sin, through death and the grave, through principalities and powers, right through to heaven itself, through to the holy place of the face of God, through to the right hand of the throne of the Majesty on high. Hallelujah! What a Saviour! Then steadfastly and continuously pull your eyes away from frail men, be they patriarchs, prophets, or priests, who, though their testimony of faith may inspire to nobler effort, yet, if they be imitated, will lead to breakdown and failure; but let your vision be full of Jesus, and the clods will change to wings.

Our great pattern had incentive for His race of faith. "Who for the joy that was set before him endured the cross, despising the shame, and is set down at the right hand of the throne of God" (Heb 12:2*b*). What was "the joy set before him," for the sake of which He "endured the cross, despising the shame"? Was it the joy of being "set down at the right hand of the throne of God" (12:2*c*)? That doubtless entered into it, but there was something more. To be able to stand before the Father and say, "I have finished the work which thou gavest me to do" (John 17:4), and to greet the multitude of the redeemed with, "Come, ye blessed of my Father, inherit the kingdom prepared for you from the foundation of the world" (Matt 25:34): that was the joy set before Him. That was the great incentive of our Captain's race. The throne is for the one who will make these his goal.

Do we know this incentive in life's great race? Is the accomplishment of the will of God the highest joy to which we aspire, so that we are ready to go with our Captain the way of the cross and the shame to attain it? And do we so share heaven's joy over one sinner that repenteth that we shall gladly go the thorny way with the Saviour to save some? That is real overcoming, and "to him that overcometh will I grant to sit with me in my throne" (Rev 3:21).

34

DISCIPLINE

HEBREWS 12:3-13

In this study we consider:

1. The divine principle of discipline
2. The human practice of discipline
3. The ultimate product of discipline

WHY? Did you ever ask that question? We practiced it in childhood. "Why do I have to?" "Why can't I?" These were the persistent questions with which we vexed our parents, and now we are vexed in our turn. Strangely enough, we turn from telling our children that they must not say "why?" to throw the same question at God! As if our children must accept our wisdom as infallible and our judgment as beyond dispute, while we are privileged to argue the ways of the Almighty!

Yet it is not always wrong to ask "why?" All depends on the spirit. If our question is asked in a spirit of resentment, if its import is that God has no right to deal with us thus, then we are dead wrong, and ripe for some stern dealing. If, on the other hand, our "why?" comes from a submissive, trustful heart that seeks to know the divine purpose in order to cooperate with it, then we are in the way of blessing.

One little statement in our text (which unfortunately is not brought out in the King James Version) gives a comprehensive answer to our urgent "why?" "It is for discipline that ye endure," says verse seven (author's trans.). That is the secret of these sore temptations, these bitter trials, these grim conflicts.

Discipline is a divine principle. Always the preparation of a chosen vessel involves discipline. It was so even in the case of our divine and sinless Saviour. "For it became him, for whom are all things, and through whom are all things, in bringing many sons unto glory, to make the author of their salvation perfect through sufferings" (Heb 2:10, ASV) ; and again, "though he was a son, yet learned [he] obedience by the things which he suffered" (5:8, ASV) . If it were so of the perfect Son, how much more shall we expect a heap of discipline in the process of "bringing many sons unto glory," transforming sinners into saints who bear the very image of the Son of God!

When, therefore, we are tempted to wax weary and faint in our souls because of the pressure of God's disciplinary measures, it is our salvation to "consider him that hath endured such gainsaying of sinners" as part of His discipline. We have been earlier called to "consider the Apostle and High Priest of our confession" (3:1, ASV) in His vast superiority over Moses, Aaron, and all others, lest we should abide in the shadows and miss the true light; now we are invited to consider Him as our Partner in suffering, to sustain us when the hand of God is heavy upon us, or when we are exposed to the fury of our adversary. However fierce our contest with the wild beast of sin may become, it will never reach the proportions of our Lord's resistance, when "his sweat was as it were great drops of blood falling down to the ground" (Luke 22:44) .

"Ye have not yet resisted unto blood, striving against sin" (Heb 12:4) , writes our inspired author to the early Hebrew Christians, suggesting that it might even come to that. Did he mean that martyrdom was on the way? Or that they might have fiercer conflicts within themselves for which the present discipline was preparing them? I have just been reading of Chinese opium victims who, on coming to the knowledge of Christ, were willing to endure untold agonies, and death itself, rather than yield to the awful craving. Koh, owner of an opium den, was one who resisted unto death, and his friend Cheng was ready to follow his example, but after much suffering, was taken to a mission hospital and lived, a victor. God could have lifted the craving from these men immediately, and taken care of the physical reactions miraculously, but, for these men at least, it was a matter of enduring for discipline. The harvest of it will be reaped in heaven.

What will be our attitude to the disciplines of God? Resentment? Indifference? Discouragement? Not if we remember the exhortation from Proverbs: "My son, do not regard lightly the Lord's discipline, nor faint when you are rebuked by him; for whom the Lord loves he disciplines" (3:11-12, author's trans.; cf. Heb 12:5-6). It is the discipline of infinite love. A mother once told me that she loved her boy far too much to whip him. He showed it, in disrespect, disobedience, selfishness, and other traits that would cause him much more suffering later on than a few good whippings at the right time. She was not a loving parent, but a *fond* parent, in the older sense of the word. She foolishly doted on her boy, spoiling him to the point of making him a nuisance to the community. Love does not spare the rod, and when we remember that chastening is an expression of divine love, we shall be ready to say with Eli, "It is the LORD: let him do what seemeth him good" (1 Sam 3:18).

This principle of discipline operates within the family. God "scourgeth every son whom he receiveth. . . . God dealeth with you as with sons" (Heb 12:6*b*-7). It is not only love that dictates the chastening, then, but the love of the Father. Here is infinite comfort—not only that fatherly love will impose no more discipline than is required, but that fatherly love will impose all the discipline required to assure my fitness for that place in the family which He has appointed for me.

God's dealings with sinners are very different from His dealings with His sons. He is not disciplining *them* toward some high destiny. Therefore, though He may at times warn sinners in mercy by foretastes of judgment, if perchance they may repent and turn to Him, He on the whole allows them to heap up wrath against the day of wrath. False professors may thus seem to have soft south winds blow for them when God's true children are battling the tempest. If God's disciplines are conspicuously absent from your life, "examine yourself, whether ye be in the faith" (2 Cor 13:5). For "if ye are without chastening, whereof all have been made partakers, then are ye bastards, and not sons" (Heb 12:8, ASV). Sinners do indeed share the common lot of men, and reap the natural harvest of their evil ways, but the discipline of God's sons is quite a different matter, which the spiritual man clearly discerns. The flesh shrinks from it, but the spirit welcomes it, not only for its wholesome effects, but for the added assurance that we are not bastards, false professors among the saints, but true children, born from above.

This divine principle of discipline is practiced among men. How is a raw recruit made into a soldier who, in face of enemy fire, will do exactly as he is told, with courage, precision, and determination? By rigorous discipline. And wherever men are to be made something other than they are, or rise to achievements beyond their present attainment, discipline is the open secret. So to help us grow from childhood to manhood, in mind and character as well as stature, "we had the fathers of our flesh who disciplined us" (Heb 12:9, author's trans.). Most of us can vouch for the truth of that!

But discipline as practiced among men is always defective. "They verily for a few days chastened us after their own pleasure" (12:10), says the King James Version, which I have always thought a bit of a slander on our good fathers. The revisers are closer to the thought: "They indeed for a few days chastened us as seemed good to them" (v. 10, ASV). They had a more or less clear picture of what they wanted us to become, and they imposed the sort and amount of discipline they thought would produce in us the end they had in mind. Now we thank God for fathers who set before them the goal of godly character and useful lives for their sons, and who diligently corrected us toward that end. It yet remains true that many fathers have lacked a true vision for their children, and their correctings have often been impulsive, explosive, rather than studied and effective. Even the best of them had but "a few days" in which to do their work, for children soon leave the parental control to fend for themselves. Little time to do a work imperfectly conceived and inadequately executed; that, at best, is the story of paternal discipline.

Not so the chastening of the Lord. His authority rests upon us all our days. He knows exactly what He would make of us, and His wisdom and resources are infinite, so that He is able to "perfect that which concerneth us" (Psalm 138:8). He knows the exact kind and the exact measure of discipline to impose—not too little or too lenient to spoil us, not too much or too severe to wound us.

What was our response to the disciplines of our earthly fathers? Whatever our feelings at the moment, we gave them respect. It is true that where chastening was just an outburst of temper, respect gradually gave place to resentment and bitterness and rebellion; but I speak of the thoughtful, firm, consistent correctings of fathers who sought to fulfill their high duty.

If, then, we gave the response of veneration and respect to the defective discipline of the fathers of our flesh, what trustful and loving submission shall we not give to the Father of our spirits, whose ways are perfect, and whose disciplines will make our ways perfect! We know that He makes no mistake. If He take away from us our health, our wealth, our home, our little empire, our best beloved; if He allow us to suffer in the long struggle with some temptation before final release comes; if He add calumny and misunderstanding and disappointment to our lot: it must be good.

> Ill that He blesses is our good,
> And unblest good is ill;
> And all is right that seems most wrong
> If it be His sweet will.

Submission—not with the growl of a helpless captive that can do no other, but with the loving trust of a child who knows that the Father's love cannot fail, nor His wisdom err—is the way of blessing. We submit—and live! The more we submit, the more grandly we live, the more nobly we live, the more fully we live. How foolish to think that submission to God means straitenment, confinement, bondage, reduction; when all the time it is the way of enlargement, release, liberty, and increase! Let us be done with putting limits to God's control in our lives; let us be done with resistance to His disciplining hand; and with the exhilaration of one who has the goal in sight, submit to the Father of our spirits, and live.

Fetis's *History of Music* carries a story of that great Italian master of the eighteenth century, Porpora, who, seeing the possibilities in a young voice pupil, challenged him to a course of rigorous discipline. The pupil assenting, Porpora wrote out on a single sheet of ruled paper the diatonic and chromatic scales, the various intervals, with trills, groups, appogiaturas, and various sorts of vocal passages. A whole year was devoted to this single sheet, then a second year, and a third. The pupil showed some impatience, but the master reminded him of his pledge. A fourth year found the two still occupied with the same exercises; and a fifth, and a sixth, with some added lessons in articulation and pronunciation. At the end of the sixth year, Porpora said to his amazed pupil: "Go, my son, you have nothing more to learn; you are the first singer of Italy and of the world!" That was Gaetano Caffarelli, the great singer of Naples. The discipline had worked.

"Nevertheless afterward!" (Heb 12:11*b*). God's disciplines may appear at times rigorous, but any less would fail of the ultimate purpose, "that we may be partakers of his holiness" (12:10*b*, ASV). God is out to produce character like His own! If we are satisfied with less than that, He is not. "Be ye holy; for I am holy" (1 Pet 1:16). "Be ye therefore perfect, even as your Father which is in heaven is perfect" (Matt 5:48). God will not have His children unlike Himself.

Two questions: considering what we are when God receives us into His family, can we expect His goal for us to be reached without much discipline? And, are we ready to accept the discipline for the sake of the product?

"What have I done to deserve all this?" asks the repining soul. That is the wrong question. Rather ask, "What is God making of me that requires all this?" And when you remember that He has predestinated you to be conformed to the image of His Son, appointed you to be a partaker of His holiness, the discipline will appear in a new light: you will not only approve it, you will call out for it. The crest of the Scottish clan from which I spring carries the motto, *Dulce Periculum.* If, for the honor of their clan, my forefathers called danger sweet, how shall we not bless the discipline which brings us ever closer to the shining image of our blessed Lord!

Character appears in conduct. Therefore, while holiness of character is being wrought within the soul by the chastenings of God, the fruit of righteousness is being manifested more and more. The processes of training may be sharp, but the fruit comes to the accompaniment of sweet peace, as a return for the travail and burnings which marked the discipline.

This is not the place to discuss the doctrine of holiness. I would only say that absolute holiness is not attained here. We do indeed possess a perfect holiness in Christ, "who of God is made unto us wisdom, and righteousness, and sanctification [holiness], and redemption" (1 Cor 1:30). The holiness of personal character, however, is definitely progressive, and as it advances, it reflects in outward conduct. The deeper the work in the soul, the finer are the points of conduct affected, till one cannot fail to sense the aroma of Christ in the much disciplined, and much sanctified, believer. The degree of holiness is not to be judged by the loudness of our claim, but by the measure in which we show "the peaceable fruit of righteousness" (Heb 12:11*b*).

If, instead of caving in under the training of the Lord, we joyfully submit, allowing it to be the gymnasium of our souls, not only shall we be blessed with inward holiness and right conduct, but our strengthened lives will be a blessing to others. The straight paths that we cut for our own feet, instead of turning weaklings out of the way, offended, stumbled, broken, will be a challenge to them to follow on, a tonic for their faith. May it be so in our disciplined lives!

35

THE PURSUIT OF HOLINESS

HEBREWS 12:14-17

In this chapter we discern:

1. Three imperatives of holiness
2. Three impediments to holiness

GOD REQUIRES HOLINESS. If He did not, He would not go to such lengths to secure it. Why the unspeakable sacrifice of Calvary? Why the high-priestly ministry of our risen, glorified Lord? Why the divine exertions of the Holy Spirit? Why the disciplines of God in the life? All to make men holy.

Someone comments: True, but God provides what He requires, and "we are sanctified through the offering of the body of Jesus Christ once for all" (Heb 10:10). That is a blessed truth. Through the efficacy of the sacrifice, through the precious blood, we become vessels of the sanctuary, set apart for the purposes of God—forever. But that is not the end of sanctification. It is the beginning; a glorious beginning, to be sure, but just the beginning. Here we are dealing with a holiness which we are commanded to pursue constantly.

Another interjects: I know all about that. Holiness is something to be sought as a second experience which completes and secures the transaction of salvation, and after which we are without sin. If that be so, then there comes a time when this exhortation no longer applies to us. It is perilous to set oneself beyond the reach of the commands of Scripture. That there are crisis experiences in the path of holiness is beyond dispute, but these never bring us to an end. The holiest people I know are still diligently following after, striving to apprehend that for which they have been apprehended of Christ Jesus.

Still another offers a thought: Holiness, he declares, is not the attainment of any man. We are holy only in Christ, "who of God is made unto us wisdom, and righteousness, and sanctification [holiness], and redemption" (1 Cor 1:30). That also is blessed truth, but not all the truth. "Christ in you the hope of glory" (Col 1:27), and if Christ our sanctification dwells in us, there will be evidence of it in increasing conformity to His character. If this is not the divine order, there is no point in the exhortation, "Keep pursuing . . . holiness" (Heb 12:14, author's trans.).

Holiness is required for the vision of God. "Pursue . . . the holiness without which no man shall see the Lord" (12:14, author's trans.). To see the Lord means to be acceptable in His presence. The story of Absalom comes before us. When this wild, willful son of David the king took judgment into his own hands, and killed his half brother Amnon, he fled to Geshur, and was there three years, yearned after by the king, but unrepentant and unforgiven. Then came the woman of Tekoah, coached by Joab, with her parable and its application, "the king doth speak this thing as one which is faulty, in that the king doth not fetch home again his banished" (2 Sam 14:13*b*). So Absalom was brought back to Jerusalem. "And the king said, Let him turn to his own house, and let him not see my face" (14:24). For all his winsomeness, he was persona non grata in the king's eyes. There was no repentance, no humility, no submission in the heart of Absalom. Therefore he "dwelt two full years in Jerusalem, and saw not the king's face" (14:28).

Whether a man be dwelling in heathen Geshur or within the walls of Jerusalem; whether he be a vagabond in the earth or abide at the gates of Eden; whether he wander at will or spend his days in the courts of the house of the Lord, without holiness no man shall see the Lord. Be his profession ever so loud, his theology ever so sound, his position in the church ever so important, without holiness he is still barred from the presence of the Lord. Let him pray with all fervor, let him preach with all eloquence, let him work notable miracles, let him control ecclesiastical councils, yet if he is not holy, the end of it all will be the desolating words, "I never knew you: depart from me" (Matt 7:23).

Those who are well acquainted with "the secret place of the Most

High" (Psalm 91:1, ASV) are keenly aware of the power of sin to interrupt communion. Not long ago a beloved brother telephoned me, asking for the privilege of making a confession before the church at the prayer meeting that evening. He had been brought face to face with what many a Christian would have called a mistake, but which he recognized as sin. He said, "I know the Lord will not speak to me out of His Word, nor can I pray anymore, until I make this thing right." The breach of communion was something he could not tolerate. Therefore, although it was painful and humiliating to make confession and take such other steps as were necessary to cancel the wrong, he counted that a small price for the preservation of unbroken fellowship with the Lord. If it be so with the true children of God, how will it fare with those who, for all their religious profession, have never pursued after holiness! "If the righteous scarcely be saved, where shall the ungodly and the sinner appear?" (1 Pet 4:18).

Does this mean that we shall never see the Lord unless we attain to sinless perfection in this life? By no means, else none of us would ever enjoy the beatific vision. The holy man is not the one who stands in the middle of the Temple court, praying with himself, "God, I thank thee that I am not as other men" (Luke 18:11)—but rather the one who will often be found in a lone corner, beating his breast and crying, "God be merciful to me, the sinner" (v. 13*b*). The man who has come to know the plague of his own heart, who condemns sin in his own life, who mourns before God for his shortcomings, who will not be satisfied with anything short of God's best, who bows his heart in loving submission to the will of God: that man has the beginnings and the essence of "the holiness, without which no man shall see the Lord" (Heb 12:14*b*). But show me a man who professes the name of Christ, yet has no concern about the sin in his life, is quite satisfied to walk as a man of the world, and is full of self-justification; and I will show you a man who has not seen the Lord in salvation, is not seeing the Lord in communion, and, except he repent, will never see the Lord in acceptance.

Then is salvation the reward of holiness? We always thought that salvation was purely of grace! But so much is holiness the inevitable work of grace, that unless it appear, the presence of saving grace is brought into question. Do you see the order here? "Pursue . . . the holiness without which no man can see the Lord, looking diligently lest any one fall short of the grace of God" (12:14-15, author's trans.).

There are various ways of falling short of the grace of God. One may have the proposition of the gospel clearly presented. He knows that following Christ would involve radical changes in his life. For these he is unwilling, and, like the rich young ruler who "turned away sorrowing, for he had great possessions" (Matt 19:22, author's trans.), falls short of the grace of God, sacrificing his soul for trifles of the passing hour.

Another is brought up in a Christian home and under the influences of a Christian community. He does not dispute the testimony of Christ, but on the other hand takes no action toward personal acceptance of the Saviour, assuming that as a member of this Christian circle he is a child of God. Yet all he has is hereditary religion. He is in the case of the Pharisees to whom John the Baptist said: "Begin not to say within yourselves, We have Abraham to our father: for I say unto you, That God is able of these stones to raise up children unto Abraham" (Luke 3:8). He is also missing the grace of God, by presumption.

Here is one of another sort, roused to a certain sense of sinnerhood, but not to the point of realizing his own helplessness and his need for a salvation that is all of grace. He resolves on self-improvement, finds a church to his liking, learns and adopts its creed, receives its rites, supports its services, and professes to be a Christian. Both he and his friends are highly pleased, yet the entire procedure is utterly devoid of the grace of God.

Our text tells us of yet a fourth kind of failure, the man who falls short through the antinomian error, "turning the grace of our God into lasciviousness" (Jude 4). This man is in the Christian church. He is thoroughly indoctrinated. He will expound grace with any theologian. Election and predestination are no problem to him. He calls himself a believer. But his faith has no relation to the sin question. He has never cried out in anguish of soul, "Woe is me! for I am undone; because I am a man of unclean lips" (Isa 6:5). Salvation to him has no bearing on character and conduct. His conversion, whatever it was, did not mark the beginning of a pursuit after holiness. If you challenge him, he will tell you that salvation is by grace, and grace takes no account of personal merit. He will tell you that your insistence on holy living is legalistic, while he, being more advanced in grace, is free. Our text tells us that that man, instead of being far advanced in grace, is far from grace; he has not yet come into grace. As evidence of one's standing in grace, a tender conscience and a longing for likeness to Christ cannot be surpassed. Holiness, then, is a command of God, a requisite for communion with God, and a necessary product of grace. Therefore, let us "follow . . . [after] holiness" (Heb 12:14).

Three sorts of men are now mentioned as being not only unholy themselves, but a detriment to holiness in the church, so that all have a duty to watch against their presence. The first is called "a root of bitterness" (12:15), which grows up into a noxious weed, and produces widespread defilement.

This phrase "root of bitterness" appears in the Septuagint version of Deuteronomy 29:18, where Moses is warning against defection in the camp of Israel: "lest there should be among you man, or woman, or family, or tribe, whose heart turneth away this day from the LORD our God, to go and serve the gods of those nations; lest there should be among you a root [of bitterness] that beareth gall and wormwood." Such a man or woman or family or tribe was to be dealt with without pity, because of the danger of defiling the whole nation. It is amazing how defection can spread. It is a malignant disease, before which holiness withers.

Such a root of bitterness in the Christian church would be one opposed to a spiritual ministry, using every pretext to stir dissension; or one seized with jealousy, creating faction; or one aggravating an unimportant difference into a vital issue, and establishing a camp of recalcitrants. These are roots of bitterness springing up and causing trouble, till the many, the people as a whole, are defiled with contention. That is fatal to true holiness, and must be carefully guarded against.

The next impediment to holiness is impurity. "Watch carefully . . . lest there be a fornicator" (Heb 12:15-16, author's trans.). This is no needless warning. Indeed, the emphasis on moral purity in the exhortations to believers is suggestive of the danger which continually lurks in this sphere. No man, no woman, can say, "Because I am a

Christian, I am immune to this temptation." "Let him that thinketh he standeth take heed lest he fall" (1 Cor 10:12).

Sin in this realm stands in a class by itself, because it is sin against the body, which is the temple of the Holy Spirit. It is perhaps for that reason that nothing so disqualifies one for the service of God. No wonder the apostle Paul wrote, "I buffet my body, and bring it into bondage: lest by any means, after that I have preached to others, I myself should be rejected" (9:27, ASV). And we cannot escape the passionate appeals which the aged apostle makes to young Timothy to keep himself pure. The bitterest penitence cannot restore confidence in a Christian who has fallen here, while the testimony of the church is sorely wounded.

The way to avoid sin is not to court it. The man who does not go in that direction is not likely to arrive there; but let him play with fire, and he is in danger of being burned. Giving rein to the flesh is apt to end in a stampede.

Spurgeon used to tell of the lady who advertised for a coachman. Three men applied for the position, and she asked them all the same question: "How close could you drive to a sheer precipice without losing control?" The first, moderately confident in his ability, believed he could go within six inches of the edge and be safe. The second, having no lack of self-assurance, boasted that he would drive to a hairsbreadth of the edge and have no difficulty. The third said: "Lady, if you want a daredevil for your coachman, I am not your man. My policy has always been, Keep as far away from the precipice as possible." The third man was hired! And with respect to sin, he had the only sound practice. If we would preserve purity, we had better not indulge habits that lead into temptation.

If we are going to take oversight that there be no fornicator in the church, we had better begin farther back. Do we take oversight of our children's reading, the pictures they look at, the radio programs they listen to? Hosts of young people in the thrall of evil thoughts and unclean practices are just reaping the harvest of careless sowing in earlier years. Nor can we who are older afford to feed our minds on the vulgarities and obscenities that are offered on the air, on the printed page, and through other popular channels. "As [a man] . . . thinketh in his heart, so is he" (Prov 23:7) and as he feeds, so he thinks. We cannot exercise the mind in impurity, and expect to exercise the body in purity.

The third impediment to holiness is profanity, which is not foul language, but just downright worldliness. Esau was the man of this world. Such a thing as the right of the firstborn in the patriarchal, covenant household held no attraction for him over against the satisfaction of his natural appetites. He lived in the realm of immediates, not of ultimates. Such worldliness is incompatible with holiness.

There is all too much worldliness in our churches, and too many worldlings. I do not speak of churches which sponsor dances and bridge parties, but of churches where these would be deemed a scandal; not of church members who frequent the theater and other "worldly" amusements, but of those who practice "separation" in regard to all these. Worldliness is not confined to such popular pleasures. Esau knew none of them, yet was a confirmed worldling. Christians who are so engrossed in their business affairs that the affairs of the Kingdom of God receive scant attention are worldlings. Christians who are more concerned with the furnishing of their homes than the furnishing of their souls are worldlings. Christians who have big appetites for turkey and little appetite for the Word of God are worldlings. Christians who have more pleasure in the social gathering than in the prayer meeting are worldlings. Christians who think more of a bank account than of treasures in heaven are worldlings. Christians who covet popularity more than communion with God are worldlings. Are there not too many Esaus among us, sacrificing so much of our spiritual heritage for passing trifles? Then, when blessing bypasses us as it did Esau, we wonder why! A worldly spirit is the blight of holiness.

How, then, shall we follow after holiness? By avoiding the malignant influences of unbelief, envy, division, and such; by giving a wide berth to all that would inflame the lusts; by setting our "affection on things above, not on things on the earth" (Col 3:2). So much we learn from our text, and if we learn this well, it is enough for one lesson.

36

NOT SINAI, BUT SION

HEBREWS 12:18-29

This passage presents to us:

1. Stern jurisdiction from Sinai
2. Sweet consolation from Sion
3. Solemn admonition from the sky

DO NOT OVERLOOK conjunctions. Insignificant and humble as they are, they have an important function, making a connected whole where otherwise we should have so many disjointed phrases. The "for" at the beginning of our present passage links with the exhortation to holiness, giving another reason for such lofty pursuit. Our high privilege under the new covenant makes more imperious the call to holy living.

"Ye are not come unto the mount that might be touched" (Heb 12:18), says the King James Version; and although there is no word for "mount" in the best manuscripts, the most ancient versions, or the finest patristic texts, I am satisfied that that is what is meant. Whether a very early copyist dropped the word by mistake, or whether the apostle purposely omitted it, the context seems to demand that we supply it, in order to sustain the evident contrast between Sinai and Sion.

"For ye have not come to a tangible [mount], and a kindled fire, and a wrack of clouds, and gloomy darkness, and storm, and a sound of trumpet, and an articulate voice whose hearers begged off from having any further word spoken to them" (12:18, author's trans.). Here we have a vivid picture of the terrifying accompaniments of the giving of the Law at Sinai. Even Moses, the mediator of the covenant being then enacted, was shaken with fear at the sights and sounds. There is little comfort for sinners here, only dire threatenings.

John Bunyan has given us a glimpse of Sinai in *Pilgrim's Progress.* As Christian is plodding his weary way toward the Wicket Gate, laden with his burden, he meets one Mr. Worldly Wiseman, who directs him to the home of Mr. Legality in the town of Morality, where, he assures the pilgrim, he will be rid of his great load. To reach the house of Mr. Legality, Christian must pass by a certain high hill, which was none other than Sinai. So we read: "When he was now hard by the hill, it seemed so high, and also that side of it that was next the wayside did hang so much over, that Christian was afraid to venture farther, lest the hill should fall on his head; wherefore there he stood still, and wotted not what to do. Also his burden now seemed heavier to him than while he was in the way. There came also flashes of fire out of the hill, that made Christian afraid that he should be burnt: here, therefore, he sweat and did quake for fear."

The picture that accompanied this text in my boyhood copy helped to stamp the truth of Sinai on my mind. The Law, with its thunders and lightnings and clouds and darkness, has no release for sinners. "Cursed is every one that continueth not in all things which are written in the book of the law to do them" (Gal 3:10). That will not quiet the terrors of the soul, nor give peace to the stricken conscience. Yet it is amazing how many awakened sinners seek refuge in the Law, which offers none. So it was with Major André, who on the eve of his execution as a spy, expressed his spiritual experience in a few powerful verses, including these:

> And thus th' eternal counsels ran,
> "Almighty Love, arrest that man!"
> I felt the arrows of distress,
> And found I had no hiding place.
>
> Indignant Justice stood in view;
> To Sinai's fiery mount I flew;
> But Justice cried with frowning face,
> "This mountain is no hiding place!"

The children of Israel were brought nigh to the mount to meet with God, but bounds were set, beyond which they might not go. The voice of God was fearful, so that the people begged that His word should be brought to them by an intermediary, and no longer spoken directly. The fire and the smoke and the gloom and the darkness and the tempest and the trumpet crescendo were enough to impress Israel with the majesty and power of God, and the authority of His word, but they also were in keeping with the general fearfulness of the revelation. The Law is the ministration of condemnation and death. It provides no access, secures no acceptance, offers no communion. "This mountain is no hiding place."

Terror gives place to tranquillity as we turn from Sinai to Sion. Here is a study in antitheses—a cluster of *heavenlies* over against a group of *earthlies,* seven against seven (Heb 12:18-19, 22-24). Do you count eight? So do I, but we must make them seven somehow! Saphir makes seven by combining "God the Judge of all" (in parenthesis!) with "the church of the firstborn, which are written in heaven." Delitzsch makes seven by uniting the angels and the church of the firstborn in the "innumerable hosts" (v. 22, ASV). I prefer to join "mount Sion" and "the city of the living God, the heavenly Jerusalem," as essentially the same, with some difference of emphasis. It seems a little happier and more natural.

Leaving this little friendly disputation, we consider the blessedness of these *heavenlies.* First notice that we have come to them. Sinai says, "Keep back, no admittance!" Sion says, "Come, for all things are now ready!" The Law says, "Your iniquities have separated between you and your God" (Isa 59:2); the gospel cries, "We are brought nigh!" (see Eph 2:13). Nor is the access merely a promise for the future, but a realization for the present. We have come, our perfect tense tells us, and we stand in the acceptance of that coming.

The hill of Sion is the place of the throne. It was the stronghold which David set apart for the royal dwelling in Jerusalem, and its name was taken up into the vocabulary of the Kingdom of God. "Yet have I set my king upon my holy hill of Zion," we read in the second psalm, and we turn to Revelation to see that same King walking as the Shepherd-Lamb upon the mount Sion in the company of the redeemed. Sion is the place of the sanctuary also, where our great Melchisedec, "great David's greater Son," engages His holy priesthood in the power of divine sovereignty. "We have come unto the hill of

Sion." We have been brought nigh, into the Holy of Holies, to the throne of grace.

Franz Delitzsch admits that "mount Sion" and "the city of the living God, the heavenly Jerusalem" are "practically and essentially one and the same." We may, however, think of it in this light. While Sion speaks of the essential dwelling place of the Most High, where our glorious Lord exercises His priestly and kingly ministries, Jerusalem is the habitation of God *with His people.* The heavenly Jerusalem is our place of abode, where we walk in the light of God's countenance, and abide under the shadow of His wings. When the Holy City, the New Jerusalem, comes down from heaven, the cry goes forth, "Behold, the tabernacle of God is with men, and he will dwell with them, and they shall be his people" (Rev 21:3). This is the city that is lighted by the glory of God and the Lamb. Sion and Jerusalem are here merged. There is no division of sacred and profane. The sanctuary is not a place apart. "I saw no temple therein: for the Lord God Almighty and the Lamb are the temple of it" (Rev 21:22).

Jerusalem the golden,
With milk and honey blest!
Beneath thy contemplation
Sink heart and voice opprest;
I know not, O I know not
What joys await us there;
What radiancy of glory,
What bliss beyond compare!

They stand, those halls of Zion,
All jubilant with song,
And bright with many an angel,
And all the martyr throng:
The Prince is ever in them;
The daylight is serene;
The pastures of the blessed
Are decked in glorious sheen.

So we could go on with Bernard of Cluny, the twelfth-century saint, through stanza after stanza of anticipation. And indeed such contemplation will sanctify and ennoble our pilgrimage; but let us remember, that so far as position is concerned, we have already come to the hill of Sion and to the heavenly Jerusalem, and we might be sipping more of its nectar and drinking more deeply of its river.

> The hill of Sion yields
> A thousand sacred sweets,
> Before we reach the heavenly fields,
> Or walk the golden streets.

"Ye have come . . . to an innumerable host of angels in festal gathering" (Heb 12:22, author's trans.). The angels shared the solemnities of the giving of the Law; they now celebrate the glories of grace. They have already been presented as "sent forth to do service for the heirs of salvation" (1:14). Here they constitute part of the holy fellowship into which the heirs of salvation enter. They minister to us on our pilgrim way; they rejoice with wonder over the grace of God to rebel sinners; they are our fellow servants unto the Kingdom of God.

These holy, heavenly spirits are here depicted as engaged in a fiesta, in which we are invited to participate. How do they conduct their festivities? They are feasts of praise, celebrating the glories of God and the triumphs of the Lamb. Are we quite at home in the festal assembly of the angels? Can we lose ourselves in the lofty paeans which they raise to God? Would we dare to invite the angels to our socials?

"Ye have come . . . to the assembly [church] of the firstborn ones who are enrolled in heaven" (12:22-23, author's trans.). Here petty distinctions have no place. Perhaps I exclude from fellowship one down here whose name stands right next to mine in the register of the church above! "I must have four things in my life," said John Wesley. "I must have a whole Christ for my salvation, a whole Bible for my staff, a whole Church for my fellowship, and a whole world for my parish!" It may be more comfortable to worship in groups where sharply divergent viewpoints do not distract and annoy, but unless we recognize the fellowship of the whole company of the redeemed, we are impoverishing ourselves and creating schism in the body. Herein is one of the great values of the Keswick movement, with its motto, "All one in Christ Jesus," that we learn to appreciate saints as saints, to recognize the marks of Christ in those who differ somewhat from us. Narrow sectarianism withers under a cosmic verse like this: "Ye are come . . . to the assembly of the firstborn ones enrolled in heaven" (12:22-23, author's trans.). Our local church rolls look small in comparison!

Stop on that word "firstborn" for a moment. It has no reference to priority of time, but to priority of privilege. Among the sons of Abraham, Isaac, not Ishmael, occupied the seat of the firstborn. Esau, by his profanity, forfeited his right, so fulfilling the divine decree that Jacob should have precedence. Among the sons of Jacob, not Reuben but Joseph received the portion of the firstborn. In point of time, angels are before men, and they are referred to as "sons of God." Yet they are not given the place of the firstborn. That is reserved for redeemed men, for the sake of the only-begotten Son, who "took not on him the nature of angels; but he took on him the seed of Abraham" (2:16). We have indeed come into the fellowship of a great company of rejoicing angels, but we ourselves are of higher rank than they. Being received into the adoption of sons by Jesus Christ, we are ranked as "firstborn ones" and so enrolled in the registers of heaven.

"Ye have come . . . to the God of all as Judge" (12:22-23, author's trans.). Rather remarkable, is it not, that the inspired writer should introduce the thought of God the Judge into this statement of the lofty privileges of the Christian! It would seem to be a terrorizing element of the economy of Law clashing with the comforts of the gospel. Yet indeed there is as much consolation here as in any other item in our list of new covenant blessings.

In the first place, is not this the very boon that Job craved? He felt that God was his Adversary, his Prosecutor, who was refusing him a hearing. "He is not a man, as I am, that I should answer him, and we should come together in judgment" (Job 9:32). "Behold, I cry out of wrong, but I am not heard: I cry aloud, but there is no judgment" (19:7). Such cries can never be ours. "Ye have come . . . to the God of all as Judge" (Heb 12:22-23, author's trans.). We stand before Him, accepted in His beloved Son, assured that perfect judgment will be passed on all that enters into our lives. When we sin, it will not be overlooked and so become a cancer of corruption. When we are falsely judged of man, we shall know His vindication. "Judge me, O God, and plead my cause against an ungodly nation" (Psalm

43:1). That prayer of the psalmist is answered for us in this access to God as Judge.

Then look at the phrase in its setting. The God of all is judging us, not as rebels, but as firstborn sons. His judgment is not for destruction, but for perfection, as those who have gone before bear witness. He judges, too, on the basis of a covenant with His own Son, a covenant of blood by which He is pledged to the remission of our sins, and our complete redemption. Apart from the covenantal mediation of our great High Priest, the thought of the God of all as Judge should strike terror into our hearts, but to know Him as Judge within the sphere of the covenant is consolation beyond words to express.

"Ye have come . . . to the spirits of righteous men made perfect" (Heb 12:22-23, author's trans.). "I believe in . . . the communion of saints," says the Apostles' Creed, and here we learn that that communion ignores the veil we call death. Patriarchs, prophets, apostles, martyrs, and all the justified beyond the grave: we have come to them, we have joined their company; we are as much part of them as we shall be when we too are perfected. We are always a "little flock" here, a despised people, but we belong to a noble company, an innumerable company, the multitude of the redeemed.

One family we dwell in Him,
 One Church, above, beneath,
Though now divided by the stream,
 The narrow stream of death.

One army of the living God,
 To His command we bow;
Part of His host hath crossed the flood,
 And part is crossing now.

All this because "ye have come . . . to Jesus, Mediator of the new covenant, and to the sprinkled blood which speaketh better things than that of Abel" (Heb 12:22-24, author's trans.). Apart from Jesus, and His blood of the new covenant, there should be no such blessed access to the presence and throne of God, no such fellowship with rejoicing angels, no such place of privilege in the family of God, no such divine judgments of vindication and mercy, no such hope beyond the tomb. Without the redemptive provision of the blood of Jesus, our every sin would be crying out with Abel's blood for vengeance.

"See, [then,] that ye refuse not him that speaketh!" (12:25, ASV). From the peak of Sinai, God spoke in the thunders of Law; from the throne of glory, Jesus speaks in the entreaties of love. Think not that rejection of the wooings of grace is a lighter thing than a spurning of the ancient Law. Jesus is God's final Word to men, spoken in terms of covenant blood, redeeming blood, atoning blood. Turn a deaf ear to that, and there is no other provision. No appeal will save you, and it will only remain to you to discover, when it is too late, that "our God is a consuming fire" (12:29).

The voice that now speaks to you in the tender accents of Calvary is the voice of a King, whose shout will one day call the dead from their resting places, send the heavens and the earth reeling to destruction, and establish the everlasting Kingdom which cannot be moved. Will that shout mean for you, "Come, ye blessed of my Father" (Matt 25:34); or will it spell, "Depart from me, ye cursed" (v. 41)? "To day if ye will hear his voice, harden not your heart" (Heb 3:15).

37

CHRISTIAN CONDUCT IN THREE SPHERES

HEBREWS 13:1-6

Here we are exhorted to:

1. Charity in the church
2. Chastity in the home
3. Contentment everywhere

"FOLLOW AFTER LOVE" (1 Cor 14:1, ASV), exhorts the apostle Paul, concluding his panegyric on that supreme virtue. But there are specialties of love according to the sphere in which this heavenly grace is to be exercised. Here it is brotherly love, or love of brothers.

The pagan world knew this word. One of the seven churches of Revelation was situated in a city bearing this very name, Philadelphia, so called from Attalus II, who was famed for his loyalty and devotion to his brother Eumenes. The Spirit of God, then, lifts this word from the pagan vocabulary, giving it a new application and filling it with a new wealth of meaning. It now connotes, not simply the attachment of brothers after the flesh, nor the artificial, and often hypocritical, bond between members of a guild or a secret society, but "the tie that binds our hearts in Christian love." "All ye are brethren" (Matt 23:8), says our Lord to His disciples; and again, "A new commandment I give unto you, That ye love one another" (John 13:34). So our text exhorts, "Let love of the brethren abide" (Heb 13:1, author's trans.).

This love of the brethren is to be operative especially in two directions: toward strangers and toward sufferers. "Be not forgetful to entertain strangers" (Heb 13:2*a*), says our King James Version, giving a verbal turn to the original noun. "Do not be forgetful of the love of strangers" is really what our text gives, putting emphasis on the disposition which induces active hospitality. A Scottish saying runs, "Nae freens like auld freens." Some, I fear, would interpret that, "No friends *but* old friends," so raising a barrier against all newcomers. However we may value our tried and proven friends of the years, the noble soul will always have room for more. Even selfish interest would dictate largeness of heart in this regard, for the old friends of today may be gone tomorrow, while the new friends of today may be the old friends of tomorrow. That, of course, is not the thought here. Our love of the stranger is to be for his sake, at least as much as for our own sake, and above all for Christ's sake.

The children of Israel received instruction concerning the stranger: "Thou shalt neither vex a stranger, nor oppress him: for ye were strangers in the land of Egypt" (Exod 22:21). Most of us have been at some time strangers either sojourning for a season, or settling, in some new place. We ought, therefore, to know the heart of the stranger, that mingled hope and fear, that loneliness and shrinking, that sickening sense of not belonging. With some, these feelings are acute, but they can be quickly assuaged by a kindly display of genuine Christian love. Too many churches are made up of watertight cliques, little exclusive groups, whose sanctity may not be defiled by the foot of a stranger. That spirit is not of Christ. The stranger is to be received as a brother beloved, not as a tolerated intruder. Where "stranger love" is "brother love," the bond of fellowship is soon cemented.

Hospitality is a thrilling adventure, and brings rich returns. "Thereby some have entertained angels unawares" (Heb 13:2*b*). Not all! And not always! On one occasion hospitality cost us two suits, a hat, a brand-new overcoat, a suitcase, and ten dollars. Perhaps that was a bit of rash hospitality, but it is a thousand times offset by the enrichments of company that one would hesitate to exchange even for angel visitants. It was good for Abraham and Lot and Manoah that they were hospitable to strangers, who turned out to be God's messengers to them. And I am sure it is recorded in heaven how W. Y. Fullerton and Jonathan Goforth and R. V. Bingham and Max Reich and P. W. Philpott and a host of others whose names are unknown in this world, but well known above, were God's angels in our home. What blessings of encouragement, of challenge, of vision they brought to us!

Even heathen culture has its recognition of hospitality. The Chinese have a story of a poorly clad man who, entering a certain village, applied at the home of a rich woman for entertainment. She indignantly refused, and sent him on his way; whereupon he came to the mean cottage of a poor woman, who kindly received him, fed him from her meager fare, prepared a couch of straw for him, and sat up that night to make him a shirt from her small supply of homespun linen. After breakfast, the poor woman accompanied her guest to the village limits, where, on parting, he said, "May the first work you undertake last until evening." On returning home she began to measure her linen, and as she measured, the linen increased, so that she did not finish her measuring till evening, by which time both cottage and yard were full of the precious cloth, and her fortune was made. The stranger was none other than Fohi! She had entertained an angel, a god, unawares.

God does not promise such carnal reward for Christian hospitality, although we shall be none the poorer for it; but there are richer and more enduring returns, with this above all—"Inasmuch as ye have done it unto one of the least of these my brethren, ye have done it unto me" (Matt 25:40).

Sufferers also call for tokens of brotherly affection, especially those who are enduring affliction for the gospel's sake. We may not at the moment be exposed to chains and imprisonment for our faith. In this land of liberty we are protected by the First Amendment. There is, however, such a possibility as the repeal of an amendment! And there are rising forces definitely opposed to this one which guarantees our religious freedom. Apart from all this, ill-treatment is meted out to many a Christian in his home, in his place of business, and in other circles. These need to be surrounded by the love of their brethren. So long as we are in the flesh we cannot be certain that we shall not be the next to be caught in the flame of persecution. Here, then, is a call to apply the Golden Rule: "As ye would that men should do to you, do ye also to them likewise" (Luke 6:31). Give that sympathy and encouragement and help that would mean everything to you were you standing in the place of that suffering, tempted, ill-treated brother.

Charity is to mark our church relationships; chastity to characterize the home. "Let marriage be honorable" (Heb 13:4, author's trans.), or, held in honor. Purity of conduct, both within the home and beyond its bounds, will be assured by a deep sense of the sanctity and honor of the marital bond and the relationships that spring from it.

How will a group of converted Ephesians, brought up in a cult of sexual abandonment, be taught purity and faithfulness and honor? "Christ also loved the church, and gave himself for it. . . . So ought men to love their wives" (Eph 5:25-28). And again: "The husband is the head of the wife, even as Christ is the head of the church" (5:23). Husband, wife: Christ, the church. Let the analogy grip our hearts, and see if home will not become a little bit of heaven. In the light of such a conception, there can be no place for the selfish, the foul, and the gross. And when husband and wife walk so together in the grace of life, the parental duties will be performed on the same high plane, till the children rise up to call such a father, such a mother, blessed. Let marriage be held in the honor accorded it in the Christian revelation, and problems will fade out, while the glory of God rests upon the home. Degrade this divine institution, and the last props of stability will soon be gone.

Sometimes I receive complaints about wives who will not obey their husbands. One cannot always form a judgment in these matters. There are usually two sides to a story. Perhaps one might ask the complaining husband: "Do you love your wife, even as Christ also loved the church and gave himself for it; that he might sanctify it, that he might present it to himself a glorious church?" If a man loves his wife with a pure love, an unselfish love, a sanctifying love, an ennobling love, it will be hard for that wife to do other than render a loving submission to such a husband. On the other hand, whatever may be said about her duty to obey, she will find it difficult to surrender her whole personality to a man who does not hold her in honor, and for whom she has lost respect. Unless the sense of honor is recaptured—honor for each other and for the relationship in which they stand to each other—the marital problems will surely multiply. This sense of honor can be found, or rediscovered, only at the feet of Jesus.

There is a stern reminder here for those who dishonor the marriage bond, whether by breaking in without right or by breach of the sacred vow. "Fornicators and adulterers God will judge" (Heb 13:4*b*, ASV). When men debase to the level of animal passion, and worse, that which the Creator ordained for sanctification and honor, the divine wrath is stirred. It is not without significance that special shame attaches to sin in this realm, and it has a way of inducing results that are far-reaching and abiding. That ancient word of warning has peculiar appropriateness here: "Be sure your sin will find you out" (Num 32:23). It will confront you when you think you had left it far behind. For sure not everyone guilty will find himself in the throes of an incurable disease. Not all offenders will be exposed to public scandal. Yet God's judgment will be just as real, though variously executed. Even if it be nothing more than the haunting, burning memory that one has played foul, that he has defiled the holy, that he has bemeaned himself and besmirched another—that itself is anguish enough: and the more complete the repentance, the sharper is the pain. The only way to escape the judgment of self-reproach is to sink to the brute, and heap up still more awful and horrible judgment, both in this life and in a lost eternity. "Fornicators and adulterers God will judge." "Flee fornication" (1 Cor 6:18).

Charity in the church; chastity in the domestic sphere; and then contentment in regard to one's station in this life. "Let your manner [of life] be free from the love of money, being content with your lot" (Heb 13:5, author's trans.). We have been exhorted to stimulate "brother love" and "stranger love," and now we have a type of love to avoid—"money love." "They that wish to be rich fall into a temptation and a snare and many foolish and hurtful desires, such as drown men in ruin and destruction. For the love of money is a root of all sorts of evil, which some reaching for were led astray from the faith, and pierced themselves through with many griefs" (1 Tim 6:9-10, author's trans.). What a description of the get-rich-quick maniacs! Here is a superlative example of the accuracy of Holy Scripture.

It is not the legitimate effort to improve one's condition that is here condemned, but the lusting after an increase of this world's goods, resulting in a compromise of one's loyalty to Christ, and a lowering of one's ethical standards, and a forgetfulness of eternal values. Prosperity is good if it is according to the will of God, and consecrated to serve His purposes. To seek it otherwise is to seek that which never satisfies, but which, on the contrary, blights the spirit.

I think of the testimony of Lord Dewar, the whiskey magnate of Scotland, who accumulated a fortune of five million pounds, and declared shortly before his death, that "it is the greatest human delusion that wealth brings felicity." Anything more than sufficient is just surplus. The Chinese have a proverb: "A bird can roost only on one branch; a mouse can drink no more than its fill from a river." What folly to encumber ourselves with excess baggage, to leave it all behind when we take our far journey!

Covetousness is not only folly: it is idolatry. To lust after riches or power or fame or position is to set these up as our gods, and is as much a breach of the first commandment as turning to the gods of the heathen to worship them. The great commandment, as you remember, is: "Thou shalt love the Lord thy God with all thy heart, and with all thy soul, and with all thy strength" (Luke 10:27). There is no room there for the love of money. "Ye cannot serve God and mammon" (Matt 6:24).

Instead of covetousness, we are called to contentment. "Be content with your lot" (Heb 13:5*b*, author's trans.). After all, contentment is a condition of the heart, not of circumstances. We may chafe at the bit until we have ourselves all wounded and bleeding, or we may turn our necessity into a guide, and an instrument of usefulness. When Paul learned that his infirmity was an occasion of grace, he gloried in it, and triumphed. Covetousness is always counting what it wants, contentment what it has. Ian Maclaren gives us a rare picture of contentment in the blind girl of Drumtochty parish: "If I dinna see," she says, "there's naebody in the Glen can hear like me. There's no a footstep of a Drumtochty man comes to the door but I ken his name, and there's nae voice oot on the road that I canna tell. The birds sing sweeter to me than to onybody else, and I can hear them cheepin in the bushes before they go to sleep. And the flowers smell sweeter to me—the roses and the carnations and the bonny moss rose. Na, na, ye're no to think that I've been ill-treated by my God. If He didna' give me ae thing, He gave me mony things instead."

We have good reason to be content, for, whatever our necessities and privations and hardships, we have His faithful promise, "I will never leave thee, nor forsake thee" (Heb 13:5*c*). And who is this that promises His presence at all times? It is He who can take a boy's lunch and make it enough for five thousand men, besides women and children, with twelve hampers of crumbs left over; who cares about the embarrassment of a shortage at a wedding, and will make ample provision of the best wine; who goes with His disciples into the terrifying storm, and rises from His pillow to rebuke the raging of the sea and the wind. It is He who has been tempted in all points, like as we are, yet without sin; who has entered the lists with sin and death and hell, and overcome; who has pioneered the way to the throne of God and opened a highway to heaven for believing sinners. Better be poor with Him than rich without Him; better weak with Him than strong without Him; better in afflictions with Him than in prosperity without Him.

The emphatic multiplication of negatives in this promise is noticeable. When the brilliant young scholar began expounding the emphasis of the Greek negatives to his aged parishioner, explaining that it was just as if the Lord had said five times over, "I will never leave thee, nor forsake thee," she dryly replied, "Well, the Lord may have to say it five times to you scholars, but once satisfies me." Yet the dear Lord knows that, scholars or no scholars, most of us need a lot of persuading, and He condescends to such emphasis for our sakes. It does not make His promise more sure, but it makes our hearts more assured, and helps us to say with greater boldness: "The Lord is my helper; I will not fear: what shall man do unto me?" (Heb 13:6, ASV). May the Lord never allow us to be so full that we have no need of His help! There is a blessed thrill in being always needy, and always knowing His present help, His ready provision, till we sing with Francis Thompson:

> And bolder now and bolder
> I lean upon that shoulder,
>   So dear
>   He is and near;
> And with His aureole
> The tresses of my soul
>   Are blent
>   In wished content.

38

WITHOUT THE CAMP

HEBREWS 13:9-14

In this passage we discover:

1. A principle declared
2. A parallel drawn
3. A procedure directed

THE WRITER of this profound epistle never loses sight of the condition which demanded his attention. In this last chapter, with its miscellany of exhortations and encouragements, he reverts to the main topic, calling more boldly than ever for a complete break with the older economy. Many a devout Jew who believed in Jesus was finding such a separation from his former religious associations most difficult. Tradition and sentiment were strong fetters. Why could not the ancient ritual be maintained along with belief in Christ? Since it had been ordained of God, it could not be wrong! Would not more Jews support the new faith if the new faith would honor the Temple and the priesthood? The symbolism would be useful for teaching purposes, while the observance of days and the distinctions in meats, and other ordinances, would be valuable for discipline, inducing piety and order and faithfulness and sanctification. So it was argued by those who desired to cling to the old order while receiving the advantages of the new. Till it became a dogma that thus it must be, and the doctrine of admixture was spread abroad in the church, especially the Jewish church.

Beware! urges the apostolic pleader. Such reasonings belong to the teachings which carry men beyond the bounds of truth. They are deceptive, failing to take account of the true nature of the former dispensation, and of its complete abrogation through fulfillment in Christ. Meat is for the body, but cannot impart spiritual strength. That is the work of grace, not of a meticulous round of religious rites. Look at your Pharisees, he might be suggesting. Who pays more attention to the niceties of form than they? Yet what has it profited them? Are not these the very men upon whom the Lord pronounced His woes, for the hypocrites and the whited sepulchers that they are? Are they not scheming devils, blind leaders of the blind, destitute of spiritual vision, incapable of discerning true values? If religious performances can produce no better than that in the system to which they belong, what value would spring from attaching them to the new faith?

It is true that all the carnal impositions of the old covenant had spiritual significance, but they had no power to produce the spiritual results which they typified. Now that grace has mounted the throne, it does not exercise its dominion in the lives of men by means of ordinances, but "through Jesus Christ our Lord" (Rom 6:11). It is a direct operation, "Christ in you the hope of glory" (Col 1:27). The faith of Christ is not a new patch on an old garment, but a new garment. The new wine may not be carried in the old wineskin. With the true light now shining, we have no need of the flickering torches of night.

To know the liberty and fullness of the gospel, therefore, one must be free from the ordinances which are under the Law. A new citizen of the United States may continue to observe certain social customs of his homeland, but he is no longer under any law of his former home. His full allegiance and political obedience belong to the new citizenship. Otherwise he is liable to be deprived of his privileges. Even so, there can be no clinging to the "beggarly elements" (Gal 4:9) along with an enjoyment of the "spiritual blessings in the heavenlies in Christ Jesus" (Eph 1:3, author's trans.). "We have an altar from which they have no right to eat which serve the tabernacle" (Heb 13:10, author's trans.). That altar is Calvary, whose benefits are for those who recognize the weakness and unprofitableness of that which went before, and are content to let grace have her perfect work, untrammeled by the works of the Law. One cannot offer a sin offering of his own providing, and at the same time know the shelter of the cross.

One cannot seek satisfaction in the sacrifices of the Law and still feed on the heavenly manna of the perfect offering of the Son of God.

To illustrate and enforce this principle, a remarkable parallel is now drawn, between the sin offering of the tabernacle and the death of our Lord. The carcasses of the Levitical offerings were not all disposed of in the same way. Some were wholly consumed on the altar: these were the burnt offerings. Of others, the fat was burned on the altar, while the flesh was eaten by the priests and the offerers: so it was with the peace offerings. The sin offerings of the higher sort, however, were treated very differently. The blood of these was carried into the holy place and sprinkled before the veil and on the horns of the altar of incense, while the carcasses were borne beyond the limits of the camp and burned in a prepared place.

"Wherefore Jesus also, that he might sanctify the people through his own blood, suffered without the gate" (Heb 13:12). His is the precious blood that is received in the holy place above and secures our pardon, our release, our sanctification, our victory. The sin-bearing Lamb, then, cannot accomplish His redemptive sufferings in the sacred courts of the Temple or within the walls of the holy city.

What is the point of this parallel? In the first place, the carrying of the carcass of the sin offering outside the camp was a mark of shame. Out there were the outcasts and the lepers, whose reprobation the sin-bearing carcass must share. So with our Lord. The curse of a broken Law is resting upon Him who, although He had fulfilled that Law for Himself, was now taking the place of the offender.

> There is a green hill far away,
> Without a city wall,
> Where the dear Lord was crucified,
> Who died to save us all.
>
> CECIL F. ALEXANDER

That second line, "without a city wall," does not declare a mere incident in the crucifixion of Jesus. That was part of the humiliation, part of the offense, part of the reproach, part of the curse. Little did the leaders of Israel know, when they effected His death, that they were fulfilling the type of the sin offering.

Here, again, right in the heart of the Levitical system, was a remarkable witness to its own ineffectiveness, and a prophecy that the real and true and final sin offering would be accomplished outside its bounds. That burning of the carcass of the sin offering without the camp was a dramatic declaration that he who would know the putting away of sin must seek an altar and a sacrifice and a priest beyond the confines of the Jewish order, out there where Jew and Roman and Greek meet on the common ground of sinnerhood, and atonement is made on a cosmic scale. The benefits of Calvary are not for those who serve their own little altars; but for those who, acknowledging the futility of all human priesthoods and sacrifices, are prepared "not to know any thing . . . save Jesus Christ, and him crucified" (1 Cor 2:2).

See, then, the triple significance of our blessed Lord's suffering "without the gate" (Heb 13:12). It filled up the measure of reproach that He must endure as Bearer of a world's sin; it abrogated the entire service of the tabernacle, as of no further value in face of the accomplished redemption; it opened wide the gates of salvation to the whole world—the leper, the Samaritan, the Gentile.

There is only one appropriate procedure to follow after the sight of Jesus going forth out of Jerusalem, the divine Outcast. "Let us go forth therefore unto him without the camp, bearing his reproach" (13:13). To be sure, this was originally a call to Hebrew believers to identify themselves boldly with the Saviour, forsaking a system outworn and valueless, in which the shadows obscured the light, and ordinances barred them from the liberty which is in Christ. Adherence to the Temple was incompatible with the fulfilled work of Calvary.

But surely there is some relevance in this call for us. We may not have the Jewish background, rich in the traditions of the tabernacle and the Temple, the priesthood and the offerings; but the principle declared and illustrated is applicable to all who would enter the Kingdom of God.

"Let us go forth therefore unto him without the camp" (13:13). That may mean outside the religious camp, as it did for the Hebrews. The cross brooks no rival. If it would not share honors with the Jewish altar, which was a divine institution, it will certainly not stand party to any altars of human invention, whether pagan or bearing the Christian name. The cross is not satisfied to give efficacy to other altars. It stands in solitary grandeur. Any religious system which offers a substitute for, or a supplement to, the finished work of the cross, has forfeited any claim to the support of the followers of Christ.

A religious camp that has no room for the Lord Jesus is no place for His people. Many have a Christ of a sort, but not the Christ we know. Their Christ is not He "whose goings forth have been from of old, from everlasting" (Mic 5:2*b*); not the virgin-born Son of God, Son of man; not the sinner's Substitute and surety; not the risen Lord seated at the Father's right hand; not the great High Priest after the order of Melchisedec; not the coming Bridegroom of His chosen people, the appointed Judge of the quick and the dead. This Christ they have discarded, driven out from their midst, in favor of a merely human Christ, a Christ of culture and morality. Such a camp has no part in the Saviour, and we have no part in such a camp. "Let us go forth therefore unto him without the camp, bearing his reproach."

It may be a social camp from which we must go forth to company with Jesus. If our "set" has no place for Jesus, we may no more belong. Not a few have had to go forth from the camp of their own home to follow the Lord. Whatever the camp, if it will not house Him, it cannot be the habitation of His people.

"Bearing his reproach." From the world's view, there is nothing heroic about Jesus' break with Jerusalem. He does not go forth with the sound of a trumpet, beckoning all noble and adventuresome souls to follow Him in a glamorous crusade! See Him passing through the Damascus Gate, bleeding and marred beyond recognition, scarcely able to stand, much less to bear His own cross farther; till the women around weep in pity, and a stranger is forced to carry the beam.

Do you know what reproaches rest on the head of that bruised and wounded Man? Deceiver, glutton, wine-bibber, blasphemer, Samaritan, devil, Beelzebub: these are the epithets that have been heaped upon Him. But bitterest of all is the reproach of a world's sin, laid upon Him. You know how a noble father, learning of the shameful conduct of a rebellious son, will bow his head as if the guilt of it belonged to him. Think, then, of the sinless Son of God bent beneath the reproaches of all the deeds of shame and violence and deceit that have stained the history of our fallen race. No wonder it is written of Him, "Reproach hath broken my heart" (Psalm 69:20).

"Let us go forth therefore unto him without the camp, bearing his reproach." Think not for a moment that the camp of the world loves Him any better today than in the day of His humiliation. There may indeed be some admiration for Him from a distance. Let Him remain outside the gate, and today's world may concede Him a place in the roster of the great. But let Him not come too near! His presence would disturb and confuse the camp. His condemnation of sin, His call to holiness, His way of salvation are unwelcome.

To be identified with Him, then, we must be prepared to bare our heads to reproach also. "The disciple is not above his master, nor the servant above his lord. It is enough for the disciple that he be as his master, and the servant as his lord. If they have called the master of the house Beelzebub, how much more . . . them of his household?" (Matt 10:24-25).

Moses "counted the reproach of Christ greater riches than the treasures in Egypt" (Heb 11:26, author's trans.), and many have followed in his steps. I think of James Haldane, who turned his back on wealth and position and fame to carry the awakening message of the gospel throughout his native Scotland and the continent of Europe, in days when the blight of *moderatism* had well-nigh crushed out all life. In crossing Dumfriesshire in Scotland, he and his companion asked directions from a coal miner, who showed great reluctance in speaking to the missionaries, and when he did oblige them with directions, begged them not to let it be known that he had assisted them. That evening Mr. Haldane recalled that it was the anniversary of a great dinner in Calcutta, India, at which he was the personal guest of the governor-general. It was a far cry from the splendor and honor of that occasion to being shunned by the humblest miner of Sanquhar, but he too rejoiced, "counting the reproach of Christ greater riches than the treasures in Egypt."

Not all who profess the name of Christ are such expert accountants as Moses and James Haldane. Some are dazzled by the treasures in Egypt, prosperity, popularity, position, and will have none of the reproach of Christ. The more shame to us! Was it not for our sakes that Jesus "suffered without the gate"? And shall we guiltily abide in a camp that has thrust Him out? Are we such moral cowards that we cannot endure the revilings of the ungodly? Or are we prepared to stand before the eternal throne, in the presence of worlds and men and angels, and hear the Saviour say in the hearing of all: "This man was ashamed of Me. This man was ashamed of My cross. This man denied Me before men. This man refused to bear reproach for My name. I know him not"?

Let us not forget that it was by suffering "without the gate" that our Lord Jesus opened the way of life to the outcast, the leper, the barbarian, the Roman, the Greek, the Scythian, the Indian, and you and me. And when we "go forth unto him without the camp," we are not straitened, but enlarged; not impoverished, but enriched; not debased, but ennobled. We become partners in the great redemptive purposes of God. We begin to reign with our crucified, risen, exalted Saviour, and to touch men's lives with power.

What is the end of all this suffering "without the gate" and going forth "without the camp"? The end is the city of God. "For here we have no abiding city, but we seek the coming one" (Heb 13:14, author's trans.). The camp to which we so cleave is no abiding city. How foolish to forfeit eternal gain for its sake! All that it has to offer us will pass away as the morning mist, and leave us paupers at last. The eternal city lies in this other direction, outside the camp, outside the gate. Its foundations are laid in the cross. Its Architect and Framer is God. Yet He will graciously give us a share in the building of it, and in building with Him we shall be staking out our "inheritance incorruptible, and undefiled, and that fadeth not away" (1 Pet 1:4).

The end of grovelling in our own little camp is "earth to earth, ashes to ashes, dust to dust," and the fire consuming the wood, hay, and stubble of a wasted life. The end of the going forth to Him without the camp is the shout, "The kingdoms of this world are become the kingdoms of our Lord, and of his Christ; and he shall reign for ever and ever" (Rev 11:15), and this also, "Come, ye blessed of my Father, inherit the kingdom prepared for you from the foundation of the world" (Matt 25:34). For the coming city is the Kingdom of God, which cannot be moved.

39

MINISTERS–PAST AND PRESENT

HEBREWS 13:7, 8, 17

These verses enjoin two duties:

1. Remember your past leaders
2. Obey your present leaders

THREE TIMES in this chapter the ministers of the church are spoken of as *leaders*. They were clearly ministers of the Word, leaders in the spiritual realm. I take it that they were elders, or bishops, which terms are used interchangeably in the New Testament, the one to mark the maturity of the leader, and the other to indicate his responsibility as an overseer.

Two groups of ministers are in view: past and present. While the present participle is used, in place of a noun, for both groups, there can be no doubt about the reference to the past in Hebrews 13:7. The ministers there referred to are not definitely said to be deceased, but the context seems to suggest it.

A duty is enjoined toward past ministers. They are to be remembered. No question arises here as to their worthiness. They were true men, who had faithfully discharged their duty as ministers of Jesus Christ. Their memory, therefore, would have a sanctifying influence on those who had known them, and would act as a powerful restraint on such as were tempted to apostatize.

We who are charged with the care of souls cannot know how deeply we are influencing the lives of others, nor how long that influence may endure. Years after we are gone, some man in the throes of temptation may draw courage from remembrance of us; or he may go down under the memory of our failure at some critical point. Many years ago, when preaching in Pitlochry, Scotland, I visited an old lady in her nineties, who had vivid recollections of the ministry of Robert Murray McCheyne of Dundee. From her girlhood to extreme old age the memory of that godly young minister had been to her as an aroma of Christ, a constant challenge to holy living.

Three elements enter into the memory of a true minister: the word he spoke, the life he lived, and the faith he exercised. "Remember them that led you, who spoke to you the word of God" (Heb 13:7, author's trans.). The accuracy of Phillips Brooks's definition of preaching, "Truth through personality," is evidenced in the fact that we associate a truth which has become vivid to us with the man who made it so, and conversely, we associate the man with the truth which he brought home to our minds. I could not have been more than ten years old when I heard John MacNeill preach on "The Head of the Axe that Swam," yet I remember how his opening remarks, with paukie humor, established the claim of this incident to serious consideration on the ground that "it's in the Bible!" A few years later a sermon by Dr. J. Stuart Holden of London, on "Labourers Together with God," took deep root. Again, Dr. G. Campbell Morgan's passionate delivery on "Jesus Moved with Compassion," left an indelible impress. John McNeill and the authority of the Scriptures, Stuart Holden and the service of God, Campbell Morgan and the compassion of Jesus: somehow these truths are more alive for their association with the men who declared them.

I have heard ministers say, with a fine air of piety (and I have been guilty of it, too!), "Forget me, but remember the truth I am declaring to you." For one thing, it is bad psychology; for another, it is bad divinity; and besides, there is just a little bit of hypocrisy in it! When the Word of God is doing its utmost to assure our being kept in remembrance, it is false modesty on our part to invite our hearers to forget us. Rather, let us give them something vital, something precious, by which to remember us.

A minister's manner of life is also a matter for close study, even after he is gone, with special regard to its issue. Some hold that the "issue" here was the martyr death of certain Hebrew-Christian ministers, and their reward in heaven. Without saying that it cannot be so, I prefer to regard the word as pointing to the outgoing of blessing from their exemplary lives. I think of two men by way of contrast, Charles G. Finney, the great evangelist, and Robert Ingersoll, the noted agnostic. Both men toured the country. Consider the "rivers of living water" (John 7:38) that went forth from the Spirit-filled life of the man of God, and judge whether the agnostic's itineraries left such trails of blessing, uplift, and rejoicing!

And now, my brethren, I call your attention to this: that God is inviting those who wait upon our ministry to take stock of us after we are gone, to see how much blessing has issued from our lives. Does it not make us tremble? It is no light thing to be a minister of the Word of God when God challenges such public inspection of us after our voice is stilled and we can no longer answer for ourselves! Will our people be able to look back on our ministry and say, "Those were years of the right hand of God"?

The third element in a minister's memorial is his faith. It was his faith that made him such a true, fearless exponent of the Word of God; it was his faith that stamped his life with its godly character; it was his faith that opened fountains of blessing wherever he went. Therefore, remember your leaders, in order to "imitate their faith" (Heb 13:7*b*, ASV). We are not told to imitate their manner, for we might just be mimicking their mannerisms; nor their technique, for it might lack the passion they knew; nor their service, for we may not be fitted for it: but their faith.

My good friend the Reverend John Linton has told us in his informal autobiography, *From Coalpit to Pulpit,* that when he was attending Woodstock College in Ontario, there visited the school a notable preacher—notable, among other things, for his long, bushy hair, which made his pulpit presence very striking. Several of the young aspirants to the ministerial office, including John and his roommate, Albert Hughes, conceived the idea that to emulate the visitor's neglect of the barber would assure some of his mastery. A splendid picture in the book reveals the success of the experiment—outside the pulpit! John repines that he could not match the lofty crown of golden glory which Albert boasted! This is a case of imitation (innocent, we admit!) in the wrong direction.

"Imitate their faith," says the apostle. For as the exercise of faith meant the developing of their whole personality in holy living and holy serving, so it will be with our personality by the like practice of faith. The imitation of faith is safe. It will not make assembly line models of us, but will preserve the distinctive marks which make you *you,* and me *me,* glorifying them with the radiance of Christ.

Moreover, while we "imitate their faith," we shall not lose sight of that majestic Man in the forefront of the long file. For what is faith, but "looking off unto Jesus"? The faith of our former ministers will challenge us to "run . . . the race that is set before us, looking unto Jesus the author and finisher of our faith" (Heb 12:1-2). The fact is, to stand back and look at some of those spiritual giants who have ministered to us in past days is a bit discouraging. How can we hope to attain to their proportions in word, in life, in faith? But we have the answer: "Jesus Christ the same, yesterday, and to day, and for ever" (13:8). These mighty men who seem to tower like mountains above us were "subject to like passions as we are" (James 5:17), and what they became was through faith in Jesus Christ; and since He is the unchanging One, He can be to us today what He was to them yesterday, and will continue so forever. So long, then, as we "imitate their faith," "looking unto Jesus" as they did, we may hope to pass on to those who come after the same example of word and life and faith with which they have challenged us.

Do I dare to declare our duty to present ministers? You will not like it, for you do not have the conception of the minister that is presented in the New Testament; while too many of us who occupy the place lack also the biblical conception of our office, and by our triviality forfeit the prerogatives of the true minister. Well, here it is, if we are fit for it: "Obey your leaders, and submit" (Heb 13:17, author's trans.). You will come back with the reminder that the minister is not to "lord it over God's heritage" (1 Pet 5:3, author's trans.). That is one of the fine lessons for the minister to learn, but it does not cancel the obligation of the members to obey. I hear a murmur, "But the church is a democracy, not an autocracy!" Perhaps, but even so, democracy is not anarchy. I have used the term "leaders" where the King James Version has the phrase "them that have the rule over you." Actually the word in the text signifies a prince, one with regal authority. I fully appreciate the difficulty of accepting that in our democratic West, but, then, I did not write the Bible.

Three reasons for this duty are offered. First, "they watch in behalf of your souls" (Heb 13:7*b*, ASV). Now the text turns again upon us ministers. It is a veritable boomerang. That is a terrible word, "they watch." It frightens me. It carries the picture of shepherds keeping sleepless vigil over their sheep, to feed them, to fold them, to protect them, to nurture the weak, to bind up the wounded, to seek after the lost. "Who is sufficient for these things?" (2 Cor 2:16). Yet your minister, frail mortal that he is, is charged with such a duty toward your souls. And when he preaches as if eternal issues hung on his words (which they do!), and when he prays so that it is more a great sob than articulate words, and when he walks like a man borne down with a heavy burden, it is because the care of your souls is pressing sore upon him. Get a man like that for your minister, and give him the reverence and the love and the obedience that such a man demands. But alas! There are so few like that among us. We watch for the crowds; we watch for our reputation; we watch the finances; with an occasional glance at souls.

With all my heart I echo the words of G. Campbell Morgan:

> The peril is that the preacher should imagine that when he has gathered a crowd about himself he has done Christ's work. No. I know how this thing searches, how it creates the doubt as to whether there may not be failure in the very fact that men and women gather about a ministry. I must be true to God and my soul. If I do but gather here men and women to hear me, I am of all failures the most terrible; unless through the things I say I can lead you to my Lord, how do I fail! Unless I can attach you to Christ, and bring you to the one and only Shepherd of souls, then I also am a "blind mouth," the most terrible of all human failures.

The second reason for submitting to your spiritual leaders is an enlargement of the first: "they watch for your souls as those who will present a reckoning" (Heb 13:17*c*, author's trans.). I have heard and read annual reports of ministers after this order: so many sermons preached, so many pastoral calls made, so many weddings performed, so many funerals conducted, so many baptisms administered, ad infinitum. I have never given such a report. I have no criticism for those who do, whether of necessity or voluntarily. Only this, that if any succumbs to the temptation to serve with that kind of reporting in view, he has lost his calling, and is not entitled to the obedience which is a minister's due. One day I shall hand in a report. It will not be statistical, but individual. Every member of my congregation will be named in it—the measure of care he was given, and his response to that care. This is a solemn thought for every minister, every leader in the church. How shall we stand in that great day?

The minister who is accomplishing his service with that day of accounting in view is not a man to be trifled with. You had better not set lightly by his instructions and exhortations and pleadings and rebukes. For one day that man is going to stand before God and talk about you, and what he says to God about you on that day will mean for you eternal profit or eternal loss. If at mention of your name his face lights up and he says, "My Lord, the one Thou hast named was attentive to Thy Word at my lips; his heart was tender and his will submissive," then the face of the Lord will smile upon you, and great will be your reward. But if your mention causes that minister's eyes to droop, and heavily he declares, "My Lord, this was a willful and disobedient child, who heeded not Thy servant's remonstrances nor submitted to Thy Word"—listen!—"This were unprofitable for you" (Heb 13:17*d*, ASV). Yes, your minister's report will somewhat determine your place in the Kingdom of God. O my Lord, what a solemn relation is this, between the minister, the flock, and Thee!

40

THE EVERLASTING COVENANT

Hebrews 13:20-21

We close this study by considering:

1. A mighty covenant transaction
2. A costly covenant seal
3. A rich covenant blessing
4. A ringing covenant doxology

"Our God is a consuming fire," declares the last verse of chapter twelve, yet here He is designated "the God of peace" (Heb 13:20*a*). There He is the Judge, shaking earth and heaven with His terror. Here He is the God of our salvation, meeting our alienation with a great reconciliation, providing "peace . . . [that] passeth all understanding" (Phil 4:7) for our restless hearts.

God's Messenger of peace is His only begotten Son, whose native dignity and deep humiliation and supreme exaltation have been presented throughout the epistle. As the Good Shepherd, He has given His life for the sheep. The "blood of his cross" (Col 1:20) has secured the peace for estranged men. And now, as the "great shepherd" (Heb 13:20*b*), He is raised from the dead to minister that peace to the sheep of His pasture. We are accustomed to think of the resurrection of our Lord in terms of power and glory and victory. Here it is linked with peace. It is a triumphant pastoral. Because our Shepherd died and rose again, we enter into the rest and the security and the plenty and the comfort of the fold.

The New Testament rings with the message of the resurrection. The gospels relate it, the book of Acts heralds it, and the epistles expound it. But here is a light upon the raising of our Lord from the dead not found elsewhere. It was a covenant transaction. "The God of peace . . . brought up from the dead the great shepherd of the sheep by the blood of the everlasting covenant" (13:20, author's trans.).

We have read of the Noahic covenant, and the Abrahamic covenant and the Mosaic covenant and the Davidic covenant. All of these are but servants to another, known to us as the new covenant, but here designated the everlasting covenant. This is not the place to examine the relation of all these. We can only say that the new covenant was before them all, and carries through them all, and outlasts them all. It is new only in human experience, but was conceived and established in the eternal counsels, embracing the vast sweep of the divine purposes.

We generally think of the covenant as between God and man, yet that is but a consequent aspect of it. The destiny of man is indeed concerned in it, but it is essentially a divine arrangement in which the Father undertakes the exaltation of His beloved Son. The second psalm gives us the substance of the promise: "I will declare the decree: the LORD hath said unto me, Thou art my Son; this day have I begotten thee. Ask of me, and I shall give thee the heathen for thine inheritance, and the uttermost parts of the earth for thy possession" (vv. 7-8).

Earlier in our epistle, words from the prophet Isaiah are put into the mouth of our Lord as having their ultimate meaning in Him: "Behold I and the children which God hath given me" (Heb 2:13). Jesus Himself used similar expressions. "All that the Father giveth me shall come to me. And this is the Father's will which hath sent me, that of all which he hath given me I should lose nothing" (John 6:37, 39). "My Father, which gave them me, is greater than all" (10:29). "I have manifested thy name unto the men which thou gavest me out of the world: thine they were, and thou gavest them me" (17:6).

Who are these children, given in covenant to our Lord Jesus? They are sinners, children of wrath, enemies and aliens, bondslaves of sin, guilty, vile, and helpless. If these are to be the people of the Lord, "a glorious church, not having spot, or wrinkle, or any such thing" (Eph 5:27), a great redemption must be effected on their behalf. We cannot be His peculiar treasure in our sin, but only as we are saved from our sin. The promise of a seed, then, involves such a redemption. The covenant provides and secures such blessings for the children as will make them meet to be the Lord's inheritance. These blessings can no more fail to the elect than God's covenant with His Son can be broken. Thus the covenant gathers us into its mighty sweep; it becomes ours, as if God had entered into it directly and primarily with us.

The primitive tribes of the earth still engage in the ancient custom of sealing covenants with blood, and even in civilized quarters men have resorted to blood to express the irrevocableness of their undertakings. When the great National Covenant of Scotland was signed in the Greyfriars Churchyard, Edinburgh, on February 28, 1638, by those sturdy men who swore their allegiance to the kirk and the king, some "did draw their own blood and used it in place of ink." Such an act simply meant, "My life for it!"

The "precious blood of Christ" (1 Pet 1:19) at once obtained the redemption sought and sealed the everlasting covenant. The whole mystery of the incarnation of the Son of God is wrapped up in this covenant. Since it required the shedding of blood, He must have blood to shed. Therefore "he took not on him the nature of angels; but he took on him the seed of Abraham" (Heb 2:16), that He might have what the eternal covenant made over to Him—"a great multitude, which no man could number, of all nations, and kindreds, and people, and tongues . . . clothed with white robes, and palms in their hands" (Rev 7:9), redeemed, victorious sinners.

So one day He reclined with His few disciples in a large upper room, and taking the cup after supper, He gave it to them, saying, "This is my blood of the new covenant, which is shed for you" (Mark 14:24, author's trans.). "And when they had sung an hymn, they went out" (14:26). "And his sweat was as it were great drops of blood falling down to the ground" (Luke 22:44). "And when they were come to the place, which is called Calvary, there they crucified him" (23:33). "When Jesus therefore had received the vinegar, he said, It is finished" (John 19:30).

In this the covenant is sealed,
And heaven's eternal grace revealed.

Christ's inheritance of a people for His name is now assured, and likewise assured are all the saving benefits which will make that people "meet to be partakers of the inheritance of the saints in light" (Col 1:12).

To receive His portion under this covenant, sealed with His own blood, the great Shepherd was raised from the dead. For this is not as many "engagements" into which men enter, in spheres domestic, commercial, and political, quickly broken for expediency or convenience. It is the most solemn pact into which the Almighty has entered; and if His least promise will be fulfilled, we may be sure that nothing will fail of all this glorious covenant. Then, too, this differs from a "last will and testament" in the human realm, where the testator has no more interest in the document the moment it becomes valid. The death of Christ was required to validate the covenant, but His interest in it demanded His resurrection.

This raising of the great Shepherd from the dead is not only a covenant transaction; it is also a demonstration of the divine resources which are dedicated to honor the covenant in every believer, so that not one will be lacking in God's gift to His Son, and not one of the elect will lack the blessings and benefits necessary to "present [him] faultless before the presence of his glory with exceeding joy" (Jude 24). This is exactly the teaching of Paul's great prayer for the Ephesians: "That ye may know . . . what is the exceeding greatness of his power to us-ward who believe, according to the working of his mighty power, which he wrought in Christ, when he raised him from the dead, and set him at his own right hand in the heavenly places, far above all principality, and power, and might, and dominion, and every name that is named, not only in this world, but also in that which is to come" (Eph 1:18-21). Let me say this reverently, and very earnestly: God is as much committed under the covenant to land every believer safe in glory, as He was to raise Jesus from the dead and exalt Him at His own right hand; therefore He exercises the same omnipotence in the salvation of each of His redeemed ones as He did in bringing our Lord up from the grave. The resurrection and ascension of Jesus are all of a piece with the salvation of the humblest believer.

The terms of this benediction, then, are no more than might be expected under such a covenant, sealed with the precious blood of Christ, and implemented by such resources. "The God of peace . . . make you fit in every good thing to do his will, doing in us that which is well-pleasing before him, through Jesus Christ" (Heb 13:20-21, author's trans.).

There is only one permissible plan for the child of God; that is, the will of God. God promises no equipment, no resources, no enabling, no fitness, to do our own will; but for that infinitely better, bigger, nobler, more enduring thing, His will, He guarantees all provision. However we may deem ourselves unqualified, in natural gifts, in personal presence, in spiritual attainment, we need only commit ourselves to His will, and the deficiencies will begin to give place to remarkable fitness. The apostle Paul himself said concerning his ministry, "Our sufficiency is from God; who also made us sufficient as ministers of a new covenant" (2 Cor 3:5-6, ASV). It is true that there is usually some natural fitness present for whatever work the Lord would have us follow, but at times God calls men to tasks for which they seem to have no natural talent—doubtless in order that they may the more depend on Him, and escape the snare of exalting self. One of the ablest of our evangelists today was advised as a young man by his faithful pastor not to try to be a preacher, as he had neither gift nor bearing for it. Certainly no one would have suspected the Boston shoe clerk D. L. Moody of being the century's greatest evangelist, whose name would be a household word in evangelical circles for generations to come. These are only two from numberless instances. But whether there be natural gifts or not, always for doing the will of God, "our sufficiency is from God." Our Lord, whom we serve, will withhold no good thing that would increase fitness for the accomplishment of His will. Here, then, is the recipe for the fullest possible development of the whole man: swing into the current of "that good, and acceptable, and perfect, will of God" (Rom 12:2).

"Doing in you that which is well-pleasing before him." That will not necessarily be well pleasing in the eyes of men. We are not to study to be ill-pleasing to men, in the false belief that we are bound in such case to be pleasing God. There were times when the church was "having favour with all the people" (Acts 2:47), but popular favor is both dangerous and uncertain, so we had better make the good pleasure of God our lodestar, and submit to the inworkings of God, whether they please or displease men. Nothing short of the power that brought Christ Jesus from the dead and lifted Him to the highest seat of the universe, is able to make these lives of ours "a thing of beauty and a joy forever" in the eyes of God. That power is available, "through Jesus Christ," whose portion we are from God, and for whose sake God will perfect all His work in us.

Father of Peace, and God of love,
  We own Thy power to save,
That power by which our Shepherd rose
  Victorious o'er the grave;

Him from the dead Thou brought'st again,
  When by His precious blood
Confirmed and sealed for evermore
  Th' eternal covenant stood.

O may Thy Spirit seal our souls,
  And mould us to Thy will,
That our weak hearts no more may stray,
  But keep Thy precepts still;

That to perfection's sacred height
  We nearer still may rise,
And all we think, and all we do,
  Be pleasing in Thine eyes!

"To whom be glory for ever and ever. Amen" (Heb 13:21*b*). We do not praise the crude stone out of which the sculptor has fashioned his work of art; but the master receives the award. So the glory is not due to the sinner in whom the will of God has been accomplished and the likeness of Christ wrought; but "unto him that loved us, and washed us from our sins in his own blood . . . to him be glory . . . for ever and ever. Amen" (Rev 1:5-6).

41

THIS IS THE SUM

HEBREWS 8:1

In this survey we call to mind:

1. The better Person
2. The better priesthood
3. The better privileges
4. The better practice

"NOW OF THE THINGS which we have spoken this is the sum: We have . . . an high priest" (Heb 8:1*a*). So our apostolic writer declared when he was but halfway through his epistle; and the statement is as appropriate at the end. It is the head truth of the entire book. Therefore, to avoid leaving this study in the confusion of a multitude of thoughts which the individual portions have brought to light, I propose a survey.

Jesus is better than angels. Lofty though they be, they are every way inferior to Him who is the outshining of God's glory, the exact image of His substance. If they are called sons of God, it is in a sense which does not touch the unique, native sonship of our Lord, proclaimed by divine decree. If they do not share the grossness of our mortal bodies, they are yet creatures, obeying the commands of the changeless, timeless Creator, our Lord Jesus. They are the servants of the eternal throne; Jesus is its Occupant. They speed on their errands of ministry for the heirs of salvation while He sits as their Lord "on the right hand of the Majesty on high" (1:3), God the Son, God the Creator, God the King: so is Jesus better than angels in divine dignity.

He is better than angels in His relation to us. Whatever angels may do for us, it is as creatures of a different order from ourselves, but Jesus had a service to render on our behalf which only one of ourselves could accomplish, and He became one of us to accomplish it. Stooping to our flesh, He was "in all things . . . made like unto his brethren" (2:17*a*), "in all points tempted like as we are, yet without sin" (4:15*b*). Suffering, humiliation, death were His lot, for our sakes; all "that he might be a merciful and faithful high priest" (2:17*b*); "touched with the feeling of our infirmities" (2:14*a*). "He took on him the seed of Abraham" (2:16) that we might know how to sing—

> There is no place where earth's sorrows
> Are more felt than up in heaven.
> There is no place where earth's failings
> Have more kindly judgment given.

After considering the superiority of Jesus over angels, it would seem rather irrelevant to declare that He is better than Moses, who, for all his greatness, is only a man. Yet the wisdom of this order is clear. Christ's precedence over Moses is the great truth which must be conveyed to these vacillating Hebrews. Showing how vastly greater He is than angels leaves no argument on the main issue. It is really an a fortiori. Yet the writer no more slights Moses than he does the angels in the comparison. See how delicately He introduces the lawgiver as a pattern of faithfulness even for "the Apostle and High Priest of our profession, Christ Jesus!" (Heb 3:1). The superiority is pressed from the side of office and relationship rather than of character.

First, Jesus is greater than Moses as the builder is greater than the house. So Jesus is a Builder! We have already seen Him as Builder of the universe, but that is only a step in the building of the Kingdom of God. For the Kingdom of God is not built in a day; it is the work of the ages. The difference between Moses and Jesus in this house of God is just this: however honorable a place Moses may have in the building of the house, ultimately he is only a stone—a living stone—in the structure; while Jesus, although occupying the place of "chief corner stone" (1 Pet 2:6), yet stands apart as Architect, Builder, and Owner.

In addition, Jesus excels Moses, as the Son of the house is greater than the servant; and although the term applied to Moses here is neither bondservant, nor hired servant, nor household servant, but one who stands in the honorable place of rendering free, voluntary service, yet he must bow to Him who is "heir of all things" (Heb 1:2).

This more excellent Person exercises a more excellent priesthood than that which was established under the hand of Moses. It is of a different, and better, order. The Mosaic priesthood was of the order of Aaron, but Jesus is "a priest for ever after the order of Melchisedec" (5:6).

The character of the new order marks its superiority. It combines the regal with the priestly. Christ is a "priest upon his throne" (Zech 6:13), bringing to His priestly office all the ethical values suggested in the title "first King of righteousness, and then also . . . King of peace" (Heb 7:2, ASV). It is a timeless order, independent of genealogies, uninterrupted by the intrusions of death. Its sanctions are not the arbitrary commands which gave privileges to the tribe of Levi to which they had no natural claim; but the native excellence of our Lord, and the eternal decree and oath of God. Before ever the Levitical order was established, it had given its tokens of submission to the superior priesthood, in the person of the patriarch Abraham, who gave tithes to Melchisedec, and bowed to receive his benediction.

The more excellent ministry of Christ is exercised within the framework of "a better covenant, which was established upon better promises" (8:6*b*). The covenant which formed the basis of the Levitical priesthood was a covenant of Law. It was couched in terms of "Thou shalt" and "Thou shalt not," with promise of blessing for obedience and warnings of cursing for disobedience. The new covenant offered an infinitely better ground of operations, lifting the burden from the unequal shoulders of men, and laying it on the shoulders of the Almighty.

Even while the old covenant was in operation, glimpses of the better thing were given to God's servants, and our epistle defines its terms as they were given to Jeremiah, the prophet who saw the complete breakdown of the old covenant. Law was not to be voided, but was to be a thing of the heart rather than a table of enactments. That meant the bestowal of a new nature, which would create an irrefragable union between God and His people. From that there would flow a communion with God available to all His chosen, a deep, personal knowledge not confined to a privileged class. All of this was to be based on a gracious absolution, a complete putting away of sins. Surely the mediation of such a covenant, such an engagement of the grace of God, is a more excellent ministry; and with such an High Priest to mediate it, what blessings must be ours!

The priests of the Levitical order had but an earthly sanctuary in which to order their service for the people. That it was built "according to the pattern" (Heb 8:5*b*) shown to Moses in the mount, and that it was a representation of things in the heavens, did not alter the fact that it was "of the earth, earthy" (1 Cor 15:47). Solomon declared that even the magnificent Temple which he built to replace the tabernacle could not contain God, and the apostle Paul reminded the Athenians that "God . . . dwelleth not in temples made with hands" (Acts 17:24). In no ultimate sense, then, did the high priests of old have access to the very presence of God. They could only represent a coming reality. But Jesus has "passed through the heavens" (Heb 4:14, ASV), has ascended "far above all heavens" (Eph 4:10), and ministers "before the face of God" (Heb 9:24, ASV) for us. His priesthood is greater than the Mosaic order as the heavens surpass a woven curtain, and as the throne of God exceeds in glory a box of human craftsmanship.

The place of the sanctuary is the throne of glory. Our High Priest is "set on the right hand of the throne of the Majesty in the heavens" (8:1*b*). His priestly tasks are executed with all the authority of universal sovereignty. No resources can be lacking to realize the ends of His priesthood.

The superiority of our Lord's priesthood further and ultimately rests on the better sacrifice which He has offered. "For every high priest is ordained to offer gifts and sacrifices: wherefore it is of necessity that this man have somewhat also to offer" (8:3). But He did not come to repeat the inadequate and ineffective offerings of the priests who were before Him. "When he cometh into the world, he saith, Sacrifice and offering thou wouldest not, but a body hast thou prepared me" (10:5). Instead of the carcasses of bulls and goats and heifers, we have the divinely prepared body of our Lord Jesus. The high priest of old offered for the people what cost him nothing; the offering of Jesus for us cost Him everything. He "through the eternal Spirit offered himself without spot to God" (9:14), His body being the instrument of that perfect sacrifice.

The offerings of the former priesthood were multiplied without number, repeated daily, weekly, monthly, yearly. This in itself marked their ineffectiveness: "But this man, after he had offered one sacrifice for sins for ever, sat down on the right hand of God" (10:12). The finality of the offering declares its efficacy. It is the all-covering sacrifice, and any attempt at repetition is nothing short of blasphemy!

So our better High Priest, of a better order, ministers under a better covenant, in a better sanctuary, on the ground of a better sacrifice. Better privileges are surely to be expected!

The better product of Christ's ministry is a worshiper cleansed from his sins. "Every priest standeth daily ministering and offering oftentimes the same sacrifices, which can never take away sins" (10:11). "In those sacrifices there is a remembrance again made of sins every year" (10:3), says our writer, speaking even of the great Day of Atonement. But our Lord and High Priest has "put away sin by the sacrifice of himself" (9:26*b*). The best the old sacrifices could offer was a ceremonial cleanness, while they taught the great principles of true cleansing. In Jesus the principles became effectual. "For if the blood of bulls and of goats, and the ashes of an heifer sprinkling the unclean, sanctifieth to the purifying of the flesh: how much more shall the blood of Christ . . . purge your conscience from dead works to serve the living God?" (9:13-14).

Not all the blood of beasts
On Jewish altars slain
Could give the guilty conscience peace
Or wash away the stain;

But Christ the heavenly Lamb
Takes all our guilt away,
A sacrifice of nobler name
And richer blood than they.

Following on from the cleansing is the sanctifying and perfecting of the worshiper. "We have been sanctified through the offering of the body of Jesus Christ once for all. For by one offering he hath perfected for ever them that are [being] sanctified" (10:10, 14, ASV). The product of the priesthood of Christ is a worshiper permanently established in right relation with God, for fellowship, for service, for obedience; a worshiper given a standing of perfection which makes possible His drawing nigh to God; a worshiper being brought in practical character ever closer to that perfection which is his by virtue of the blood of Christ.

As a result of all this cleansing and sanctifying and perfecting, the worshiper in Christ has access to the Holy of Holies. This is in striking contrast with the former order, in which the constant ministrations of the priests never secured entrance for the people into the holy place, much less into the Holy of Holies, into which only the high priest was permitted to go, one day in the year, in the prescribed manner. No Admittance was the sign on the first veil and the great veil, and if the priests of Levi had continued to minister for ten thousand years, the first tent would still have borne its mute witness that "the way into the holiest was not yet manifest" (9:8). But when "the veil, that is to say, his flesh" (10:20), was rent for us, the veil of the Temple also was rent in the midst, the Holy Ghost thus signifying that the new and living way was now established, "by the which we draw nigh unto God" (7:19).

When the better Person has obtained a better priesthood to secure better privileges, there must follow a better practice for those who hear the glad tidings. Our epistle has not forgotten this practical side of the matter. For one thing, it has repeatedly given warning that the higher privileges carry weightier responsibility, and that the penal sanctions of grace are even heavier than those of the Law. We must therefore give heed more abundantly, lest we be carried away by the fatal drift. The example of the Israelites who fell in the wilderness is intended to stir in us holy determination not to fall short of the grace of God and lose the rest which He has prepared for His people. The finality of the offering of Christ makes more imperative our abandoning every other trust, and holding fast our confidence in Him. A falling away from Him would mean the end of all hope.

In more positive vein, we are reminded of obligations which do not come in a catalog of commandments, but which rather rise from our happy lot in Christ. It is the principle of noblesse oblige. Our "boldness to enter into the holiest by the blood of Jesus" (Heb 10:19) calls us to take advantage of our dearly bought right: "let us draw near with a true heart in fulness of faith" (10:22, ASV). Again, honor demands that those who know the blessings of the open highway into the presence of God sustain an unbending confession, for Christ's sake who opened the way, and for sinners' sakes who need the way. And, having been introduced to the great "high priest over the house of God" (10:21), we must remember our place in that house, helping one another by our presence in the assembly and by mutual encouragement.

To assure the better practice we are taught the way of faith. "The just shall live by faith" (10:38) is the great working principle of the Christian life, illustrated so vividly and with so much challenge from the saints of old, who, though they lived in the first glimmerings of revelation, yet are witnesses of heavenly realities. See the worship of faith in Abel, the walk of faith in Enoch, and the work of faith in Noah; then consider faith's early adventure, faith's long patience, and faith's noble sacrifice in the patriarch Abraham; examine the inner workings of faith in the man Moses, leading to personal renunciation and national redemption; follow on to the triumphs of faith, the trials of faith, and the endurance of faith in those who came after. Finally see the principle of faith fully wrought out in our blessed Lord, "who for the joy that was set before him endured the cross, despising the shame, and is set down at the right hand of the throne of God" (12:2*b*). For us, faith is summed up in the phrase, "looking unto Jesus" (12:2*a*). He is both chief Exemplar and object of faith.

All Christian conduct—in the church, in the home, in the world—will stem from this practice of faith. By it we shall "go . . . unto him without the camp, bearing his reproach" (13:13), loosed from the uncertainties of this world, our vision lifted to "the city which hath the foundations" (11:10, ASV), the eternal city of God.

So the message of our wonderful epistle is just this: We have a better Person engaged in a better priesthood, securing better privileges that call for better practice and point to a better prospect. "To whom be glory for ever and ever. Amen" (13:21).